D0822619

Table of Content

Good in the Beginning
Aspire

May all family and book-loving friends gather and join in sharing their unique stories and life truths.

May we listen, talk and learn, be genuine and have fun.

May we dive deep into memories and be inspired by our recollections of people and events, both present and past.

May questions be openly asked and answers be lightheartedly explored.

May our stories spark personal insights and meaningful, conversations.

And, may we create a space for feeling right, good and grateful about the preciousness of our human lives and the experiences of our existence.

Please note

I encourage any discussion to begin with a reading aloud of these aspirations and any of your own.
Thank you. Likewise,

Do

Good in the Middle
Do

Breathe.

Slowly inhale, follow your breath.
Exhale, follow your breath.

Be aware of your body in all regards.
Calm the mind.

Allow thoughts to flow freely, without judgment or
attachment. Welcome ideas, perhaps different from your
own.

Realize and respect all others and yourself.
Act mindfully.

Slowly inhale.
Follow your breath.
Exhale, follow your breath.
Be mindful.

Please note

*I encourage us to begin any reading of this book with a
review of these instructions and* **Aspire** *at the start.
Thank you. Likewise,*

Dedicate
personally at the end.

Preface

Each of us has an origin, a story, a unique and swirling confluence of time and place, of people and processes, of causes and conditions that bubble and burst forth into life. Some stories recount loving parents under the most fortunate of circumstances, for others not so much.

From the sloshing, watery, warm and nurturing existence of our mother's lightless womb, into the bright, noisy, reality of our harsh, new worlds made manifest, we are here.

As we grow and mature, a boundless variety of life experiences ebb and flow. Lessons are learned, and re-learned; often and only to be learned yet again, until we more fully understand.

Over the years, I have been to, seen, and encountered many places, things, and perspectives. I have been taught that our capacity to comprehend is expansive, bound solely by our habits of body, speech and mind.

Life in Tens streams my earliest memories with on-going life lessons. Issues of physicality, good health, family, friendship, joy, depression, food, culture, acceptance, rejection, sexuality, emotionality, spirituality, travel, lives both past and present, and death.

Each and more inform and compose uniquely my tales.

In recounting behaviors and events, the larger lessons are the focus of my tales, not particular individuals cast among the many who co-created these shared histories.

I am grateful for all with malice towards none.

I honor my grandparents' and parents' by using their

given names. May happiness ripple everywhere, each time future readers speak their names. I have respectfully changed all others.

"Violet, Robert, Arlene, Carolyn, Bill."

As the title *Life in Tens* suggests, these stories are scripted in decades, 10 year spans.

Chapter One ('64 – '73): *Childhood* speaks to the wide-eyed, inquisitive and guarded pathway of my youth, as seen through the eyes of a child who always felt and inhabited a ponderous, state of different - a child constantly asking *"Why?"* only to be frustrated by unsatisfying replies. The routines of life, family, school, and church, were my foundations. Inklings of an uncommon sexuality bubbled young.

Chapter Two ('74 – '83): *Adolescence* shares the transition from child to adulthood. Family and the larger, familial bonds of neighborhood and community had profound influence. Stories of hijinks, uncertainty, intoxicants and experimentation are recalled.

Unexpected independence taught me much.

Throughout the text, you will find italicized paragraphs beginning, *"One thing:"* or *"Two things; one: ..."* They provide tangential flavor. For example:

One thing; I periodically kept journals during my 20s and 30s. As I prepared to read them for the first time since they were written, I was anxious and a bit ambivalent. What would they reflect of me?

I inputted journal content on first speak/read, seeking to keep the tone and truth of my words as immediate and fresh, as real and raw as the days they were penned. Incorrect grammar and poor word choices were not edited.

In some cases, I have no idea the context in which I was writing – so many random thoughts.

Also, I share cassette transcriptions from some hypnotherapy sessions I underwent during my 30s, plus a few other surprises.

Chapter Three ('84 – '93): *My 20's* details significant passages of learning as I attained my Bachelor and Masters' degrees, then went on holiday to relax and returned stateside 18 years later.

Travelling first to Australia then to Japan and elsewhere, everything intrigued my mind and effortlessly motivated my moments. At times, they seemed to melt. I met wonderful people and experienced wondrous things. I worked as a bartender and later as an English teacher who fell in love.

Chapters Four and Five ('94 – '03): *My 30's Nepal* and *My 30's Hong Kong* recount further Asian adventures. I was blessed to meet and serve extraordinary spiritual Masters – men and women who have devoted their lives to studying and passing on an ancient wisdom that traces its' unbroken lineage back 1,000+ years.

For the benefit of all sentient beings, may these teachings be applied, preserved, and forever forward shared.

I worked for a trekking agency, had a restaurant with friends and blossomed professionally. Opportunities allowed me to play in academia and the world of corporate training. I lived on a small island full of exemplary folks.

Sadly, underlying the joy of these activities, I navigated family pains from afar and love again within.

Chapter Six ('04 –'14): *My 40's* details my return to Australia for school and then to America. A shift in my professional focus and attempts at navigating personal relationships are shared.

My 40's reflects on my struggles to re-establish myself in a country vastly different from the one I had left. Attitudes and energies were not the same. I too was different.

In striving to live with compassionate integrity, I was reminded that American culture remains discomforted by the advancement of particular ideals and the enacting of certain ideas.

Personally, unhealthy habits teased and took shallow root as mindfulness waned. Disgruntled cynicism percolated. I got lost and hurt and I was ok.

Chapter Seven ('15 – now): *My 50's* end, and are again unfolding.

For decades, friends have commented, *"Peter, write that down,"* and time availed. I wrote, knowing that no one, at any time or place, has ever experienced life in the exact manner by which you have lived yours or, me mine.

We are all swept up in the streams of our experiences whatever their levels of rage and saturation.

Some streams are swift and strewn with boulders to re-direct the currents – challenges to integrate and transform. Other streams are trickling and tranquil, gently swirling eddies where we relax, refresh and reconnect.

We all thrive and survive in this state where being is the constancy of change.

I share my stories so that you may dive deep and re-surface to breathe life into tales of your own.

"For a life examined," some claim, *"is a life well lived."*

Throughout the book, you will find **two (2) question types**.

Questions to Ponder (QtoP) are for pause and private reflection.

They appear throughout the text, margined right in groups of three (3). If they interrupt your reading flow, please skip them and return later. The questions are direct, and the answers as private as you see fit. Let them percolate honestly over time throughout your heart and mind.

Reflect and Share questions end each chapter and aim to spark fun, meaningful conversations.

Someone yells out a letter (A-Z) and the corresponding question is read aloud. Stories begin as you dive deep into the pools and puddles of your mind. Please applaud the many tales and opinions until they are exhausted. Then, yell out another letter.

QtoP1: Where are Reflect and Share questions?

QtoP2: When can I pause and privately reflect?

QtoP3: What do I want from reading this book?

One thing: Questions to Ponder (QtoP) were placed based on immediately preceding stories. The photos are caption free to encourage discussion and were inserted amidst their corresponding tales.

And with that, may you enjoy reading *Life in Tens*. Together, let us:

- Bring about laughter and smiles;
- Generate respectful discussions;
- Encourage self and mutual understanding; and,
- Tend to our inter-connectedness. Peace

August 11, 1956

1

Chapter One: Childhood

I was born during a frigid, frenzied, Buffalo blizzard. The third of three (3) boys, my mother says the pregnancy was easy and uneventful. Birthed at 3:06am, doctors quickly decided my fragile, too small body and newly re-realized consciousness needed some alone time before fully making their world debut.

Therefore, they placed me in the incubator ward for seven (7) days of nourishment and nurturing. Word is, I turned my back to anyone visiting.

One thing: I believe now that everything we experience forever etches an impression on our mind. Some experiences etch deep like letters chiseled into stone, seemingly permanent. Others gently impress like writing on sand – easily smoothed away, while others still, are experienced fleetingly with barely perceptible impact, like scripting your name on the surface of still, cool water.

I wonder how these initial days impacted my frail, newborn sense of self. What and how deep are the imprints from those tentative times? Perhaps those seven (7) days are the source of my highly independent streak – my strong sense of "I can go it alone. Thanks."

Perhaps, they are cause for my occasional bouts of social awkwardness? Perhaps they are both or neither, one or the other. I do not know. Whatever the cases may be, "It is what it was. I am who I am."

On day eight (8), doctors declared me sufficiently strong so my mother wrapped me in a small, white blanket and carried me home to my two (2) older brothers - Adam, born 1957, and Todd, born 1962. Years later, the same blanket was used to swaddle and warm Charlie, our pound rescued puppy.

Famous in the annals of our family history, Adam's initial reaction on seeing me was, *"Mom, you need to take him back to the hospital. His head is a way too big for his body."* Looking at my two (2) day old picture (*see the cover*), you may well agree. I am all head, covered in thick, black, mowhawked hair, atop a tiny, pretzel thin body that said, *"This fragile child must be handled with tender attention."* Thus began my Kenmore home life.

One thing: About my head, I hit it on everything. Nothing seems to phase it and one day something will. I once dove into our backyard pool, eyes closed, and landed on my brother's head. He got five stitches. I got a lump. When retrieving jars of homemade sauce from our fruit cellar, I repeatedly hit my head on the low door frame. The story, "Falling Head First Off My Bicycle" names itself. My childhood nickname quickly became "Lumpy" and I felt it an aptly earned, wholly appropriate, moniker. To this day, when speaking with a childhood friend, our phone conversation begins:

Friend: Hey, Lumps, how's it going?

My first home was a duplex dwelling, It was located in Buffalo's first suburb, Kenmore, New York. I admire cities and am intrigued by the ways people adapt and organize themselves to their environmental surroundings. In this, Buffalo is rather unique. Comparing urban inspirations and developments, the city has an intriguing history.

In 1825, the 365 mile Erie Canal opened, linking New York City to Buffalo through a series of 36 locks that raise and lower ships a total of 565 feet. It established easy, inexpensive access to the Great Lakes region, Canada and the West, spurring industrial growth. Thousands of immigrants who built the canal settled in Buffalo, while tens of thousands more subsequently followed its gently flowing waters. Neighborhoods were ethnic smorgasbords.

At Easter, Mom always visited the Polish section of town to purchase a butter lamb. After grace was said and the meal commenced, my brothers and I would gleefully fight to behead the lamb, slicing cruelly through the red ribbon placed around its' neck then smothering our roll.

3

Buffalo is home to 13 centers of higher education and hosts seven (7) buildings designed by world renowned architect, Frank Lloyd Wright, including the Albright Knox Art Gallery. The city has irreplaceable architecture such as the 1926 Shea's Theater. It is a city with a historical buzz and diversity that inspired me to dream of the world beyond my immediate surroundings.

I first experienced culture in these iconic, performance venues. At Shea's, the booming percussion and driving brass still vibrate as the curtain opens and the Director commands – "*Step. Kick. Kick. Leap. Kick. Touch. Again*" – in the Tony and Pulitzer Prize winning musical, *A Chorus Line* – my favorite. At Kleinhans, our family saw Art Garfunkel's first, public performance after going solo. Monthly we saw plays at Studio Arena Theater.

On Fridays nights, we joined family friends for a German fish fry, or Italian pizza, or fresh corn on the cob and buckets of original, Anchor Bar chicken wings, Buffalo's famous, world culinary contribution. As an adult, post-work breakfast was often had at a Greek café where I intriguingly heard snippets of an unknown language.

In 2015, *National Geographic* identified Buffalo as the 3rd best food city in the world.

We moved from Kenmore to the Town of Tonawanda (ToT) in 1969. I was four (4). Over the years our family would go back to visit former Kenmore neighbors and my parents would point out our old house and share rarely voiced stories of my toddler days.

The Town of Tonawanda

The Town of Tonawanda's general tranquility, well-manicured lawns and friendly ways found reflective truth in the iconic television sitcom, *Leave It to Beaver* and its' depiction of suburban, domestic bliss.

Both Ward Cleaver and my Dad departed for work daily in a suit and remained in their professional attire through the dinner hour. Unlike Ward however, my Dad enjoyed a *"scotch on the rocks, two cubes"* and the newspaper on arrival home. When he was done reading, we were called to the table. *"Boys,"* Mom yelled, *"dinner is ready."*

One thing: I now appreciate how special this personal and private transition time must have been for Dad. He talked and managed folks all day; then, he fathered three boys, and was a husband all night. A few minutes to simply relax had to be a welcomed pause.

My mother, like June Cleaver, ensured smooth domesticity, but differed in that she also worked full time. This meant her sons contributed to household upkeep in ways Wally and the Beaver were never scripted to experience. Early television certainly failed to portray humanity as I saw and felt it being lived around me.

Imagine Wally one day paying Beaver to stay outside so he and his girlfriend could enjoy a forbidden round of teenage exploration, or, Eddie Haskell puffing on an illegal herb, or, a pre-pubescent Beaver, stealing knick knacks on a dare from the local pharmacy.

The ToT was American newness. Not at all a city with the attributes of a vibrant, diverse center, bustling sidewalks and café hideaways, nor, a rural existence embedded in nature with the smells of Mother Earth and the twinkle of limitless, night stars. It was neither.

The ToT and the thousands of communities just like it that sprouted post-WWII were neutered hybrids. Not quite city, not quite country, they developed around the conveniences of comfort, commerce, autos, and the security of sameness.

Recognizing these neutered qualities, I was very fortunate that my parents constantly and consistently introduced us to wide array of cultural experiences, both urban and rural. From an early age, though, I always felt *"there's got to be more than the sameness of this place."* That all said, I am so grateful for and loved where I grew up.

One thing: I would feel remiss, not mentioning the impact of Native American cultures on this area. The Haudenosaunee, or Iroquois Confederacy, consisting of seven (7) tribes, dominated much of New York and the northeast area prior to European settlers. Names like Tonawanda, Cheektowaga, and Onondaga speak to this rich history.

Moreover, the Confederacy's constitution strongly influenced Thomas Jefferson (my favorite) and others as they drafted the Declaration of Independence and the Constitution. Meaning, the core documents that define us as a nation and people are directly linked to the indigenous inhabitants. Teaching ourselves a complete and proper recounting of history is important. There is much to understand about our present situations by acknowledging the past grounds from which they arose.

My Parents

Before neighborhood and home, I'd like to introduce you to my parents: Robert Kenneth and Carolyn Ann. I consider it an extraordinary blessing to be borne unto them. They are kind hearted, caring, funny, genuine, spiritual people within the Lutheran tradition. If all people of faith manifested the fundamental goodness of their religions in the manner by which my parents realize theirs, the world would be forever balancing a welcoming peace.

QtoP1: Do I have with a strong sense of my ethnicity? How does this influence my behaviors?

QtoP2: Is there someone whose mere presence upsets me? Why?

QtoP3: Did my parents set a strong religious example?

Certain Eastern traditions posit that we incarnate to our parents for a variety of reasons. Perhaps a karmic debt, or attaching ourselves to the familiar, or incarnating with folks in whom we see the possibility for enhanced personal growth and the potentiality for enlightenment. Whether or not one believes this, please consider how such thinking shifts the dynamic of parental responsibility - from parents being the fundamental creators, to parents as on-going caretakers and guides.

I am an inquisitive adult, and am told that, I was even more so as a child. My constant chant was, *"Why?"* Unfortunately, the most common and utterly unsatisfactory replies were, *"Because I said so,"* or *"That just how things are,"* particularly relating to matters of physicality.

One year, a local pharmacy delivered a box of napkins to each front porch. My mother's birthday was the following day so I took the box, wrapped it, and presented it as my gift. On opening, her face displayed an uncomfortable uncertainty. I asked, *"Don't you like them?"* She countered, *"Do you know what they are?"* I answered, *"Yes. They are dinner napkins."* She seemed to sigh and then smile a bit, *"Thank you."* No more was said. It was only later that I realized they were feminine hygiene napkins.

Matters of sex and sensuality were never spoken of. They were cloaked in the humility and modesty that infuses the way my parents live their lives. My brothers and I never had the *"talk."* And, while I would have welcomed such conversations, it has been my journey to uncover such matters on my own. I am grateful that age and many challenges have forged closer bonds among all family members and created space for more honest and satisfying conversations.

I know surprisingly little about my parents' childhoods. My dad was born in December 1930 and raised in Niagara Falls, New York. His biological father died of a brain tumor when he was 12; his mother had two further husbands. Dad had two (2) older sisters, one of whom has since passed. Their upbringings were influenced profoundly by the challenges of the Great Depression and WWII. Our ethnicity traces to northern England and southern Scotland.

My father served in the Navy between World War II and the Korean War, and later went to Cornell University in Ithica, New York, where he attained his Bachelor's degree in Industrial Relations. He worked as a human resource manager with the same company for nearly 50 years. His lifetime commitment, rare in today's world, yielded a comfortable retirement.

I know he loved his mother, Violet - my Grandma Trask - very much. Every Sunday for nearly 17 years I witnessed his devotion when our extended family gathered at her home for dinner. To this day, his voice fills with a gentle kindness when he speaks of her. He was a good, and only, son. Through his compassionate words and deeds, he has passed on to my brothers and me, the fine, caring, and respectful manner of his youth.

My mother was born in 1935 and also raised in Niagara Falls, in a house her father helped build; he passed in 1967. She had one younger sister who has passed. Her mother, Arlene, remained a widow until she died peacefully at the age of 102. Our ethnicity from this side is mainly German.

Two things: one: In her late 90s, she moved to a facility near my parents. Here, we had a reunion that brought together five (5) generations - Grandma Feeley and he nine (9) month old, great, great grandchild. Gram sparkled, clapped and played as he laughed and flailed his arms. They were a bundle of pure, giggling, goo-goo talk joy.

Two: Grandma Feeley passed exactly as ancient, Eastern teachings describe a peaceful, fortunate death, borne of a life well lived. Slowly, all energy gravitated towards her heart.

Ascending from the feet, blood slowed and her skin became cold. Control of urinary and digestive functions diminished. Breathing became labored. Descending from the head, hearing, eyesight, and the capacity to speak faded. Until one day, she fell sleep and quietly transited to whatever comes next.

Mom attained her BA in Education at Buffalo State and taught for nearly 35 years at the grammar and junior high levels. The patience and love my mother brought to her classroom were shared equally at home. She strongly instilled the value of education as an end in and of itself.

My father once told me, "*Your Mom is as sweet as apple pie.*" I could not agree more.

Wanting to ensure his return, Mom proposed to Dad shortly before he went off to college and he accepted. I only learned of this unusual fact on December 3rd, 2016. They married in August of 1956.

One thing: In my 30's, I lived in Hong Kong on Lamma Island, a 25 minute ferry boat trip and a world away, from the hustle and bustle of Hong Kong's glittering, urban vibrancy. During this time, my parents visited for two (2) weeks. One day I came home from work and they were gone. I was worried and headed down to the village, eventually finding them at a waterfront restaurant enjoying some wine and the glorious sunset.

Joining them, I experienced something unexpectedly extraordinary in its' matter of factness. I began asking them questions about their lives, how they met, what they remember, etc... and I witnessed two (2) people who had shared over 50 (now 60) plus, loving years together, negotiate the timeline of their lives. I love them so.

Once, for an undergraduate research project I interviewed people with the question, "*When do you become an adult?*" I received many different answers from biological age to experiences All interesting, yet my favorite answer was:

"You fully become an adult when both your parents pass."

No matter experiences, when I visit my parents, I am first and foremost, their child.

Our Neighborhood

Our neighborhood's relative safety made for terrific summers filled with endless daytime adventures and nighttime pleasures – bike riding, swimming, and warm weather fun, and back yard sleep outs, games of kick the can and hide-n-seek. In later years, this last game morphed into uncomfortable bouts of baseball – *"I got to second base. What did you do?"* Me? I embellished.

I spent countless days exploring the Dewey decimal listings and endless rows of books at Brighton Public library. One of my favorites was *A Wrinkle in Time*. Others were: *Charolette's Web, Treasure Island*, and the stories of Roland Dahl.

With free time, friends and I would wake at an early hour and bike for miles to get purposefully lost then return home before the street lights came on at dusk. Swimming at the town pool – Brighton Pool - required, first, showering, and second, getting our feet checked for plantar warts. We spent many summers here.

To this day, the sounds of *Waterloo* by Abba and early Mr. RK Dwight transport me back to fun, splash and Captain Fantastic sun. For several summers, we joined the town diving team. Local TV sports once broadcast me diving at a meet where I performed the wrong dive. I came in sixth (6th) place and earned an aptly awarded, pink ribbon.

One summer, my brother was a ticket taker at a *Fun & Games*, a small, local amusement park *where* he met his future wife. Our favorite rides were the bumper cars, Tilt-a-Whirl, and Might Mouse roller coaster. We rode them anytime because Adam brought home un-torn tickets for our free re-use. Adjacent to the park was a drive-in theater where we first saw *Ghostbusters*. I love you, Mr. Murray.

We fished for carp at Ellicott Creek Park and went to Saturday matinee movies at Boulevard Cinemas. Short films always preceded the main feature. This is where *Willy Wonka and the Chocolate Factory* forever captured my imagination. Peace, Mr. Wilder. And, I fell in love with Ms. Cicely Tyson in *Sounder*. Such a remarkable woman.

Mr. Softy, the ice cream man, appeared regularly on our street, announcing his arrival with a distinctive jingle that had us begging our parents for money. We then ran quickly curbside for a chilly, tasty treat. Dreamsicles were my favorite – vanilla and orange ice creams on a stick. Years later, I added vodka and this became the signature drink at my college graduation party.

Plump, dressed in a bakers' white, tall, ribbed hat and a red scarf, Tony appeared less commonly. He pushed his wooden cart down the street and sang opera-like announcements: *"Hot bread for you!" Made fresh, come to!"*

A milkman regularly delivered fresh half gallons to our doorstep with decidedly less fanfare, actually none. When I was real little, I would go knocking door to door asking, *"Can I have a cookie?"* The nice lady in the brown house at the end of the street always gave me something special.

In winter, we went to bed dreaming for a powerful, snow dumping, school closing storm. Hovering over the radio, we hoped to hear, *"Erie Country Public Schools."* If uttered, we cheered wildly. It meant snowball fights, fun and shoveling for money.

When we got older, it also meant the slick streets and slow, moving cars were a perfect way to *"pogee."* We waited on corners for a passing vehicle, then ducked quickly and grabbed the back right wheel well or bumper. This was *"pogeeing."* Stupid, huh?

In 1977, Buffalo experienced the legendary *"Blizzard of '77."* It closed the city for a week as we dug our way out. That morning, confirmation of our day off was accompanied by news of snowy expectations. At approximately 10:30am, Adam and I were shoveling the driveway when the wind started blowing. I looked up. Both Adam and the house were gone in a howling white out.

We rushed inside and watched from the living room window as the snow fell for hours in wave after horizontal wave.

13

Accumulation totaled over seven (7) feet. Cars and houses were buried. 20+ foot drifting allowed us to walk above the traffic lights. Mom and neighboring families cooked pots of soup. We had one big, impromptu party.

> *QtoP4: How was my parents talk about sex?*
> *Did they teach me what I needed to know?*

> *QtoP5: How do I view my parents' time together?*
> *Would I like to experience the type of relationship they*
> *share(d)?*

> *QtoP6: Did I like or not my neighbors?*
> *Did any significantly influence my childhood?*

Both Brighton and Kenmore East (my elementary and senior high respectively), were on Fries Road close to home. The schools were separated by a huge playing field. At one point, we treated this field as our own, private driving range and fired off golf balls in the wrong direction for the wrong reasons. My apology.

Annually, the field hosted a big bonfire on the Friday night, preceding the homecoming football game against our rival, Kenmore West. The crowds went wild as a huge effigy of their mascot was burned.

On game day, crabapples collected from front yard trees found throughout the neighborhood became ammunition as folks drove around and randomly threw them at unsuspecting targets. In later years, the game and rivalry were voided due to increasing recklessness.

I lived on Calvin Court South where the lives of baby boom children played out in approximately 50 homes. Within a 10 home radius, there were 28 children, spanning the full range of boomer years (1946 to '64). Dozens and dozens more populated the street. There was always something abuzz somewhere.

Each housing lot was identical, with the exception of large

corner lots. From the curb to every white, blue, brown, and off-green house, there was:

- a small rectangular patch of grass with a maple tree planted center;
- a public sidewalk;
- a well-attended front lawn;
- a private sidewalk leading to the rarely used front porch and door, beside which hung commonly the American flag;
- another small angular patch of grass to the right; and,
- a garden area that abutted the foundation, always made pretty and welcoming.

Most homeowners landscaped this with an array of flowers. In our case, Dad planted rose bushes, pine like shrubs, and some sort of covering vine. Every spring our front yard smelled of mulch and manure. On warm summer nights, hose in hand, Mom and Dad sat on the porch and watered the lawn and shrubbery by the light of a midnight moon. As Autumn approached, Dad would prune the rose bushes back to nubs. I was always amazed that they sprang back in Spring with such speed and vigor. I think of this every time I cut back the roses bushes that beautify my front yard.

In our backyard, for many summers, Dad tended a garden of cherry tomatoes, peppers, cucumbers, and more, just as his mother, cultivated her larger garden in Lewiston, New York. There was a huge, climbable tree growing center back, while another arched over from an adjacent property. Occasionally, a friend and I sat amidst the tree branches and sang *Born Free*, from the wonderful film by the same name.

Above ground pools, 18 to 24 feet in diameter and five (5) feet deep, dotted many yards. They were a constant source of summer fun. In 1975, after the premier of *Jaws*, I was terrified of night swimming when I realized the shark was bigger than our pool. For all your cinematic visions filled with wonder, humanity and inspiring potentialities,

15

thank you, Mr. Spielberg.

To quench the muggy thirst of summer heat, we ran through the sprinkler, or created slippery slides by laying out long strips of plastic and dousing them with the water hose. My Dad was constantly aggravated by the inevitable damage to his well-tended lawn. One winter, our neighbors built an ice rink. They set up a wood frame, filled and froze layers of plastic sheets, then hosted ice skating parties. When spring arrived and the rink melted, the lawn was damaged beyond repair. Expensive new sod was planted. I loved the smell and barefooted feel of it.

At night, we used to go fence hopping. Starting in someone's backyard, we ran stealthily hopping fence after fence. There was no malicious intent. We did it solely for the thrill. Dogs would go crazy and people would occasionally come out and shout. Granted, some things did get trampled and we sometimes ate from random gardens, but no harm was ever intended. It was fun - pure and simple. Nowadays, I would fear getting shot.

Our Home

Driveways led to unattached single or double, backyard garages. Chain link fences, four or five (4 to 5) feet high, marked property lines. The closest home entrance was the side door. Entering here, a small landing led stairs directly down to the basement, or, stairs up to the kitchen and first floor, then onwards to the second. Either way, I go - stairs down, or stairs up - I arrive at so many stories, so much life and learning and love.

Stairs down. Our basement.

At the base of the staircase, to the immediate right is a door. Straight ahead is another. These link an L-shaped area that houses the home heating oil tank, a furnace, a workshop, a washer and dryer, two (2) utility sinks and a storage area. The floor is rough and unfinished. Small, rectangular windows originate at ground level and meet the ceiling, allowing in very little light.

Three things about this area; one: When the only bathroom in the house was occupied, my brothers and I would pee in, but not rinse or clean, the cement utility sinks. "Boys, stop peeing in the basement sinks!" Mom would yell.

Two: A laundry chute connected the first floor bathroom to the basement. I always thought it cool to drop our dirty clothes into a basket placed one floor below.

Three: At one point, my parents kicked my brother out of the house. I would be home alone from school for lunch and find him trying to break-in via these small, ground level windows. I experienced such conflicting loyalties between my parents and my brother, eventually siding with the former and not letting in the latter.

At the base of the staircase to the left, is a large, semi-finished room, darkly tiled. On the far wall, a short, door-less frame marks entrance to the fruit cellar; it is dank and musty smelling, lit by a single bulb, hanging on a pull chain.

A dart board, kitchen style table and a few chairs are in the corner. Annually, my father would spend a weekend here calculating taxes. *"Boys,"* my Mom would say, *"don't disturb your Father. He's really busy downstairs."*

I wish I inherited more of my father's fiscal discipline. He and Mom have a lovely, comfortable life. Not always the case, I remember overhearing a parental argument that led to Mom cutting up her credit cards in a severe bout of self- aggravation, scissored with a conquering energy that fueled her affirmation, *"Enough is enough. Carolyn."* Like mother like son. I have made similar declarations to the Universe about a myriad of topics.

There was a simple wooden bench with black, faux leather seats and a buffet cabinet; on it sits a small, rabbit eared, black and white television.

It was July, 1969 and upstairs and outside, the sticky, humid heat of summer permeated while our new

17

basement was cool. We had just moved in and were surrounded by unpacked boxes. My brothers and I were roughhousing as the television emitted a fritzy, sporadic picture.

"*Boys, come on,*" my parents admonished, "*This is important. Stop playing and watch. It is history.*" We did and it was. Neil Armstrong stepped out of a lunar module and onto the moon, just as I spilled a milkshake all over my brother.

I am so happy my parents instilled an appreciation for events and world history. Like the lunar landing, they ensured we witnessed the news surrounding Robert Kennedy's assassination, Nixon's resignation, presidential inaugurals, and other civic events, excluding civil rights unrest. I remember my cloudy uncertainty over news coverage related to Vietnam and what it all meant, and I know exactly where I was when the space shuttle Challenger exploded in 1986.

For certain personal happenings, however, my parents presented a united front in shielding us from perceived sufferings. Several instances come to mind, one in particular, regarding our dog, Charlie.

Dad surprised us one Sunday after church, by stopping at the animal rescue shelter... "*Boys,*" he said, "*Let's get a dog.*" We were ecstatic. Charlie was the mixed matched runt of the litter.

Years later, he suffered from severe epileptic fits and became a danger to himself and others so he was put down. We woke up one Saturday morning and he was gone. Dad had taken him to the veterinarian one final time; we never had the chance to say goodbye. I remain uncertain as to how I feel about this. I can understand Dad's rationale for avoiding the pain and tear filled fest such goodbyes would have created, nevertheless.

One thing: Decades later, while living in Nepal, I did some work with a publisher named Lal. One day I walked into his compound and spied a docile dog curled up in the corner. Knowing that Lal did not have a dog, I asked him about this particular puppy; he said he did not know. It had simply and unassumingly appeared the preceding day. I began recounting that we had a childhood pet named Charlie. With the utterance of this sound, this name – Charlie - the stray dog went positively apocalyptic. His head quickly turned. He up and ran at me wildly, tail wagging in a blur – kissing, jumping, licking and loving.

Every time I said, "Charlie," his frenzy increased. I visited three (3) days running and each day the same occurred. When I was not there, Lal said that the dog barely moved.

The fourth day I went, he was gone. Thank you, Charlie, for allowing me the opportunity to finally say goodbye. And, hello, again.

Stairs up. I am in the kitchen.

Sun from the front window illuminated the lime green wallpaper, olive green linoleum floor, and maple colored dining table where we religiously shared family meals. A white phone with a long, overstretched and twisted cord hung just before the entrance to the living room.

For years, we had a two (2) party, shared line. Either a dial tone or a voice greeted you when lifting the receiver. At some point, we got a private line.

A counter divided the kitchen. To my right, a Frigidaire met the counters and the cupboards where I used to hide and play. A mirror hung above two (2) sinks. There was no dishwasher. Hand washing was one of our chores. Even now, I hand wash as my dishwasher sits, unused. To my left were a white draped window and an electric stove.

One day, Mom was two (2) doors down and I decided unsupervised candle making was in order. I started melting wax on the stove and somehow spilled it on the electric heating element. Flames quickly leapt as smoke spiraled upwards, then hovered. I doused the fire with the baking soda kept in the fridge to eliminate odors. Rushing to clean it up and thinking that Mom would never know was a fantasy.

To this day, I have a love of fresh food, simple cooking and healthy eating due to the many wonderful memories prepped and prepared in this kitchen.

On cold winter mornings before school, we stayed warm by sitting in front of the stove as we ate. I remember grace at dinner: *"Bless us O Lord and these thy gifts which we are about to receive from thy bounty. Through Christ our Lord, Amen."*

I remember Mom's signature dish, lasagna, and helping stuff the Thanksgiving turkey, then placing it in the oven at 250 degrees to cook overnight. Mom basted it every two (2) hours. By morning, the skin was a perfect, crinkly, crusty, tasty brown and the entire house smelled delicious. I woke up literally drooling, although truth be known, I am a drooler anyways.

I remember capturing all the goodness of the fresh fruit and tomatoes we had picked joyously on excursions to surrounding farms.

Early June marked the start of the Summer and Fall, fruit and vegetable picking seasons. Peaches, cherries, blueberries, pears, apples, cucumbers and tomatoes followed the first strawberries. Our family would pick, freeze, mash, cut and can everything. In the ensuing months, when eating spaghetti topped with her home-made sauce, Mom would always warn,

"Watch out for the bay leaves."

Bottom line: an endless stream of jar sterilization, cutting, peeling, and mashing led to the ultimate pay off – running to the fruit cellar in the dead of winter and retrieving a quart of our hard work – applesauce for our pork chops, or peaches with cottage cheese for breakfast. Nothing ever tasted better, ever.

My parents periodically hosted Friday night cocktail parties for upwards of 30 guests - mainly Dad's work colleagues and their spouses. The preceding week, I loved helping Mom roll dozens of Swedish meatballs and cutting strips of beef for a big pot of bourguignon. Fresh shrimp, crab with cream cheese, fruit platters, cheese and crackers, and all sorts of other nibbly bits were served. We placed special slats to extend the dining table and used the silver cutlery and china. Shiny, copper serving trays lit by the glow of sterno-lamps warmed the meatballs.

As an adult, I trace my love of hosting parties to these special nights and I realize now how Mom was contributing to my Dad's success. Also, one of these parties was the source of my first scandalous memory.

At some point during every party, my brothers and I were sent upstairs to bed but I could never sleep. I would sneak down to the bottom stair, sit knees curled, and listen. Here is what I once heard.

Unknown man: *"Violet, how did you get such a fine son (my Dad)?"*

Grandma Trask: *"Well, that's easy,"* she replied, pausing *for dramatic effect in a room suddenly silent, "A long... Slow... Screw."*

Everyone erupted in laughter and I was shocked, knowing that I was privy to an utterance so clearly adults only.

> *QtoP7: Did I ever vandalize or deface public property?*
> *What did I do and how do I feel about it now?*

> *QtoP8: What is my view of money?*
> *Has my view changed over the years?*

> *QtoP9: From what did my parents' shield me?*
> *Did I feel always safe?*

Many of the same men who attended these parties were also members of the Clammers Club. The Clammers built a halved, 55 gallon drum steamer and hosted a rotating garage party. They bought clams by the 50lb bag, lots of beer and party foods, then steamed, shucked and consumed all day into the night. The stinky steam wafted through nearby yards. One year, Dad hosted a January session as a snow storm raged. They celebrated in their t-shirts while the world froze beyond the walls. The fun and camaraderie was palpable.

One thing: Fizzy drinks only made a home appearance at events like this and holidays, otherwise it was fresh juices, milk and water. It pains me to see anyone, particularly kids, drinking sodas for breakfast. It creates such unhealthy habits that ripple negatively throughout our bodies.

At 17, I began working in a supermarket so I sometimes brought lobsters home and cooked them up with Mom. She brought out her linen napkins and rings. We would talk over a glass of wine. They were such special moments, love plumped for a mother and her son.

One thing: Growing up, the drinking age was 18. In 1984, President Reagan, at the urging of MADD (Mothers Against Drunk Driving), coerced States into raising their legal drinking age to 21 by threatening to withhold federal highway funding. It totally worked. Grandfathered in, I was the last year for the 18 designation.

As I share stories about drinking at what now seems a very early age, this is the reason. Further, as a socially acceptable intoxicant, alcohol was a topic of responsible conversation. Its' use was relatively balanced and woven into our family life. The same could not be said for the arrival of other substances during adolescence.

An archway marks the transition from the kitchen to the light blue carpeted living room. The front door, a rocking chair and a large picture window was to the left. Opposite was a large, patterned, sofa bed couch with lacquered end tables either side. In the far corner was a grayish lounge chair on which I befriended a hand-held Swedish massager when no one else was home. This same chair was the designated site for corporal punishment.

When we misbehaved, Mom would place us over her knees and say, *"This hurts me more than it hurts you,"* while smacking our butt, always and only, with her hand. Her statement still intrigues me.

Lots of family photos and several paintings hung on the walls, including a nature inspired watercolor, painted by a neighbor who displayed at the Albright Knox Art Gallery and painted in Monet's garden. A wooden bench for sitting and storage marked the hallway that lead to my parents' bedroom, the bathroom and the family TV room. Stairs ascended to the second floor.

Together with the parties, I most remember our living room as the place for annual Christmas joy. A fresh cut tree, illuminated by a string of colored lights and draped in twinkling tinsel and ornaments, bathed the space. Each year, our family frequented a local tree farm to select and cut two (2), short needled, blue spruce pines - one for our home and one for Grandma Trask's.

The living room was the place where I danced for my Grandma Feeley when she babysat. Swooping in from the kitchen, twisting and flailing about, Gram would clap and cheer me on, *"Ooooooooo,"* she crooned, *"you are quite the little dancer."* At bath time, she would sit tub side and sweetly ask with a rising intonation, *"Did you wash your dinghy?"* Tucking me into bed, she would practice this weird form of back massage that was at once, both a gentle pinch and a cringe inducing slap. Her unconditional love and support were priceless.

Two things; one: Genuine self–acceptance has been an on-going challenge. In a culture which inundates us with messages of self-loathing, it can be difficult. While I never ever doubted her love, Mom often told me when I was recounting something I had accomplished, "Peter, SPS," meaning, "self -praise stinks." As a child, this befuddled me. What was the boundary between doing well, taking pride, then speaking about it, while simultaneously avoiding the stank of arrogance? How does one promote one's accomplishments while remaining modest, humble? The challenge posed by these questions remains.

Two: I have always been thin; some say skinny. I prefer the word lean. I have allowed matters of physicality to sometimes overwhelm me. At one point, my brothers and I cruelly took to calling Mom, "Big C" because she had gained some weight. This rightfully hurt and Dad quickly squelched such talk. Shortly thereafter though, I would pass through the living room and find Mom doing floor exercises in the dark, seemingly, somehow embarrassed. And, while I cannot know exactly what she was feeling or thinking, I believe that there have been times when I have thought and felt exactly the self-same.

I always wanted a piano but we lacked space so one year we got a small electronic keyboard. Your right hand struck the keys while the left pressed cord buttons to provide harmony. I would play and sing for hours. Mom has always had a good ear and could find a tune quite easily. Sometimes, during the parties, she would lead everyone in song.

On cold winter mornings, we sat in front of the furnace vent to get warm. My Dad kept our house about 62 degrees at night and when no one was home, otherwise, 70 degrees. We always wore warm clothing. As a matter of fact, my parents slept with their bedroom window cracked an inch, even in the freezing cold of winter believing it improved sleep. I agree.

Proceeding down the hallway, the bathroom and parental bedroom doors met at a 90 degree angle. Numerous times when sick, I rushed downstairs and fell a few feet short of the toilet and vomited in front of their door. "*Gads, Peter,*" Dad would say, "*Can't you just make it another three feet?* I guess I could not.

My mother had a thing about having a carpeted bathroom. With three (3) boys who insisted on peeing upright, I never understood her futile, unending battle to keep the carpet clean and fresh.

My parents' bedroom was off limits. Dad is a coin collector and I once stole some old coins he kept in a small, felt lined wooden box atop their dresser. I bought candy at the local convenience store. When caught, Dad was angry, and yet acknowledged the good fortune of the clerk in finding such valuable coins.

One thing: This is so wonderfully typical of my Dad – always seeing multiple perspectives surrounding a single issue, always expanding his thoughts to include the impacts of a given circumstance on those involved. When I came out of the closet, he first expressed love and support, then turned to my Mom and said (paraphrasing), "Well, Carolyn, we need to be more aware of the things are friends might say and call them on any slurs." Thank you so very much, Dad and Mom.

In the back corner of our home, a couch, a chair, a throw rug and a small black and white television furnished the TV room. We had five (5) channels. ABC, NBC, and CBS with local #29 being the source for Saturday morning wrestling and roller derby, while PBS broadcasts at #17 included the British classics *Monty Python's Flying Circus* and *Fawlty Towers.*

Dad would watch sports while ironing his work clothes. Every night, the late news began with the statement and question, *"It is 11 o'clock. Do you know where your children are?"*

On Friday nights, we could watch the 11:30 movie, often a *Planet of the Apes*, or classic Universal such as *Dracula, the Mummy, or the Werewolf.* Hammer Studios made a vampire film with Christopher Lee that scared me for years. I loved these films so much that I built an extensive model collection. I was later upset when we blew them up and scared all the neighborhood dogs.

We got Home Box Office (HBO) in 1981.

25

During my senior year, I skipped school with a friend. We got drunk on 151 Rum and Coke and watched *The Way We Were* over and over again. I do not remember much of what happened, but the next morning as I lie anxiously and sick in bed, I overheard my Mom and Dad discussing me. My Dad saying, *"Carolyn, I guarantee he has learned his lesson. Nothing we can do would make it worse."* He was correct. I have never done anything like that again.

The staircase to the second floor reached a landing and turned right 90° up four (4) more steps. Here was Adam's bedroom through which you passed to reach the larger room Todd and I shared. At the landing was a wall space cupboard where my Mom stored her teaching supplies, including a mimeograph machine with stacks of carbon paper. To this day, I easily recall the smell of the ink and the *kerchunk, kerchunk* sound as you hand cranked the copies.

Adam's room had a small clothes closet, and in it, another smaller door leading to an unfinished attic where luggage and stuff were stored. For the longest time, due to Hammer Films, I could not pass by these doors in the dark for fear that harm was lurking just beyond sight.

Once older and employed, Adam would spend money on *Playboy* and *Penthouse* magazines, later, the more hardcore *Hustler*. He kept them under his mattress. Yes, I actually read *Playboy*. The pictures were nice, but relatively uninteresting. *Penthouse* and *Hustler*, though, always had at least one (1), male included photo shoot. I would tuck the issue into my back pants and sneak it into the bathroom.

QtoP10: What do I think of magazines like these?

I remember hearing Adam and Mom fight when she would find his magazines and tear them up. I was too young at the time to understand more fully the many issues at play. It was my parents' way, regardless, to segment or compartmentalize topics like this. *"This is between your older brother and us,*" they would tell me. In today's jargon, a teachable moment was missed.

Years later, Adam moved out and I took over his room. One night HBO broadcast *Personal Best*, a groundbreaking, lesbian themed film starring Mariel Hemmingway, set in the world of track and field. I watched upstairs while my Mom obviously watched downstairs because the next day she tried to engage me in a conversation about it. Primarily influenced by my fear of full disclosure, the conversation did not go far. I greatly appreciated her effort, though, in speaking to such a mutually discomforting topic.

Todd and I shared a bedroom with a single closet, two (2) twin beds, dressers in opposing corners, and Aunt Ruthie's old, large, white corner desk.

One Easter, Dad won a three (3) foot chocolate bunny and I consumed a solid ear. That night, I swam in chocolate vomit and my parents had to buy a new mattress. Similarly, I once over indulged while cherry picking and did the exact same thing.

Twenty-fine years later, I received a massage modality that subtly shifted my cranial bones with the help of the therapist's pinky finger, a baby condom and a dab of Vaseline. Vivid memories surfaced and flooded my taste buds with a fresh cherry flavor.

One for the bucket, two for me.

There was a window near my bed. Sometimes, Adam would stay out too late, forget his key, and be locked out. Hoping to get in, he would throw snowballs at the window and try to wake me up. Rather than heading downstairs, I would pull the covers tight over my head, scared. This happened more than once and I really do not know why.

In 1976, *Charlie's Angels* premiered and changed the world in their own ways. I loved them all. Three (3) women starred as private detectives in this cheesy, groundbreaking show. Farrah Fawcett, in her first, and only, year on the show, became a cultural phenomenon. I loved her stunning, free spirited beauty. Her swimsuit poster remains the best-selling poster of all time.

I bought it, and an extra-large, poster imprinted, yellow t-shirt at KMart. Both hung on the wall near my bed. Shortly after putting them up, Dad came in and took them down, telling me they were inappropriate. Was it her nipples?

Todd loved drumming. At one point, he studied with the lead percussionist for the Buffalo Philharmonic Orchestra. He practiced his rhythms on a 5" x 5" practice pad and shook the house when he played the complete set in the basement. Each night in bed, headphones on and records playing, Todd concerted wild, air band sessions.

Several times, I came home from school and found him and a female classmate barricaded inside our room. He had moved his bed to block the door and would yell, "Go away," amidst new and unfamiliar, real life sounds. I never really sat and listened. I just went downstairs.

Weekday Routine

Growing up, our family had only one car. Around this fact, routine was built. It is amazing how routines become so quickly, unquestionably common. When we know nothing different, we have nothing against which to compare. You simply make do with what you have.

My father worked at a factory in downtown Buffalo as a Human Resources Manager. My mother taught in Niagara Falls. Both were 40 minute commutes. Although technically a substitute teacher, Mom taught consistently.

She regularly took long term, maternity leave positions, or extended PTOs postings. For years, the following was a basic time line of our weekday routine.

<u>Between 6 – 8:05am</u>

Mom and Dad got up and ready. Mom came upstairs, woke us up, and then took Dad to the bus stop. My brothers and I got ourselves and our breakfasts ready.

Two things; one: Mom returned and made sure we were underway. She would usually prepare something for dinner, often a crock pot meal. It was during this time that I loved watching Barbara Walters, Tom Brokaw, Bryant Gumbel, Jane Pauley and Gene Shalit on the Today show.

Two: From the Today show, to the network news, to The View, I have always loved the strength, humor and intelligence of Ms. Walters. She is a groundbreaking woman with an extraordinary life history, Ms. Goldberg, I love you, too. Such a legacy these ladies are. We are all so very fortunate. And, to see Ms. Pauley now on Sunday Morning!

7:45: Mom left for work; and,
8:05: We left for school.

<u>Between 3:15 – 6ish</u>

We came home;

Two things; one: When younger, we were caretaken at a neighbor's house after school. Here, I learned about soap operas and General Hospital (GH). The creator of GH was a Buffalo native and our city was the fictional setting of Port Charles. Wildly popular, local pubs ran GH Happy Hours from 3-4 and college classes were empty. The marriage of Luke and Laura rivaled that of Charles and Diana.

Two: When older, we went directly home and were in charge of getting dinner in the oven. During their 4pm broadcast, I fell in love with classic Elvis movies and was inspired by Ms. Winfrey. Her groundbreaking, town hall style shows about HIV and racism etched deep and profound memories. Thank you, Ms. Winfrey, for all you are, have shared, and are still becoming. For years, you have been my friend. May you live a continually long,

31

blessed and bountiful life that radiates understanding and happiness for the benefit all sentient beings.

4:15: Mom came home and left to pick up Dad;
5:30: Mom and Dad arrived home; and,
6ish: Mom finalized dinner and we ate when Dad was
ready.

One thing: If my father worked late, I often joined my mother on the drive downtown to pick him up. I loved that she waited in the car and let me go into the factory alone. I would excitedly check-in with the security guard and pass down a bland, uninspiring hallway and break area to my father's office. On the way out, he would buy me an ice cream sandwich – vanilla with chocolate wafers. It cost a dime.

On reflection, I realize how much my parents were doing and wonder their levels of exhaustion. Moreover, I see now how this routine taught me about organizing time, the need to work together, about cooking and personal responsibility. For years, my mother and two (2) colleagues carpooled to Niagara Falls. They rotated driving duties weekly. I remember being impressed by the cooperation, money saving and decreased driving hassles.

One thing: A lesson in civil disobedience; travel from the ToT to Niagara Falls means crossing over Grand Island via toll bridges. At four (4) tolls per day, five (5) days per week it got pricey. One year, the state authority announced it was doubling the toll and people were very angry. In protest, drivers began paying their toll fee in large bills or pockets full of small change. Toll collectors were overwhelmed by the backed-up chaos. If only for a while, the changes were rescinded. The power of peaceful, polite civil disobedience is great when unified voices are heard.

The following weekend routine rarely wavered for the first 16 years of my life. Saturday was a free day filled with friends and fun. Sunday was church, scrambled eggs cooked by Dad, lunch at Grandma Feeley's, and dinner at Grandma Trask's where my favorite Aunt and cousins

32

often joined us. On the 50 minute, late night drive home we listened to classic, radio programs like *The Shadow* and *Orson Wells Theater*.

Elementary School

Before reminiscing more about this routine, my weekday school experience at Brighton Elementary school (now a senior living facility) deserves a proper mention. For starters, this is how my mother taught me to walk to school alone. We first walked together the entire way. As the days passed, she stopped short and I continued as she waited and watched. One day, I proceeded then turned back to look. She was gone and it was alright. I continued onward.

> *QtoP11: Did I ever receive corporal punishment?*
> *What do I think of it?*

> *QtoP12: What aspects of my personality do I*
> *easily accept? Perhaps dislike? Reject?*

> *QtoP13: At which interpersonal skills do I excel?*
> *Which need improvement?*

I attended Brighton from Kindergarten to Grade Six. It was a typical three (3) floor, red brick school building with a flag pole out front, and endless marbled rows of wall lockers inside.

In my first few years, I remember our *"Duck and Cover"* drills. When a siren squealed, we stopped what we were doing and ducked under our desks, or, filed into the hallway and sat on the ground facing our lockers. What an extraordinarily false way of engendering a sense of protection and survivability in the event of nuclear horror. Such were the fearful days of cold war living.

Reflecting on my childhood, I realize how much I loved learning and the teachers who made it possible. My kindergarten teacher was Ms. Hammond. I remember her name because she was plump and I associated that with ham. I crushed on my first grade teacher, Ms. Kerwin. Years later, when The *Mary Tyler Moore Show* began, I thought, "*She is just like Ms. Kerwin!*" The thing I most remember about my second-grade teacher, Ms. Barnett, was her height. She was really tall for a lady, 6'ish.

My third-grade teacher, and lover of ice hockey, Ms. Pearl Bouche, deserves special mention because her Alaskan travel stories and mesmerizing photos. I loved when she shared them because I sensed a future of exciting places and inspiring adventures.

One thing: Years later, Grandma Feeley gave me a round trip ticket to Alaska for graduation. My best friend, Craig, who was living in Kansas at the time, hitchhiked to Seattle where he boarded a plane for Anchorage. We arrived within two (2) hours of each other and set off on an extraordinary, one (1) month backpacking experience through the Alaskan wilderness.

We went north two (2) weeks to Mt. Denali (formerly Mt. McKinley), then south to Kenai Fjords National Park. Within the first 24 hours of landing, we were face to face with a moose, 150 feet from a black bear sitting on its' hind side, plucking berries from a bush, and bald eagles soaring with my plucked heart.

In third-grade, I experienced something unusual for it speaks to my earliest inkling of spirituality. I recounted this tale several years ago (*Realizing a Spiritual Path*) in an anthology series entitled, *Life Choices: It's Never Too Late*, compiled by my dear friend and mentor Judi Moreo. It is with utmost gratitude that I share an abbreviated section:

****

"Line up single file, everyone. Count off and make sure all your classmates are here," called out my 3rd grade teacher, Ms. Pearl Broche. 'We don't want to leave anyone behind....'

Thousands of us marched single file that day, out the many exits.... Students from schools across the city on a field trip to Kleinhans Music Hall had just seen the Buffalo Philharmonic Orchestra perform a sampling of classics such as Beethoven's 9th.... As we boarded the standard yellow bus for our 30 minute return to Brighton, I took the window seat in the back right corner, and tried to meditate by uninterruptedly counting to ten as I breathed slowly....

Every Sunday, for the first 16 years of my life, my mother woke my two older brothers and me up around 8 am for breakfast and the 9:30 service. We were members of a Lutheran church in Kenmore.... I was baptized and took my 1st communion there, served as an altar boy, sang in the choir, joined in youth group activities, and went to an affiliated summer church camp along the shores of Lake Cayuga in southwest New York State.... Sometime in the early 80s, during "Seniors Week" at camp, along the shores of Lake Cayuga, something happened to forever both my religious understanding and self-perception ... A group of us were circled on the grass in front of the main lodge.... The presiding Pastor approached and sat with us (and asked)..., 'Why are you all really here this week?

What is the point of our gathering?'

Immediately, my mind answered, "to be with my friends," but I choose not to speak, nor did anyone else. A long, awkward silence ensued. Our eyes darted around, each of us not sure what to say, not knowing the desired response.... In the workings of my mind, I suddenly understood what he wanted to hear.... What Pastor wanted to hear was,

'We are here to worship God.'

"Wow. Sorry," I thought, "I cannot speak for others, but, I am surely not here for that reason," at least not in the manner by which I had been raised; at least not in the manner by which I had been ushered to believe; at least not in the manner by which I had yet to reflect on life

35

through the prism of my own experiences and perspectives. I was there for friends and fun.

For me, this was the start of realizing my spiritual path – looking at life as a thinking, feeling, cognizant and self-aware human being. This is where I began to cultivate the personal skills and steady resolve needed to genuinely question and explore the inner unfolding of my own, unique spirit.... I knew then, that I needed to make a conscious decision to distill and reflect on the veracity of the truths instilled within.

Sometimes we must ask difficult questions of ourselves and others, facing uncomfortable truths about how we may truly feel. We must grapple with the seeming hypocrisy and apparent contradictions that abound. But, this is the work required if we are to arrive at a place that satisfactorily answers our larger questions of life, ultimately making us more peaceful, loving people.

As we boarded the bus for our 30 minute return to Brighton Elementary, I took the window seat in the back right corner, and tried to meditate by uninterruptedly counting to ten as I breathed slowly.

Fifteen years passed before I remembered the significance of this simple and profound action; before I sought out and found answers that resonated with my unique, human constellation; before I began realizing a spiritual path that supports, sustains, inspires and guides the swirl of my re-occurring lives (www.judimoreo.com).

****

I do not remember my fourth grade teacher. My fifth grade teacher was some man who once got angry and threw a desk and a student across a room. He got fired.

My sixth-grade teacher, Ms. Geraldine Batt, was exceptional. My mother had heard of her teaching talents and successfully petitioned the Principal for my admittance into her class. I am so fortunate she did. I was ten. Why was she so amazing? Here's why: the entire year was a journey of self-directed learning with Ms. Batt as the guide.

At the start of each school day, the around-the-room chalkboards listed all the class work we needed to accomplish. We had the choice of doing whatever we wanted, whenever we wanted, with whomever we wished, as long as we successfully completed everything by day's end. Along the way, Ms. Batt constantly monitored our progress and was in total control, while putting us in charge.

She filled the classroom with posters and pictures, and lined the shelves with plants, pets and experiments. She constantly ran contests whose prizes included pop rocks, raving neon glow sticks, even a ride in her VW drop top "*Thing.*" Imagine the liabilities of doing as such today.

We brought in cardboard boxes and cut them to make a three (3) sided cubby that surrounded our standard, wooden desk. We personalized it with pictures and things that inspired – an early version of an office carol.

One time, she had us run throughout our neighborhoods and collect crabapples from front yard trees – the same trees that years later provided homecoming ammunition.

We brought them to school and made crabapple jelly and fruit rolls. We also made strawberry jam. I started learning French. We visited museums and went on hiking field trips. I remember on one such trip, she stressed we were not allowed to take anything - just enjoy the nature and leave only footprints. Thinking myself special, I took a stick and stored it in the sleeve of my jacket.

On the way home, Ms. Batt conducted a surprise inspection and found that another student had taken something. I do not remember what it was. All I knew was my shaky fear of being caught. Luckily, I was not. Should I have been?

One final thing before speaking of our weekend routine; I felt then, that Ms. Batt and Ms. Hope, a fifth grade teacher, resonated as life partners. I believe it to this day. They owned property and traveled extensively together. They lunched and bantered in the halls and left school together. I admired them both. Surely their friendship was more than platonic.

Fast forward to the 21st century and some still advocate prohibiting gay and lesbian folks from teaching children. It would be funny, were it not so sad, the thought. To said advocates, please wake up. Chances are high that your educational history included gay and lesbian teachers, whether you knew it or not.

Ms. Batt and Ms. Hope positively impacted the hearts and minds of thousands of young lives. They planted the seeds of success and encouraged our potentials. Through them, we better understood our emerging senses of self. We should all experience the good fortune of being guided by such exceptional teachers.

Two final, and first, memories related to Brighton are etched deep. Many years later when I shared them with my Mom, she asked, *"How do you remember that?"* I do not know. I just do. She asked the same of my bus, meditation memory.

Gym class was held in a large room, commonly halved by retractable walls. Boys and girls played separately. Two (2) week blocks rotated throughout the year – volleyball, basketball, etc.... During the square dance section, some boys were forced to wear special smocks to mark them as the female in the dance partnership. A huge ruckus always ensued as young egos were threatened. It never bothered me.

One thing: Decades later, a dear friend and very manly man would cause me to ponder seriously what I thought of men – gay or straight – and their relationship to womens' clothing.

During the obstacle course section, the walls opened and girls and boys played together. One day, as class finished and we all ran to our respective locker rooms, chatter centered on girls and getting married and having kids. I remained quiet, thinking,

"Hmmmm.... I do not want to marry a girl. Why would you ever do that?" I did not experience this in a *"oooo.... yucky girls"* kind of young, boy way. No, the answer felt self-evident. I was in first grade and five (5) years old.

Weekend Routine

My weekend routine rarely wavered. On special occasions, instead of visiting Grandma Feeley, we brunched at a local restaurant where a Lionel, toy train choo-chooed overhead. Mom sometimes prevented my brothers and me from returning to the food line because she was embarrassed by our excessive consumption. *"No, boys,"* she would say, *"You do not need an eighth plate."* Sunday brunch is my favorite meal - friends, good food, drink and a bit of lazy jazz followed by a mid-afternoon nap.

Everything changed one fateful Sunday morning when Mom shouted, *"Get up boys. Time for church,"* and Adam replied, *"I am not going."* Todd soon stopped and I was the sole child to join my parents at church. Sunday school, youth group, special holiday breakfasts: all were fine by me. I made dear friends and enjoyed my time there. I derived deviate pleasure from the Sunday school teacher who taught us the following dinner grace: *"Rub a dub, dub. Thanks for the grub, yeah God!"* Some folks were upset.

The pungent beauty of Easter's purple, pink and white lilacs lingers still. I can hear the choir's glorious, uplifting performance of Handel's Messiah. One year, their rendition was so inspiring that the congregation gave it a standing ovation and some people were offended.

"You do not applaud in Church," they argued. *"Please,"* I say, *"The world needs all of the joy we can muster."*

39

Goose bumps precede my tears when feeling this magnificent piece purely performed.

On Christmas Eve, the fresh cut, 25 foot, long-needled, pine glowed white. Hundreds of hand-held candles flickered at the beauty of *Silent Night* and quivered to a rousing chorus of *Joy to the World* as we processed out. What was not to like? To this I answer:

The suffering of hypocrisy discomforts me. The superior judgments people render in the name of their God while they themselves, are internally struggling and succumbing to the common frailties of human existence.

Devout followers of differing religions steal or rail against sexual deviancy while committing sexual abuse, or, kill in a said name. These are obvious examples. So many subtle ones exist. It is all so very sad. May the dogma of religion give way to authentic and universal spirituality. May genuine compassion and wisdom soon and forever enlighten and uplift.

The Niagara River links Lake Erie and Lake Ontario with the Niagara and Horseshoe waterfalls cascading in between on the American and Canadian sides, respectively. Below this spectacle, the mighty river flows swiftly onward, taking a 90 degree turn before entering Lake Ontario. In doing so, it creates a giant whirlpool.

Grandmas Feeley and Trask both lived nearby, in Niagara Falls and Lewiston.

Four things; one: Horseshoe Falls is often deemed the more picturesque of the two. Therefore, many movies commonly depict Horseshoe Falls as Niagara Falls. Arghhh...

Two: One day on his way to work, Dad tells of witnessing a person, just above the Falls in the middle of the river clinging to a rock and screaming; they had recanted on their suicidal impulse. A helicopter attempted a rescue, only to be pulled into the river by the panicked outreach of this terrified soul. Dad says he sat there for hours watching it unfold. Thankfully, it ended safely for all, except the helicopter.

Three: One weekend a year, along the narrow banks of the Niagara before it opens wide into Lake Ontario, the smelt run. Smelt are eight to ten (8 to 10) inch, sardine like fish. In the dark of night, hundreds of us made the trek riverside with metal, meshed baskets attached to a long wooden pole. One dunk into the smelt running river and it was filled with unlimited free fish. We would pack a Coleman cooler then lug it back up. Mom would clean and freeze them. Honestly, I liked the catching and not so much the eating. They tasted far too fishy for me.

Four: Artpark is a stunning, state funded performance venue downstream from Whirlpool State Park. It has both indoor and outdoor lawn seating for concerts, philharmonic performances and musicals. In summer it hosted extended art events and theater study groups. My dear junior and senior high friend, Catherine Shane, spent a summer there studying musical theater. I loved the place.

Maternal Grandmother

Grandma Feeley was quite a looker. Born in 1905, a flapper era photo shows Gram dressed in a full length fur coat with pearls, capturing her elegance and class. Mom says that she never wore a pair of pants in her life - always and only a skirt. Gram worked full time as a telephone operator. Aligned with dozens of women and donning headphones and hands free microphones, they patched through incoming calls by appropriately matching the correct retractable cord with the proper plug, much like Ernestine on *Laugh In*. I love you, Ms. Tomlin and you too, Ms. Hawn. Both such blessed, radiant spirits.

At some point, she met and married Grandpa Bill. He worked for the Port Authority for 30 years as a toll collector at the bridge between the United States and Canada; he passed in 1967. My earliest memory is standing on Grandpa Bill's lap and pulling at his nose. Gram's cooking was love. Apple pies were weekly treats.

On special occasions, she made lemon meringue and coconut cream pies. I honor my Grandma Feeley whenever possible, by finishing my meal with an always 2nd place slice of coconut cream.

Each Sunday, we arrived around one. After hellos and grandma kisses, my brothers and I ran to her wooden candy dish. Over the years, it contained a variety of sweets but my favorite was always the caramel strip candy that hugged a sugary white filling. Occasionally, there was a variety box of chocolates and we would poke the bottom of each candy to see what was inside. Coconut rocked. Those with pink cream were returned to the box for consideration by others and a scolding.

While always immaculately clean, sparingly decorated, and forever smelling good, the house had a pervasive feeling of *do not touch*. All items sat in regularly dusted spots. Nothing ever seemed disturbed or out of place. Decades later, Mom told me she was fearful that we might knock something over, or somehow mess something up. Luckily, to my recollection, we never did.

A big, cutting edge Zenith color television sat in one corner of the living room. Gram loved *The Lawrence Welk Show*. As lunch cooked, my brothers and I enjoyed football and regular, Sunday re-broadcasts of: *Jason and the Argonaughts,* all the Don Knott's films, especially *The Incredible Mr. Limpet,* and a rotating selection of family friendly films deemed appropriate for Sunday afternoons. Sometimes we played Checkers or Chinese Checkers with marbles.

There was a screened in porch, a steep staircase to the basement, a kitchen, a living room, two (2) bedrooms, and an unfinished attic with a finished spare room. Each Spring and Autumn we prepped Gram's house for the coming Summer and Winter by cleaning and swapping out the 15, hand-made, house screens and windows.

The house itself was aluminum sided. It shared a two (2) lane, blacktop driveway with Lebanese neighbors on one side, and a tall, white picket fence marking Italian neighbors opposite. Gram lived in this house until her mid 90's.

During her last few years there, a lady came two (2) times a week to check on her, clean, and do laundry in the basement. Gram could no longer climb the stairs. One day, my Mom got a call from the helper who declared that until a new washer and dryer were purchased, she would no longer do the laundry. Why?

Gram's washing machine was circa 1940 and had no spin cycle. You had to hand feed the wet clothes into cranked rolling bars and squeeze them dry. Gram was distraught, "*But it works fine,*" she adamantly declared on its' removal and replacement. She said the same when her 1950ish refrigerator was replaced.

As vividly as the Sunday it occurred, I remember hearing the next door neighbor yelling loudly in Italian so I ran to Gram's backyard. In the middle of the neighbor's driveway, just in front of their garage door, I saw a tree stump. Shortly thereafter, the yelling lady came outside with a flailing burlap bag in one hand and her resistive young son in the other. He was screaming, "*No.*"

They approached the stump. She reached down and produced a hatchet, then into the bag for a live chicken. In an instant, it was beheaded. The son and I were astonished. Fear rippled as she thrust the hatchet and another chicken into his hands. After much fussing, he chopped its' head off but failed to retain control. The headless chicken, as they do, ran amok, spewing and splashing blood all over Gram's white sided house. Dad hosed it down.

QtoP14: What was my most impactful, grammar school experience? What did it teach me?

QtoP15: Am I an emotional person? What moves me to tears? Joy? Sadness? Anger?

Twice a year, my Aunt Sandy (Mom's sister), Uncle Jed and my cousins Keith and Jon would visit Grandma Feeley. Our visits always unnerved me a bit as some family members sniped immediately and incessantly on meeting. Others got caught in the swirl.

One thing: I love my cousin Keith, and Jon and I are brotherly. We visit our respective homes and often talk on the phone. He is a vegetarian and leans Buddhist. Dad once told me that he felt Jon was born into the wrong, immediate family.

As a child, I loved and respected my Aunt Sandy and Uncle Jed very much. Uncle Jed owned cool cars and German Shepherds. He drove an ambulance, kayaked, shot guns and arrows and loved to hike. In 1979, at 14, they took me on a life changing, camping adventure. Picking me up in Buffalo, we went west through Canada, down into Detroit, across the Dakotas, up through the Canadian Rockies and down to the Grand Canyon then back home.

We covered 10,000 miles and 35 states in five (5) weeks.

During this time, the country's economic health was poor. The government had loaned an auto company $1.2 billion dollars and I found myself arguing in favor of the bailout. Uncle Jed disagreed. He was adamant that we should let the company and the livelihood of thousands go under for the sake of mythical *"free market"* principles. Markets are never *"free,"* some are simply less impeded than others for a variety of reasons.

A similar scenario unfolded in 2009.

"Promote the general welfare at hand?"
"Of, by, and for the people?"

What do the answers mean? We must pay closer and more constant, informed attention, to our representatives.

44

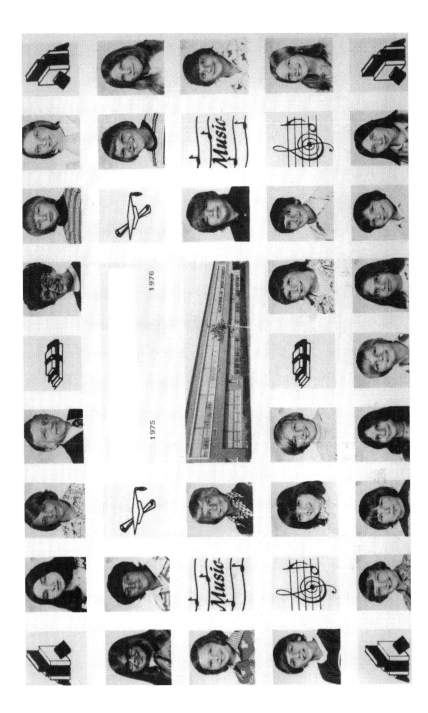

45

46

Paternal Grandmother

After our reserved and tempered lunch at Grandma Feeley's, later Sundays at Grandma Trask's were festive and fun. The dusk and dark were dedicated to the outdoors, extended family, food, and games.

Gram's Trask's ranch style, 2B/2B home house sat well back from the road, on a long, grassy plot that became a backyard and garden then a hill.

Buying meat by the whole, she had an industrial sized freezer in the pantry. Not believing in banks, the freezer held her "*cold cash*" so she had thousands of dollars foil wrapped and stored amidst the meat and vegetables.

Outside, a huge rose trellis seemed in perpetual bloom and lilac trees abounded. Mom would bring home bouquets as wide and grand as your biggest hug. The drive home smelled glorious, as did our kitchen for the week to follow.

Behind the house was a garden where Gram grew corn, raspberries, peas, squash, tomatoes, brussel sprouts, and more. We swung from the weeping willows that marked the end of the garden and the start of a forested hill where we hiked. We tossed pebbles into a crumbling, Native American water well listening for the watery, kerplunk. Occasionally, we found arrow heads.

Further uphill were moss covered rocks, a stream and an abandoned railroad track. After each snowfall, it became an idyllic, breathtaking wonderland as the willow limbs wept gracefully under the gentle weight of an exquisite snowfall.

Grandma Trask was 100 pounds and stood no more than 5'2". Her spirit and sass were beyond compare. Her laugh was an infectious type of grovel. She forever smoked Parliament cigarettes and enjoyed her scotch. She worked as a cashier and loved Grape Nuts breakfast cereal. She was an extraordinary cook. Her Yorkshire pudding with home grown & made raspberry jam, kidney steak pie, and fresh mint lamb dishes were perfection. Gram jarred pickled onions and Dad would check with Mom before eating them because his breath would get so skanky.

Meals were served on two (2) tables set in a T. During one meal, our dog, Charlie, and Butch, my cousins' terrier got into a huge fight causing the table to quake, spilling everything. Red wine ruined the table cloth. Gram just laughed and laughed, saying, *"Don't worry. We can get a new one. Those dogs are pissed."*

Most weeks we were joined by Aunt Ruthie (Dad's sister) and our cousins, Sasha and Merv. I never met their father. Aunt Bonnie, Uncle Erick and our cousin Karina joined us once or twice a year at holidays. I remember Uncle Erick as a smooth talking man.

I have no idea what occurred nor does Mom. And Dad, if he knows, has never spoken about it. But, warring parties held a truce long enough for our three (3) families to celebrate Christmas day together, and an occasional Easter. Sometimes tempers flared and Gram would cry.

One thing: Mom once bought a beautiful, full length fake fur coat at Sears for the upcoming Christmas holiday season. Shortly thereafter, I found her replacing the jacket's label with one from Jenss, a high end, luxury clothing store. Her soon-to-be daughter in-law, Kat, had sold the label to her. When I asked Mom why, she told me to wait and see.

Sure enough, on Christmas day, Uncle Erick greeted us at Gram's and offered to take Mom's coat, in doing so he checked the label before hanging it up, commenting, "Nice, Carolyn, from Jenss."

Everyone should have an aunt like my Aunt Ruthie. I love her so much. She was my role model when I became Uncle Peter to Adam's first child, Trisha. Aunt Ruthie lives with Sasha and her family in Texas. Interestingly, Sasha writes and enjoys photography, same as me. Merv lives in Connecticut with his family.

49

Aunt Ruthie's infectious laugh filled the house as we joked and played. She joined us in blowing up balloons, rubbing them on our hair to generate static electricity and then sticking them on the ceiling. We had Nerf Ball wars and enjoyed horseshoes or Jarts outside. No matter what it was, Aunt Ruthie played. After dinner we watched the Mutual of Omaha's *Wild Kingdom* and *60 Minutes*. One very special Sunday each year, we watched *The Wizard of Oz*.

Prior to VHS and the digital age, CBS owned the broadcast rights to this iconic film. If you wanted to see it, you had to watch CBS. If you missed it, you waited a full year for the next viewing opportunity. It was a cultural event and always shown on a Sunday night. I have seen this film more than any other, easily over 20 times. I still love it. My last viewing was atop a Vegas casino roof while floating in their swimming pool.

Annually, *Cabaret* was also broadcast. There was an extended discussion over whether or not it was appropriate viewing; my parents decided yes. I saw it simply as a Nazi movie and missed entirely the abortion, homosexuality and bi-sexuality issues that compose the story's core. Go Liza!

Similarly, when *All in the Family* first aired, my parents hesitated in allowing me to watch. Years later, I understood its' issues of bigotry and racism. Then, I simply loved Edith. Go Norman Lear. Thank you for subsequent decades of integrity and social activism.

We sometimes visited Aunt Ruthie at her mobile home on Grand Island. During one visit, we laughed so hard we cried. As things quieted down and we caught our collective breath, Aunt Ruthie excused herself for a minute. Leaning forward, Mom then whispered, *"I can't believe it. I just peed my pants."* She stood to reveal a wet spot on the chair. Laughter erupted once again.

One thing: Aunt Ruthie's home became my touchstone for what a trailer park is; her location was pretty, peaceful,

manicured and lovely. Years later, when I encountered the trailer park stereotype that pervades American culture, I had trouble reconciling what I knew from experience with the image commonly portrayed; a lesson in perception.

QtoP17: Do I dislike any of my relatives? Why?

QtoP18: Do I hold any positive or negative stereotypes? What are they? Towards whom?

QtoP19: On a scale of 1-10, how concerned am I about what people think of me? Any examples?

Christmas

Our family has so many wonderful memories associated with Christmas, all culminating at Grandma Trask's. Annually, a week before Christmas, our family and Charlie visited a local tree farm to seek out and obtain two (2) trees deemed perfect. Sometimes we spent hours searching, other years not. We cut and tied them rooftop and headed to Lewiston where we dropped off Gram's tree for Christmas day decorating. Family folklore recounts that one year no Christmas trees were to be had so a family member went to a state park and acquired a hot tree for the sake of tradition.

Returning home we shook off the snow and put it in the basement to warm and settle. Soon thereafter, Dad carried it to the living room, cut an inch or two off the trunk and set it up in a green and red stand with water and aspirin.

The 55 gallon cardboard drum that housed our special decorations and handmade ornaments collected over the years was carried up from the basement and we began. Lights first, ornaments second, garland last. Some years we made popcorn and cranberry garland strings (at a ratio of 10 to 1.) To this day, my Mom declares that year's tree, "*The prettiest!*"

Putting us to bed was always a challenge. The Christmas energy of three (3) boys is pretty powerful. Of course we woke up early and ran excitedly downstairs where we were allowed to open our stockings. Made of felt and individually handcrafted by Mom, they were always hung orderly on the shutters, filled with candies, toys, and useful gadgets. Opening the gifts was done together one-by-one, round-robinly.

Per Sunday routine, we went to both Grams. The sheer specialness of the day made it bigger, broader, and more fun. I cherish the holiday as a practice of cultivating seeds of generosity and joy.

I finish with a letter to my brothers.

Dear Adam and Todd,

May this find you well. I hope you have enjoyed remembering and reliving these childhood adventures. I look forward to hearing your additions and unique remembrances of our worlds.

There are so many stories to be shared; our summer holidays in Letchworth State Park; our fishing trips to the Thousand Islands; our long weekends in Toronto with dinner at the Spaghetti Factory and visits to that hands-on science museum.

Adam, you were a terrific big brother. You taught me to drive your MG Midget and took me to my first concert, Styx, and R rated film, Midnight Express.

Todd, you always took care of me and defended me in the neighborhood and at school. We played, laughed, and acted as good brothers do. Do you remember the Sunday at Grandma Trask's when we swapped clothes and pretended to be twins? So silly we were. Thank you.

As they always and perpetually do, things changed. Adam, you moved out, got married, had children. You faced the deepest, darkest depths of life unimaginable, hovering at the edge, cloaked in sadness, touched the void and gratefully returned to us.

Todd, somewhere along the way you got lost and we await your return. And, as for me, I had my own experiences to attract and embrace, or hesitate and avoid. Whatever our circumstances, one indisputable truth is the good fortune of our childhood experiences. We lived well and were loved. For now, we all remain.

Your little brother,
peter

These were tales of my childhood.

***

I encourage all groups to begin chapter discussions with the following three (3) questions, then reflect and share.

What is my overall impression of the chapter?
Which story did I most prefer? Least?
What is a theme of the chapter?

Reflect and Share: Childhood

A suggested way to proceed*: Someone call out a letter (A-Z). Read aloud that question and answer it until conversation is exhausted, then, continue with another letter. Enjoy.*

a) Where were you born? What were the causes and condition surrounding your birth?

b) Do you agree or disagree? (pg. 3) *"I know now that everything we experience forever etches an impression on our mind."*

c) Do you have any habits that tend to bother those around you? If yes, what are they?

d) Where did you grow up? Did you like it? Why or why not? What was the neighborhood like? Describe your house and share any special memories.

e) What do you know of your parents' upbringings? Was family history commonly discussed? If yes, what stories do you most remember?

f) What do you think of this concept? (pg. 8) "*Certain Eastern traditions posit that we incarnate to parents of our choice for we see in them the potentiality of fostering more advantageous causes and conditions for personal growth.* "

g) What three (3) adjectives best describe your general childhood disposition/ nature? Why these words? Give examples in support.

h) When do you become an adult?

i) What were you favorite forms of entertainment? What things were prohibited?

j) Who were your childhood friends? What adventures did you share? Do you remain in contact? Why or why not?

k) Were you exposed to news events? If yes, what do you remember?

l) Did you have pet(s)? If yes, share stories. If not, did you want one? If yes, what?

m) Did your parents instill in you a love of any particular thing or activity? If yes, what?

n) What were your favorite/ least favorite foods growing up? Have your tastes changed over the years? How so?

o) What are your thoughts on reincarnation?

p) When did you first realize that adults say things NOT intended for children's ears? What did you hear?

q) What were your earliest sexual inklings? When did you first realize gender differences? Sexual attraction?

r) How do you answer these questions? (pg. 28) *"What was the boundary between doing well, taking pride, then speaking about it, while simultaneously avoiding the stank of arrogance? How does one promote one's accomplishments while remaining modest, humble?"*

s) What are your fondest family memories? Holidays? Parties? Vacations?

t) What things elicited fear? Why? How did you cope *then and now?*

u) What routines shaped your childhood?

v) Which stories from this chapter are most memorable? From them, what are you taking?

w) What is learning? Who was your favorite teacher? Least? Why?

x) Were you regularly involved in a religious tradition as a child? Does it continue today? As an adult, has it changed?

y) Did you have a favorite relative? Who was it? What made them so special in your life?

z) Overall, on a scale of 1-10, how do you rank your childhood? Why?

Chapter Two: Adolescence

Introduction

Adolescence is many things.

From infant to toddler, from child to teenager, to young and responsible adult; from family to friend focused, from innocent to questioning and finding one's own way. These compose adolescence. Growth, learning, experimentation and an impending sense of independence, do too.

The confluence and impacts of physical maturation, the demands of socialization, the arousal of intellectual curiosity and the fulfilling of cultural expectations stir up powerful, behavioral streams that pre-curse and co-create of our futures. These also compose adolescence.

In earlier times and simpler days, the influences that shaped adolescence were more prevalent and pervasive, more prominent and exemplary. Nowadays, limitless exposure to different ways of being makes navigating adolescence considerably more turbulent. The breadth of acceptable behaviors is wider and the guidelines less certain. We best adapt accordingly to this new truth, while at the same time, pass on the enduring truths understood by preceding generations. These being the powers of:

- a caring, compassionate heart that cultivates helpful actions;
- a patient, reasoning mind reflected in the utterance of well-chosen words and actions; and,
- an expansive, open spirit that embraces the many, much more than the me.

The social landscape of my adolescent schooling peaked with 7th & 8th grade popularity based on academic success and friendliness towards others. From 9th grade, the currents flowed quicker and rougher as ignorant, youthful certainty led to social fracturing. Cliques arose and social groups formulated. Friendships shifted as

58

priorities changed, degrees of innocence lost. Along the way, memorable teachers provided illumination.

Among my community of Calvin Court neighbors, I recognized that each family personified attitudes and qualities that we embody as individuals. Each family broadly reflected differing aspects of the human condition in both inspiring and worrisome ways. The tributary life of each individual streamed into our collective family. By our energetic nature, we seek to blend. Our *inter*dependence is as undeniable as the fleeting and false nature of our perceived *in*dependence.

Friends and I expanded personal boundaries in daringly stupid ways as life's increasingly muddied waters lapped the shores of our existence.

At home, brotherly issues planted seeds of challenging discord. Dad, Mom and Todd re-located out-of-state so I became independent and remained in Buffalo with Adam.

Admittedly, being on my own shifted parts of my life for the better, at least in the sense of avoidance. Subtle fears about complicity regarding my brother's circumstances abated. Space opened and the pressure to come out was avoided and delayed.

Adam, his in-laws, my friends and workmates all became my guides through the rocky rapids and remaining years of adolescence, cascading me into my twenties. Two (2) significant, death related experiences mark this period of life.

These are tales of my adolescence.

***

A Tragic Accident

I was eleven years old and spending a week at Lake Cayuga summer camp. We hiked through the woods on our way to a small, local amusement park. As the forest ended and we began crossing a meadow, a two (2) lane,

59

road cut the landscape. A family car led a large, garbage-like truck that shifted left and began passing. Approaching the park, the car slowed to turn. The truck did not. My eyes were sadly poised. I watched as the car was struck and a young girl was thrown through the window. Surrounding adults consoled as we said a prayer shocked and silent. The police came and I told my story.

Months later, an insurance agent arrived at our home. I re-told my story and learned two things; one: the young girl was a summer exchange student from the Soviet Union, and two: the garbage-like truck was illegally carrying nuclear waste across state borders.

Junior & Senior High Schools

I entered Grade Seven (7) at Benjamin Franklin Junior High School at age 11. The joys of learning cultivated during my grammar school days initially continued. My classes and teachers were great. Being smart and kind hearted remained inspiring, aspiring and popular. I befriended Jake Weldon and we were voted Student Council President and VP, respectively. We were best friends and he was my first tidal crush.

I often slept over at his farm style house and played innocent games of touch and tickle, as young boys are prone to do, before sharing a bed. I found Jake's three-story, brick house as alluring as Jake. It was positioned well back from the street and sat atop a rustically, manicured slope on a near acre plot of land. By grade 9, Jake's good looks drew him to a different crowd and our friendship waned.

One thing: Oh, the irony of it all. Jake and I re-connected senior year. We skipped school and drank copiously 151 Rum. I think about us drunk, my crush persistent and strong, watching The Way We Were on HBO, fearing and feeling all sorts of something, only to experience a little less than nothing.

Having started in 6th grade, I completed two (2) more years

of French. I love the culture, and languages, in general. Ms. Harper, our French teacher, was friends with Mr. Jacque Renaut, owner of a French restaurant. They arranged a magical, French dining experience. The memory has yet to fade in personally profound ways.

The next class day, classmates teased me for something I knew to be true. That is, Mr. Renaut had showcased my language skills and encouraged me over others. That special evening, he let me know this truth - *"don't worry, it will all be ok."*

As adults, we see many wonderful qualities within our children. Our hearts instinctively overflow with compassionate aspirations: May our actions aid this child in realizing fully their courage and potentialities. That night, for me, a flag unfurled and an unstated legacy had been passed. I felt it then and better get it now.

In wild and decidedly creepy contrast, our 9th grade gym teacher forbade swimwear. We swam and showered mandatorily naked. A thin, wiry man with a loud voice spent hours watching 50 to 60 boys, at various stages of maturation, frolic in the school pool. Something was not right.

One thing: Until I moved abroad, I thought a circumcised penis was the natural state of man. It was all I had ever seen. Foreskin? What was that?

Without hesitation, Mr. Roberts was my favorite junior high school teacher. Joining the profession straight from college, he was inspired by President John F. Kennedy. They even looked alike. Mr. Roberts, with his blonde hair, blue eyes was the embodiment of JFK's vision.

Twenty years later, I visited Mr. Roberts in the same school, and in the same classroom, while he was teaching another batch of seventh graders. I do not remember the specific topic, but he was holding up the iconic, *Life* magazine picture of JFK Jr. saluting his father; informing and inspiring another generation, exactly as he had done with ours.

Our Social Studies teacher was Mr. Maury. I have absolutely no idea the trigger, but one day, he went crazy on our class. He called students out by name, lambasted them, criticized them, told them their faults, yelled and then stormed out of the room.

The principal was inundated with phone calls from concerned parents, including mine. Absent for several days, Mr. Maury returned and apologized, then resigned shortly thereafter.

Years later, I sat next to him on an airplane. We talked politely and I could not muster the courage to ask the question obvious.

Lunchtime in the cafeteria was always a cautionary tale.

Hundreds of students all dining on crappy, processed food made the impossible anonymously possible.

There was one table where sat the nerd, the pimple faced outcast, the gravelly, baritone voiced boy, and the kid deemed negatively something. I would stop by to say hello and inwardly applauded their individuality and uniqueness.

One thing: I have always perceived myself as hovering just the other side of the undefined and uncertain line that made them gather in such a way. I have little doubt that each one has attained great success as an adult.

One day while I was sitting and chatting, a peeled navel orange sailed through the air and disintegrated in a shattering sunburst of sticky citrus flesh, right upside my head. Time stopped. Can moments freeze?

Hundreds of students watched as silence ensued. It was a pregnant pause, that feeling of "oh no!," The fear of what may be next, amidst uncertain glances and wavering eyes that asked, *"Who did that?"* and *"Did you throw that?"* The cafeteria monitor, Ms. Dubois, approached me with kind, understanding words and escorted me to the lavatory for clean-up. She was Serene's aunt.

Serene was the young lady with whom I attended junior high prom. It was an embarrassing, unsettling experience. I did not dance with anyone the entire night for fear of what it might have meant. Similarly, I once found myself at an 8th grade Halloween party uncomfortably French kissing a girl who had painted her face Hulk green. I am not sure which one caused me more discomfort: the obligated kissing or the slippery, sweaty paint.

It was during my mid-teens that *Saturday Night Live,* disco and the film *Saturday Night Fever* re-defined music and fashion. Yes, I did buy a white suit. And, yes, I did wear pig skin, thick heeled shoes with plaid, bell bottomed pants. I was adorable. And, yes, I wore Swedish clogs with my pastel, light cotton blazer a' la *Miami Vice.* Cue music. *Roots* made real the resiliency of wronged peoples reclaiming their lives, families and histories. As art, it touched hearts and shifted minds. Likewise, *Mash.*

Saturday morning roller skating sessions at the local rink were weekly events. Stevie Wonder's iconic album, *Songs in the Key of Life* fueled my slick 8 wheeled moves. *Sir, Duke* guaranteed me skating backwards and doing twirly jumps. Thank you for the inspiration, Dorothy Hamill. I will never forget seeing Diana Ross at the height of her *Endless Love* era. She is history, beauty and grace personified. Decades later, I re-saw her when she headlined the opening of the Palazzo Hotel in Las Vegas. *"Ain't No Mountain High Enough,"* truth. Thank you.

QtoP1: Am I afraid of death? What concerns me?

QtoP2: Do I slow down to peer at crashes? Why or why not?

QtoP3: On a scale of 1-10, how vain am I? How much am I influenced by others' perceptions of me?

As I entered 9th grade at the age of 13, *Rumours* by Fleetwood Mac dominated music as the newly pubescent pecking order was emerging. I sensed the judgmental habit that often accompanies adolescence taking root. *The Breakfast Club*, one of my favorite films, is iconic for so accurately capturing the misguided fallacies of this age. As the facade of each character crumbles, we empathize with the human truths revealed and learn a bit more about ourselves if we so allow.

Flash forward to the 21st century and I am teaching massage to recent high school graduates. Many of them are same sex coupled and the class vibe is welcoming and comfortable; their union is a public, non-event. I can only wonder my life had I been raised in such a positively evolving, social atmosphere.

One thing: I remember my ninth grade English teacher as a beautiful woman. I do not recall her name. I know that post-graduation, she quit her job and started living with, Doug, one of my classmates. He was a sexy ball of testosterone. I admired him from afar, never really wanting to touch, preferring rather to simply appreciate, free from notice or reverberations.

Overall, I found high school academically easy and did well. Maximal effort not required. I am grateful for all I learned.

My 11th grade Western Civilization teacher was the best. An avid, story filled, world traveller. Ms. Florence was motivating, engaging, tremendously insightful and intelligent. She was passionate about her teaching. I understand now that she practiced the Socratic Method; she responded with questions and required us to dig deep prior to answering. Clichéd, pat, unsupported replies were rejected. Logical, reasoned responses were demanded. I will always remember the day I stood up and openly challenged Ms. Florence's provocation. The topic was the 52 Americans taken hostage by Iran in 1979.

This national drama played out for 444 days. She stirred

the pot by broadly gesticulating and feigning disgust at how *"horrible it was that these poor Americans are being held. They are the most important people in the world. We must do everything in our power for them. Everything must stop so we can get them back."*

Standing, I retorted in screaming disbelief at her attitude and tone. *"They were Americans. They deserved our best efforts at release. How could you think or say things like that?"* She listened fully and when I finished, thanked me. She then reviewed and discussed my points with the class. After which, she highlighted ongoing injustices around the world that raised not a ripple of concern among the general populace, nor the government at large - situations far more severe, and possibly catastrophic, than the unlawful holding of 52 people that captured our national focus for over one year. She had a good point in illuminating an uncomfortable truth. Sometimes life is like that. Over the years, when re-visiting Buffalo, I would meet Ms. Florence, finding her as feisty as ever.

My 11th grade science teacher was a laid back, slightly disheveled, mad scientist type who once mixed the wrong chemicals and created a toxic cloud that caused the entire school to evacuate. Seeing as no one got hurt, I always thought that was sort of cool in a perverse kind of way. His name was Mr. Rizzor and he lived on Calvin Court North. I had been his paperboy.

Calvin Courts South and North formed a block of around 100 homes, 60-70 of which got the daily newspaper – *The Buffalo Evening News*. My brother, Todd, first had the route and then passed it to me. Beyond my weekly allowance for household chores, it was my first proper source of money. This, and collecting cans and bottles for the recycling deposit.

Every weekday after school, and early weekend mornings, I wagonned up the papers, or slung them over my shoulder in a burlap sack for door-to-door delivery. On exceptionally cold, winter mornings, Mom was kind enough to put the newspapers in the backseat of the car and follow slowly along. Twice a month, I collected subscription fees. I do not remember how much I actually made.

At 15, I went from being a newspaper boy to tossing bundles out the back of the delivery truck, weekdays after school and at 3:30 am on weekends. I worked out of a camper-like, plywood structure on the bed of his Ford truck. In winter, a bone chilling breeze blew through the cabin. We drove 25 minutes to pick up wire wrapped bundles of 50-count each. One bundle was the newspapers, the second, advertisements. Per need, I divided the bundles accordingly. The last day I ever did this job, three (3) stops before our final delivery, I had no more newspapers or inserts. What a complete and utter mess. I blamed it on the sleepless sleepover from which I had come.

High school clique-wise, I most identified with the theater crowd. I performed in *Fiddler on the Roof* and *The Boys from Syracuse*. I opened the latter dressed as an old man, pleading and begging for my life, then spent the rest of the show being dragged around in shackles. A story about twins, our production starred actual, identical twins, one who went on to Broadway acclaim in *Hairspray* and appeared on *Glee*.

My 11th and 12th grade English teacher directed the school musicals so he assigned creative, thought provoking, theatrical projects. One saw us interpret popular music as poetry. The most memorable was one group's dramatic reading of *The Wall* by Pink Floyd, complete with flashing colored lights and a gradual stacking of school desks on their sides to build the wall. I don't recall what our group did.

One thing: I feel that the Stanley Kubrick film, A Clockwork Orange, is one of the most powerful cinematic experiences ever realized. Its' vividly violent reckoning of a rapist and his thieving gang, while incredibly difficult and discomforting to watch, tells a cautionary tale worthy of consideration and thoughtful, honest discussion across a range of topics. My parents forbade me to see it. I saw it numerous times at midnight showings.

During this time, my Grandma Trask was in the hospital where she subsequently passed. I was a chorus member in a community production of *Bye Bye Birdie*. The day of Gram's funeral, per her desires, friends and family gathered at her house for a festive wake celebrating her life. Here, I heard my Aunt Batty declare that Gram would have liked her coffin appearance because the mortician *"had given her tits."*

My parents went home early and I remained. After drinking too many screwdrivers, I felt compelled not to miss rehearsal. A cab ride later, I was a drunken mess on stage. As news spread of my why, the director halted things and led my friends and me to a fire escape stairwell. Here, I cried for the first time over Grandma Trask's death. I cried tears for her passing and all she meant to me. I also cried tears of guilt.

I had used my rehearsals as an excuse to never visit Gram. Please forgive me, Gram, for my fear and ignorance. When Mom picked me up, I got in trouble for having been drunk. If a consoling word was uttered regarding my grief, I do not recall.

Two things; one: In both these instances (not visiting Gram and going to rehearsal drunk), I wonder my persuasive powers in convincing the adults around me, to let me do as I had done. My actions were so very selfish.

Two: I recently found the program for this show. Signed by someone named Libby, she wrote, "Thanks for teaching me all you know about meditation." Surprised and long forgotten, I do not remember it at all.

In my late teens, our church staged a production of *Godspell* with a nearby parish. During production, I gravitated to the maturity of new friends. Edward and Liza, who played Christ and Mary Magdalene, were a beautiful couple that split after the show, followed by her tragic, auto related death within a year. I think of her often. She was so radiant.

Tim and Daryl became the main source of my social life.

The energy was a welcome change from my high school existence. Tim was the first man with whom I consciously shared a bed for simple and safe experimentation. With time, our attraction faded. Essentially, they were new older brothers, though, admittedly, we sometimes acted immaturely.

- In winter, Darryl and I drove around honking and waving at strangers as if they were friends, hoping that they would fall on the icy sidewalks in surprised response. Many did;

- The bus ride home from our final *Godspell* performance was a beverage enhanced, "*Christian Youth Gone Wild*" scenario; Pastor had a stern group meeting over this happenstance; and,

- One summer, Tim and Darryl served as counselors and me the dishwasher, at Lake Cayuga camp. When a lay pastor found us puffing on herb, in that moment of shocked capture, of undeniable illegality, Darryl says, "*Don't worry, Peter, it is not God, just one of his helpers.*" I burst out laughing. It was the last time I did that for quite a while.

The best part of my high school experience was 12th grade because: the end was near, I got my first tax paying job, and I got to take Advanced Placement (AP) English and US History classes for college credit. Both classes were small, and terrific.

My class placement was 27th out of 550 students in the Kenmore East Senior High graduating class of 1982.

From these years, I am blessed to remain in regular contact with Ms. Catherine Shane, the talented friend who studied drama at Artpark.

GODSPELL

"Well [...] quite like a good [...] Have a good [...] Peter Grutt"

"[...] you're a [...] + I love you [...] Laurie"

"Dearest Peter, [...] love [...] I hope [...] and I [...] know you [...] later, I'll keep in [...] DENISE & I'M OFF WEEK IN!"

Dear Peter,

i really don't know what to write. it's been such a far-out cosmic, deep, moving, motavating experience

Andrew Denler — working
Monica Bartlo
Rick Stepien — with you
Denise Hahn — thanks
Susan Fischer — for
Cindy Morgante — teaching
James Kluge — me all
Mary Beth Bona
Maria Fletch — you know
Tina Runfola — about
Kathryn Fahmer
Chet Swiatek — meditation.
Peter Kirchgraber
Mike Barnes
Dave Dolce
Jay Cady
Paula Miceli — i hope
Karen Wieland — we can
Barry Hibbert — work
Libby Morsheimer — together
Sean Fitzgibbons
Peggy Wilson — again
Daniel Hess — Sean

From the beginning, our energies resonated. Her the eldest of three daughters, me the youngest of three sons; our mutual love of theater and our concurrent searches for a sustaining and inspiring spiritual path strengthen our bond. Our friendship was once again incarnate. It is a blessing that our lives still dabble and blend.

Work: Digmons

I joined Digmons during my '81/'82 senior year. The wonderful people, experiences, and life lessons learned here over the course of four and one half (4 ½) years, still teach. It was a family-owned, upscale supermarket chain based in Rochester, New York. As a part-time employee, I enjoyed a prescription program, paid holidays and a partial college scholarship. They are consistently voted one of the best private employers in America, an accolade well deserved.

On initial hire, I worked three (3) days collecting shopping carts then got moved to the produce department. Here, I generally worked morning shifts, anywhere between 5am and 2pm, for 35 to 40 hours per week. Occasionally, I worked graveyard. This routine afforded me flexibility to work as the church janitor, and allowed time for afternoon and evening classes.

My sophomore academic year suffered as I sought balance amidst the surging and eddied currents of my new experiences. My yearly grade point averages were: 3.0/2.75/3.25/3.5; memorable freshman and sophomore classes, included:

- Rome 44BC to AD476: A plethora of names and places, I got my first "D" ever and squeaked out a "C" for the class. I was devastated;

- Writing Criticism 386: I enrolled in my freshman semester, second quarter. The teacher publically chided my presence in a junior level class. I managed a "B;"

- Modern Drama: Taught by an eccentric, older woman who had lived and breathed Broadway. She loved Bertolt Brecht. I had a sense of voyeuristic guilt as she recounted backstage tales; and,

- Psych 101: My first "en mass" class with 350 other students in an auditorium setting, taught by a bombastic professor.

I absolutely loved my job at Digmons. My childhood joys of picking and canning expanded to care and sale. I loved the constantly shifting, seasonal produce. The work was fast paced and never boring. Work divided into three main categories: the back room, "*the rack,*" or "*the floor.*"

Back room work kept everything clean and flowing. You accepted deliveries, organized the incoming stock, and prepped it for sale. Once, I nearly asphyxiated myself with bleach while hosing down the cooler walls without proper ventilation.

When working "*the rack,*" you pruned all the leafy greens and herbs. You wrapped alfalfa sprouts, put up broccoli and periodically squirted it all with water.

One thing: A small section of the rack was dedicated to exotic salad dressings and lesser known Asian edibles that required refrigeration. One day, someone broke a bottle that had been sitting, unsold for years. The smell was a tidal assault on the nose. It was a jar of Korean kim chee – spicy, pickled cabbage. It is an acquired taste - one that would return to my palate in later years.

Working "*the floor*" entailed many tasks such as rotating through the dry good items - onions, potatoes, etc..., putting out cases of fruit and bagging citrus. Several times, when tightly stacking asparagus bundles in large trays, I had visions of crammed, Tokyo subway commuters during rush hour. Years later, I was the commuter.

Every task was timed and you marked it down. For example, preparing a case of lettuce was allotted 7.5

minutes, while putting up a case of bananas nabbed you three (3). An ideal day saw your tally sheet match hours worked. Because of this, I still have an affinity for tallying up numbers.

The Digmon family regularly toured each store. It was always an event prior to their arrival as you sought perfection in presenting your department. The family was friendly, accessible and caring. I remember the son, Dennis Digmon, as a blue-eyed, curly, blonde haired well-built, rich, handsome and sexy man, about whom all the ladies talked. I always listened.

Our manager, Dan, oversaw his staff like a proud father and elicited our best work. He was fun, friendly, with an infectious zest for life. His wife and children always expressed great kindness and happiness towards me. We shared many, many good times, including a camping and river rafting trip to Colorado.

He loved the hands-on aspect of the many jobs we performed. Our 15,000+ square foot selling area averaged weekly six-figure sales. Whenever and wherever needed, Dan joined in the chaos of a busy, shopping day; Tuesday, coupon day, was the worst. The regional manager constantly chastised Dan for not restricting his work solely to operational matters such as ordering, staffing, paperwork etc...

While I appreciate the need for rules and guidelines, I prefer policies that break down barriers among people, support individual and common goals, and encourage others by example. These actions lead to greater, long term successes. A leader's willingness to invest the necessary time, personal attention and empathy into employees, yields a healthier, more satisfying work culture, leading to higher productivity and decreased absenteeism. Show people respect, support, and a decent wage, then watch what happens.

One thing: Dan once caught me in the back corner of the produce cooler as the following scenario unfolded: To my

73

left sat hundreds of boxes of fresh, locally grown strawberries, to my right was a bakery vat of fresh whipped cream, sitting center was me in a dipping orgy of red and white My capacity to consume was only limited by my stomach's ability to stretch and contain. And, Dan.

Silly behaviors aside, working at Digmons taught me about taking responsibility, prioritizing, and balancing one's many and varied lives as I adjusted to my new independence and explored my burgeoning adult self. Church and neighborhood friends supported me in my late teens while my work friends took on greater significance in my early 20's.

QtoP4: What is my most embarrassing life moment?

QtoP5: Did I enjoy my first overt sexual experience?

Qto6: Am I more comfortable being a boss or a follower?

Calvin Court South

The Calvin Court South community of families was truly a microcosm of humanity. Each family represented different aspects of the macrocosm's potentialities - all the possibilities that we embody individually and collectively. I saw and felt reflected:

- culture in the form of music, art, culture and education; they were ballet dancers, viola players, writers, musicians and librarians;

- *"salt of the Earth"* goodness; they owned several farms and would invite our family for winter weekends of ice skating and summer stay overs that saw us navigating a pitch black, scratchy tunnel of forebodingly stacked hay bales in the barn; their Scottish relative visited and stood on the front lawn in full traditional regalia and played the bagpipes;

- anger and the roughness of racial views that were

74

never publically challenged, their attitude and behaviors proved themselves unhealthy for many in the neighborhood; we were all irresponsible;

- power in the form of information and control; they scanned the police frequency nightly to find out who did what to whom and always had their minds in the happenings of others;

- machismo and the need for meticulous order; they ensured their home and everything in it was perfectly placed;

- simplicity in living; they had a wedding free of alcohol and asked guests to gift only white, paper products; and,

- abuse internalized, then released and revitalized by anger driven, painful whacks of a rubber hose to the back of a child's legs; we sometimes hovered outside their windows and incredulously listened.

Amongst all, two (2) families particularly impacted the dynamics and energies of the neighborhood. One, over time, was essentially ostracized, while the other evoked uncertainty and concern.

The Fords was an all-male, single father family whose family member moved them to the relative upgrade of suburban life. They brought with them uncommon views. In subsequent years, they gained unfairly a reputation as being the family who introduced drugs into the neighborhood. They were and did not.

That being said, years later, the water department dug up the drainpipe linking the house to the sewer line. As the giant, corkscrew drill receded from the pipe, it was covered with hundreds and hundreds of flushed and rotting baggies.

Initially, our young ages kept the boys within good graces.

75

They joined us on trips and picnics at the park. We often hung outside their home and talked fishing. They were the first family to get an Atari game console. We spent hours playing. As teenagers, we were banned unsuccessfully from hanging out.

The youngest, Stan, was Fonzie to my Richie Cunningham, a la the iconic sitcom, *Happy Days*. Stan had a presence and energy about him that made him a leader. Like me, he served as an altar boy, though at a different church and behaved in decidedly ungodly ways.

He led the way for the straight boys in getting the ladies. I had an on-going, internal debate fueled by the energy of attraction and aversion. I found myself uncertain, even frightened. Perhaps it was my first taste of the "*bad boy*" thing? You know – wanting what you should not have. Thankfully, whatever the motivation and desire nothing ever happened; only occasional thoughts.

Mr. Ford worked until midnight so post-school, the house was open and unsupervised. By 14 or 15, access was forbidden. We snuck in anyways, and sometimes did the things our parents feared we would. When leaving, we would go to the backyard, fence hop several yards down, and appear upon a distant sidewalk. Funny how an act learned joyously in childhood transformed into a manner of adolescent deception.

Dad and Mr. Ford both loved fishing. Despite the family's reputation, Dad displayed his kindhearted approach to people as he sometimes crossed the street to visit in the front yard while Mr. Ford practiced his casting.

Mom often served as the maternal surrogate for the boys. Once, Carl severely sliced his hand on a piece of glass and came to my mother for medical attention. Whatever misgivings or resentments she may have harbored, she tended to his wound with genuine kindness.

Decades later, I came home to visit and was in Digmons when I saw a family member shopping. I started to approach, then hesitated and turned away. My initial joy at seeing them quickly turned to discomfort, tainted by a twinge of fear. What could I possibly say in 30 seconds about all that had come to pass? May they be well.

The Warans was the second impactful family. Mrs. Waran was at once caring and compassionate, and, angrily combustible. Interactions invoked hesitation and concern. I never felt quite sure what would occur. She sometimes referred to me as her "*third son*" and I have always appreciated that. There were a few times when I was caught in the cross hairs of her anger but escaped, making me ever more grateful for my parents.

Having now both passed, I share the following story because it is etched like stone into my childhood memories. Compassion for the pains endured, and for all who suffer in similar ways.

Mrs. Waran stood 5'4" and weighed nearly 400 pounds. It amazed me. In the mid-70's, when diagnosed with gallstones, doctors insisted that she lose weight before surgery. Therefore, she became a pioneer in the, then experimental medical procedure, gastric stapling (nowadays modified as gastric bypass or gastric sleeve therapies).

For over two (2) years, she navigated the painful trials of having 90% of her stomach stapled shut. Several times, serious things went wrong and she was flown elsewhere for treatments.

She lost 200 pounds and the golf ball sized gallstones were successfully removed and placed in a jar, on a living room shelf for all to see. Post-surgery, however, despite the staples, she returned to the eating habits which made her so large in the first place. She often liquefied and drank an entire pizza. Within a year, she had regained her weight, plus more.

Two things; one: In light of all we have learned about human psychology since that time, I feel for all the negativity she must have suffered and survived. Peace.

She once front yard disciplined her child with a rubber hose to the back of their legs. Deep, dark bruises took weeks to fade and heal. My skin still bristles and I wince. Ouch. Nowadays, protective services would be notified in a heartbeat.

Two: Years later, I sat around their dining table and listened as the children shared with their mother how horrendous and impactful they found such actions and people were heard. They loved each other for many more years. She lived longer than one might have expected.

Friends

Church and neighborhood friends were two (2) separate, distinct groups.

Church friends and I shared a common history of first communion, weekly services, acolyte duties, movie nights, picnics, cook outs, church dances, and other youth group activities. By their nature, they were guided by Christian values and defined by an intention larger than simple fun.

I am not sure, however, that our sleep-over prank of putting a sleeping person's hand in a cup of warm water and causing them to pee was grounded in any sort of religious virtue.

For years, youth group was run by an inspiring couple, Larry and Carol. They guided us over many angst-filled, teenage dilemmas and their subsequent divorce hit us hard. Larry would later become my landlord when I rented a room in his house during my early 20's. Years later, I attended Carol's second marriage at the Frank Lloyd Wright house where President McKinley was shot.

Neighborhood friends were defined by proximity and bound by the desire to have fun, explore, push boundaries, and test authority. Within a 12 house radius, the umbrella of friendships self-organized accordingly.

79

Adam ('59-46): SuzanneS, ChrisT, MacyL, TrentK, TimS, ClarkB, JimF, JeanP, +5 others

Todd ('63-'60): BillyM, MarieP, TomV, ClaireS, SueT DebbieM, CarlJ, LaurenZ, TedK

Me (64+): BelleS, PaulV, StanJ, JuddM, RickW

Another 120-130 children resided among the other houses and I knew them too. But, as a young child, Adam and his friends looked out for our well-being as our adventures embraced greater depth and daring.

We rode our bikes farther, explored new destinations, and sought out challenges such as swimming beyond the "*Do NOT Enter*" signs at the "*chutes.*" They were an abandoned rotating, railroad crossing bridge. The wooden supports narrowed and the water catapulted you out the other side. Rusty nails and splinters the size of pencils abounded.

We jumped into snow banks off Brighton school roof and once threw a bike off. We egged and toilet papered houses. We exploded an M80 in the school bathroom.

One thing: I did not agree with this last action. Yet, I failed to act against it. I knew it would happen but silent complicity prevailed. Destruction of public property infuriates me. You own it! It is yours, ours. Respect and behave accordingly. (Yes, I know, the golf balls).

Music by *Rush* and *Van Halen* ruled. Due to his eyes, we spent hours deciding if the singer on the cover of the biggest selling, double live album ever was high.

We went to a local pancake house for their "*bottomless cup of coffee*" and drank ourselves into a twitching, agitated frenzy. We hid and sought. We kicked the can. We ignited a yard fire, four (4) houses down, with a bottle rocket gone rogue.

We made small tennis ball cannons by taping five (5) soda

cans together and shaking lighter fluid to create launching fumes that fueled balls over rooftops. We eagerly sacrificed frisbees to a good windstorm. They sailed for blocks before falling out of sight. I have, at times, wondered what we might have broken.

Time inevitably shifted the hierarchy. By my 10, Adam and his friends were in their mid to late-teens. They began doing things that younger kids did not. My immediate friends and I were to discover these things on our own. Chiefly among them were beer and marijuana

Three things; one: I feel most parents were understandably blindsided by the arrival of these types of drugs into the lives of their children. Culturally, we have a relative handle on the responsible use of alcohol. It is woven into our behaviors. We share a collective, negotiated history with this drug.

Other drugs, however, created new norms and ways of being. My generation navigated their use and abuse in numerous ways. Our parents struggled to adapt and respond within the bounds of their ignorance. Is there a similar challenge for today's parents and pharmaceuticals?

Two: Every society has a social drug of choice. For the West, alcohol; for many Native Americans tribes, peyote; for many Asian cultures, opium. In each case, unique rules and behaviors govern their relatively safe usage. Switch the drug and the culture, though, and extremes ensue.

I once spent an extraordinary evening in the jungles of north Thailand, in the "Golden Triangle," an area known for opium production. A family invited me into their forested, bamboo home where we shared an evening that included rice, fish and a communal smoking of the poppy plant.

The grandfather controlled the sharing of the pipe among the men and older boys. Kids were around this adult activity in the same way kids are exposed to alcohol in the West.

81

The first of only two (2) times I have tried opium, it was a positive, mind expansive experience (the 2nd time not so much).

In each case, however, my pounding head made the prior night's activity resoundingly less attractive. I understood how folks got so easily hooked. All you wanted was another euphoric taste to ease the downside impact.

Three: Given today's preponderance of prescriptions, I am not certain if the drugs we tried were any better or worse than those now consumed under the guise of a doctor's note. I am unsettled by the use of psycho-tropic drugs among teenagers diagnosed with attention and depression disorders. I see the issues as primarily, a matter of diet.

At 16 or 17, I obtained a laughable, yet workable, fake Ohio ID from the back of a magazine. Remnants of the first bottle of wine I ever bought were visible for years in the form of a red stain on a nearby roof.

Incredibly nervous, my first purchase was a bottle of Gallo Port. Not knowing it is a sweet dessert wine made for sipping, we certainly did not sip. He painted the white, tiles outside his upstairs window and I fertilized a friend's hedges.

One summer, we discovered that someone's parents had a large, forgotten stockpile of gifted liquors in their basement. Once discovered, Dewars & Lemonade became the senior year drink of choice during back yard sleep-outs. Games of *Spin-the-Bottle* and *Truth-or-Dare* became highly discomforting when the dares were heterosexual in nature. Obtaining weed and maintaining paraphernalia occupied much time.

Cruelly, a group of us once made a huge sign with six (6) foot letters spelling, "*SPONGE*" and placed it for all to see, on a roof. It was referencing a friend who always seemed to want our weed. So mean we were. My apology.

82

Intuitively, I feel that if you are going to intoxicate, then naturally occurring substances are more appropriate (and yes, I recognize that the wrong mushroom can kill).

Drugs manipulated in a lab (and yes we sampled some), seem different to my way of thinking.

I believe that, *"I am the environment and the environment is me."* What we find on the outside is found on the inside. Therefore, our bodies best recognize and process *moderate* amounts of nature in all its' forms, generally.

Seek to avoid excess in all endeavors, no matter the workings of body, speech and mind. Be balanced. Be peace.

As for neighborhood friends, life has followed wildly varying pathways. Some friends remain in the neighborhood, are married, have children, and are living their lives much like their parents, while others have married, moved elsewhere and divorced. Other friends:

- passed sadly due to AIDS;

- sat in prison charged with pedophilia;

- faced the challenge of raising a challenged child;

- explored beyond the borders of American culture and married inter-racially; and,

- cared compassionately for their diabetic dad throughout his declining health that saw both legs amputated.

It goes on and on.

Health, happiness, and peace for everyone who shared in creating the events and experiences recounted here. We were so blessed in so many ways and I am grateful for all we shared. Nothing can replace childhood friends. Peace

84

QtoP7: What things do I like but cannot have? Am I
attracted to the nerd or the muscle bound boy?
The virgin or the whore (see Madonna)?

QtoP8: What is the angriest I have ever been?

QtoP9: What three (3) drugs do I find acceptable?
Unacceptable?

Love simply is. Born of this truth, love does; shining with innate clarity and boundless radiance. As I write, my parents and brothers are alive and our relational bonds are at their truest, strongest and most lovingly genuine. A better place has followed decades of distance and discord.

During late adolescence, the swift currents of my personal unknowns were submerged within the Category Six rapids that dominated family life. Everyone was drenched by waves of fear, love, anger and uncertainty.

Events at home included:

- my parents' growing awareness of drug use in the neighborhood;
- their actions to understand and correct unhealthy habits;
- my desire to deflect attention from my knowledge of what transpiring and my complicit actions, as well as sexuality; and,
- Adam's departure from daily life.

"Hey, Pete, did you know that Mom was at school (Kenmore East) last night?" asked my brother, Todd. *"Nope. No idea,"* I lied.

I knew. Mom had attended a seminar on dealing with drugs and your children. Todd's troubles at school, his retreat into drums, rock & roll and drugs, his skirt with illegalities: our once dynamic, cooperative family energy now channeled conflict. We went to family counseling.

With Adam living independently, I was alone and not

entirely naïve. I knew some of what was up with Todd but not everything. Somewhere along the way, did he encounter something permanently altering? If yes, then it helps explain much of what has followed.

He got kicked out of our home in the middle of winter and his whereabouts became unknown. The constant worry and anguished tears that accompanied daily life have stained my memories. When word passed that Todd was considering an irrevocable alternative to his situation, he returned and has since lived with my parents. In later years, more and similar heartbreak would follow.

Coping with my own issues, I wanted many things. I wanted my family to be better. I wanted to better understand myself. I wanted my fears to subside. I wanted everyone's love. I wanted sex. I wanted my brother to be better. I wanted to make my parents proud. I wanted to come out and move out. I wanted more money. I wanted whatever I felt I did not have. I wanted. Want, want, want, desire.

Sons always want their father's love, yet are not old enough to appreciate that it can come in many ways and countless forms. In my youthful ignorance I failed to realize this truth. I saw physical expressions, such as hugs and kisses as the only way love plays out. During adolescence, fear of my genuine gay nature, coupled with experimenting and everything my brother, I did not see the see the larger picture in play.

When Mom kissed Dad in front of us, his slighting reaction was *"Carolyn....the kids."* When I was 15, I hugged my Dad from behind as we entered the kitchen.

Pulling away, he said, *"Why do you always have to be touching me? Keep your hands to yourself."*

How petty it seems now.

Decades later, having not met for three (3) years, Dad picked me up at the airport, shook my hand and said,

"Welcome home, son." And while it took me years, I now happily own it. I transform it.

I own the youthful ignorance these examples reveal. I transform it by knowing that when Dad says, *"Pete, let's go hit a bucket of balls,"* it is love. I know now that when Dad insists on buying me an expensive pair of Italian dress shoes for my corporate job in Hong Kong, it is love.

I know now that when he spends time with me on the phone discussing politics, it is love. I am so very grateful that, for this heart centered issue, my ignorance is dissolved and the truth enlightens. I cherish each and every moment spent with Dad, in all and every way.

At 17, I descended the basement stairs and interrupted Dad as he calculated our yearly taxes. I sought to move out and made my case accordingly. He said no. I was too young.

Within the year, my parents and Todd relocated 1,200 miles south to a beautiful home, and I moved in with Larry, our former youth group advisor.

Life in my early 20's became a balancing of:

- working at Digmons and janitoring;
- attending college;
- hanging with friends; and,
- spending time with Adam, his new wife and child.

These were tales of my adolescence.

***

I encourage all groups to begin chapter discussions with the following three (3) questions, then reflect and share.

What is my overall impression of the chapter?
Which story did I most prefer? Least?
What is a theme of the chapter?

Reflect and Share: Adolescence

A suggested way to proceed: *Someone call out a letter (A-Z). Read aloud that question and answer it until conversation is exhausted, then, continue with another letter. Enjoy.*

a) What three (3) words best describe your adolescence?

b) Which of these four (4) adolescent factors, is most impactful? (pg. 68):

"*The confluence and impacts of physical maturation, the demands of socialization, the arousal of intellectual curiosity and the fulfilling of cultural expectations stir up powerful, behavioral streams that pre-curse and co-create of our futures.*"

How do you interpret "*... pre-curse and co-create our futures*"?

c) Culturally, the concept of adolescence is relatively new. Previously, if you could procreate, you assumed adult responsibilities. Now we have 16 for driving, 18 for everything, except drinking at 21. Are these age appropriate, milestone years? Would you change any of them?

d) Where did you attend junior and senior high schools? What did you most/ least enjoy? With which "*clique*" did you most identify?

e) Which stories from this chapter are most memorable? Why?

f) Who were your best friends? What adventures did you share? Are you still in contact? Why or why not?

g) What are the top three (3) qualities in a friend?

h) What is the most uncomfortable truth you have ever faced?

i) What were your greatest challenges when navigating puberty and the transition to your late teens and early 20's?

j) I write, (pg. 76): "...*she quit her job and started living with, Doug, one of my classmates. He was a sexy ball of testosterone. I admired him from afar, never really wanting to touch, preferring rather to simply gawk and stare, free from notice or reverberations.*"

   Was there a "*Doug*" (boy or girl) in your life? Who was it? Who were your crushes?

k) Did you have household chores and an allowance? If yes, what and how much?

l) What was your first official job? Did you enjoy it? How did you spend your money?

m) What types of work do you most / least enjoy?

n) What qualities compose a successful and effective boss?

o) Do you agree or disagree? If yes, what did your neighbors embody? Give examples. (pg. 85): "*The Calvin Court South community of families was truly a microcosm of humanity. Each family represented different aspects of all the potentialities of the macrocosm - all the possibilities that we embody individually and collectively.*"

p) Did you have younger / older siblings during adolescence? Do you consider yourself close? How have your sibling relationships evolved?

q) What do you think of this idea? (pg. 69) "*Our lives, by their nature, seek to blend. Our interdependence is as undeniable as, the fleeting and false nature of our perceived independence."*

r) As you explored your emerging independence, how did you act out? Did you do anything of which your parents were not aware? Share some examples.

s) What was your earliest exposure related to matters of mortality?

t) If, when, and where were you introduced to intoxicants? What were they? What stories surround their initial use?

u) How did your parents express their love? In what ways did they offer support and guidance?

v) What are the top three (3) wants in your life?

w) Do you have a special skill or talent? Share an example.

x) Would you like to re-live your adolescence? Why or why not?

y) At what age did you become independent? What were the surrounding circumstances?

z) As an adult, have you *"seen your parents in a new light"*?

Chapter Three: My 20's

Introduction

Once unbound from the rules and regulations that guide and shape our youth, we must face adulthood. Knowing that we alone are responsible for scripting our future, that the limits which newly bind are of our own making, we proceed. Appreciating truly the power and gravity of this responsibility can seem daunting. Still young works in progress, how do we best move forward? How do we know that the decisions we make are correct?

As we analyze options and consciously establish goals, then act towards their ends, we can never know the limitless number of events and possibilities that may intervene. We must be open to these changes and adapt accordingly. Aim to:

- quiet your mind;
- open your heart;
- align every thought, word, and deed; and,
- act with positive consequence.

Along the way, we may feel uncertain as to the perfect direction and I am ok with that, though it has its' moments. I often ask myself, *"Are the consequences of my actions reflecting my better nature?"* If every choice I make is a positive reflection of who I am, then the end result must necessarily be good.

People often ask me how I decided to do the things that I have done. I do not really know. I took advantage of opportunities and paid attention to the unfolding moments therein.

From undergraduate to graduate schools, from Digmons to a teaching assistantship, from Kenmore to Asia, my 20's unfolded in a seemingly random path as a wave of foreign fascination subsumed and subdued physical desires. The world opened wide and I embraced it wholeheartedly.

I toured and worked in Australia. I played at the Great Barrier Reef and swam in a rainforest. I moved to Tokyo and swam in different cultures. I got my first taste of Asian medical practices. I had the chance to fly, or at least try, and much more.

Sadly, family events that simmered throughout my adolescence boiled over, causing my heart to collapse inwards, alone on the other side of the world.

These are tales of my 20's.

***

By November 1983, my parents and brother had moved to North Carolina. I was 19 and living on my own, attending my sophomore year at the State University of New York at Buffalo (SUNY Buffalo or UB), and working full time. I resided with Larry.

My life at Larry's house in Kenmore was a situation of much good fortune. It was conveniently close to both my college campus and the church where I worked. Also, my respect and love for Larry as an older brother was genuine in creating an excellent living arrangement. I rented a room in the back of his home and we shared the bathroom, kitchen, and living room. Over the years, various tenants occupied the 2nd floor apartment.

The street was shaded by towering Dutch Elms that succumbed to an infestation in the 80's and were cut down. Driving it now feels somehow empty, new, and naked. I love trees.

Two things; one: One day, while filling the tub and wearing only a towel, I locked myself out and had to break in. Which to damage more - the window or the floorboards?

Two: I lived on the 2nd of 3 floors during a water shortage in Nepal. The landlord privately purchased water that was stored in a rooftop tank. One morning, I forgot to close the faucet after checking for water and went to work. Water was delivered in the afternoon. That evening, my kitchen and living room were flooded. Thankfully, the marble construction prevented leaking to the floor below.

It fascinates me how the mind seeks out commonalities and links seemingly disparate and separate events distanced by time, space and experiences.

Living with Larry provided insight into the world of dating and coupledom. Except for watching my oldest brother, I had never really been privy to such happenings. Larry was a handsome and successful man, a *"good catch."* As he rebounded from his divorce, I was intrigued and entertained by the ebb and flow of the strategies employed by the vying women. He has long since married and become a fine father.

One of the benefits of being gay is often a closer attunement to, empathy for, an understanding of, both male and female energies as they influence our actions. Gay men create extraordinary couture for women, in part, because our male energy recognizes their physical and spiritual beauty, free from sexual clinging or want. And then, our female energy dresses them up.

On a deeper level, I get why straight men are often discomforted by a question starting, *"How do you feel?"* I get why women ask. I have occasionally inquired myself. Similarly, I know men frustrate women when we are lost and refuse to ask somebody for assistance. At times, I am that guy.

For each one of us, our hearts feel and our minds ponder.

They blend, reside and resound. They connect and conduct themselves in a much broader spectrum of being-ness than we habitually don't realize. This makes us infinitely more alike, than not.

Our next door neighbors were a terrific couple. She was an only child and he had eight (8) brothers and sisters who were all best friends. Each was skilled in a different area of construction so they collectively built houses for each other. I marveled at their experience as a large, tight knit family.

The husband once lent me a porno video while Larry was away. He then invited himself over and would not leave. Really? Can't a closeted gay guy have his homo moment with the man in your hetero porn?

SUNY Buffalo

UB has two (2) campuses – an older one in Buffalo, and a newer campus in the suburb of Amherst, adjacent to Tonawanda. The Amherst campus has two (2) lakes and the beautiful, green grasslands sprawls across hundreds of acres. Roman pillars sit atop tiered, stone steps along one shore. Here, Ms. Lauper performed on her *Girls Just Want to Have Fun* tour. I am so grateful for her talent, joy and lifetime of inspiring LGBTQ rights advocacy.

One thing: Adam attended Mom's alma mater, Buffalo State. One of my best fraternal memories happened on this campus. Adam, Todd and I went to a sold out show featuring Misters Shatner and Nimoy of Star Trek.

We arrived late and stood in the back as the lights went down. During Q&A, the house lights came up and Todd was gone. Capt. Kirk asked, "Who has a question?" and from the very front row Todd's voice arose. "I do," he said, as the microphone was passed. "What does the "T" in James T Kirk stand for?" he asked. Mr. Shatner replied, "Really? That is what you want to know?" Everyone laughed and no answer was given.

We now know that the answer is "Tiberius."

Given its' size, driving from one side of the UB Amherst campus to the other was common. Parking meant a long walk to class. In August 1986, I was passing through a labyrinth of connecting hallways when the space shuttle Challenger and the future both exploded across the television screen.

94

I attended UB from the fall of 1982 to mid, 1986, attaining my Bachelor's in Interpersonal Communication.

The first two (2) years I was undeclared and leaning towards Political Science but soon realized that my employment options were not intriguing, Moreover, I enjoyed the *communication* of politics, not the *topic* of politics, per se. I am so glad I switched. The program was challenging and satisfying, the instructors, excellent. Outstanding classes included:

- Advanced Interpersonal Communication: I am fascinated by the ways in which we share meaning and self-express;

- Interracial & Ethnic Communication: This included Intercultural Communication, a topic I would soon navigate first hand;

- Analysis of Face-to-Face Communication: We did an on-site, ethnographic study of behaviors at a public health clinic; and,

- Rhetorical Theory and Criticism: This became a teaser for the focus of my graduate studies.

Three things; one: I once attended a Psychology 101 class with 350 students in a big auditorium setting. A loud, bombastic teacher angrily railed about gay men, anonymous fellatio and mental illness. a) "Me thinks thou doth protest too much," and, b) the desire to receive is the providence of most men, regardless the manner of receipt.

Two: A teaching assistant once caused alecture hall uproar. He talked about the shaping of reality through the power of words and segued into our social practice of avoiding certain topics. With that, a video of a woman exploring her genitalia with a mirror and gynecological tool appeared.

People freaked out in offense. My reaction was more like, "Oh, wow, A bit more heads up would have been nice, but the topic certainly is one that ladies should know about. It is important. It is their body." I wonder. What exactly was causing the offense?

Three: Similarly, I cannot understand the uproar over public breast feeding and attempts to make it illegal. I find it one of the most natural, beautiful things in the world. Sure, use some discretion regarding time and place, and, support the new mother's natural rights to nourish her newborn, free from any shame or offense. If anything, we should be alight by the extraordinary amounts of violence we let pass as entertainment.

In 1986, I graduated with 6000 other students in one of 10 ceremonies simultaneously held across the campus. My parents flew up and Calvin neighbors hosted a terrific party. Shortly thereafter, I moved south for graduate school.

Work: Church

Working as the church janitor was the perfect, supplemental job. The pay was good and the hours highly flexible. Each week, I took pride in ensuring that the church was ship shape for Christ by the appropriate time and I was good to go. I would often sweep and vacuum the sanctuary at 2 or 3 am Sunday morning.

One thing: Our organist and choir director was a talented young woman in her late 20s. She was fun and had a terrific laugh. Sometimes, as I cleaned the sanctuary, she practiced for Sunday service and would turn up the volume, playing all sorts of requested, non-religious music - from Bach to Beethoven to rock and roll. The church would shake. Also, she took me to New York City.

Airlines deregulated in the early 1980s. For a short while you could fly round trip from Buffalo to New York for $38 so we went. We stayed at her gay friend's apartment somewhere in Manhattan. I slept on the floor. We saw the sights, visited Times Square when it was still sleazy, and spent an evening at the Copacabana Club. It was a great trip. Dad was upset when he found out.

One year, post-Christmas, I overlooked cleaning the heating vents along the floor boards that ran adjacent to the pews. Pine needles from hanging wreaths had dropped. Someone discovered this and queried both my work and the monies being paid. I soon resigned. Admittedly, there was a degree of avoidance involved – guilt induced departure - since I was taking my wage from a group with whom I no longer agreed.

QtoP1: As a teenager, was I bound by strict rules?
At what ages could I do different things?

QtoP2: Did a teacher ever shock or offend me?
What did she/ he do or say?

QtoP3: What is my view of younger/older, woman/man relationships?
Do I have a preferred age range?

<u>Family</u>

With my parents and Todd gone, Adam and I grew closer. He married in the early 80s and his in-laws became my second family. His wife became the sister I never had. His mother-in-law was a strong, kind woman who became my "*Sometimes Mom.*" Meaning, when I felt the need for maternal discipline I would go to her house and tell her, to tell me, "*Peter do this,*" or, "*Peter don't do that.*" Sometimes I listened; sometimes I didn't. Such kind love.

I soon became an uncle as Adam and Kat had their first child, Trisha. It was terrific. I mastered the art of "*uncle spoiling*" and found great joy in babysitting. The notion of marriage and children caused pause.

Several Thanksgiving holidays, our family met at Aunt Sandy and Uncle Jed's in West Virginia. My parents and Todd drove eight (8) hours north. I drove Grandma Feeley, Kat, and Trisha six (6) hours south. Adam was in the Army Reserves and could not join us. Excepting year one, I always drove safely. That year, after six (6) hours and 350+ miles, I turned into the driveway 19 feet short and down a ditch. The car angled 40 degrees just as my new niece vomited in Gram's lap.

During these long weekends, I felt myself as a father in obligations and responsibilities. At one point, my mind entertained the notion of swooning Kat from Adam, as if something like that would have ever happened. Back in Buffalo, something occurred that tragically foreshadowed a profoundly heart wrenching experience.

I went to Adam's to babysit and on arrival, he seemed somehow off, not quite himself. He was floating in his own world and asked that I care for Trisha while he went to the store. After an unusually long time, he returned in a state of mild shock and worry. He looked confused as he told me about hitting another car in the supermarket parking lot; in and of itself, not a problem. Things happen. In this case, however, Adam had no recollection of the event.

He said the police came, information was exchanged, and no one was hurt, yet, it all was now an uncertain blur – a blur induced by, and cloaked in, an unhealthy relationship with pharmaceuticals of which I was unaware. My ignorance blinded me from seeing the existing reality of Adam's life. Soon after, I left the USA.

Church Friends

While internally struggling to navigate my thoughts and desires, an experience centering on sexual attraction happened amidst my church friends that forever changed our relationships. Similar experiences re-repeated over the years. Each time, my body froze with uncertainty, as my mind raced with anticipation.

One night, friends and I attended a high school football game. We were drinking a tequila-based concoction named after a southern state when Sam became a bit amorous. While laughing and having fun, his discrete, touchy feely hands were not so discrete and caught the silent eyes of others. I was scared and ecstatic. "*Was this really happening?*" I liked Sam.

At the same time, everyone paused awkwardly. *"Did Sam really just say and do that? Could they be...."* were the discomforting and unasked questions. My eyes spoke uncertainty. *"Don't blame me. I didn't start this,"* as if there was blame to be assigned. The moment passed and we carried on but something had changed. Our energies shifted from that moment forward as the seeds of separation were planted. My *"Sam in the Car"* moment has since re-occurred.

I felt that in hushed tones others posited the possibility, and perhaps revealing truths, of what had occurred. This was fearful talk then, and sadly, still is for many today.

Digmons' Friends

Digmons was the center of my social life. Our friendships were a plethora of human kindness and suffering. Over the years, the complex and ever evolving web of relationships witnessed:

- the joys of weddings and childbirths;
- the sorrows of emotional pain and addiction;
- friends married then divorced under the strain of adultery;
- a young colleague unsuccessfully tried to extinguish his pain with pills;
- weekend cabins at Alleghany State Park;
- softball and volleyball competitions;
- colleagues fired over theft allegations and others successfully promoted;
- a friend died from homemade fireworks; and,
- parachuting from 3,000 feet and soaring with Larry.

Personally, the secret, seductive, and often times acted upon attentions of Chad, aroused physical and foreign, emotional experiences. Our secret rendezvouses in the produce cooler, always clothed, were kinetic.

One realizes, with age, that early infatuations can excitedly present as early love. Chad's attentions were heart fluttering and embarrassingly hard at times. On various occasions, our "*wrestling matches*" exhibited a roughness and struggle for control that went beyond friendly fun. The energies of dominance and submission fluctuated. The casting of a knowing glance clashed with the seeming demands of discretion and secrecy. The first Christmas morning I ever spent away from family, I passed with him. Wherever and whatever has unfolded in his life, may he be well and happy.

One thing: Around this time, whispers throughout the gay world of a new and deadly disease – Acquired Immune Deficiency Syndrome - AIDS – were being uttered. Millions became sick. It scared the celibate right into me. Please see Philadelphia with Tom Hanks.

I met my best friend, Craig, at Digmons. He is a straight man and has always captured my highest regards. There is just something about us. An effortless smile suffices to acknowledge the certainty of our connection. I have never experienced even a hint of sexual attraction towards Craig. We are just simply, gratefully, playfully best friends, like Oprah and Gayle. Later in life, Mom once asked me if he was gay. Looking from the outside in, I would have wondered the same.

One thing: Straight and gay men can be best of friends when two (2) factors are fulfilled: 1) no carnal energy exists from the gay side and, 2) the straight man embodies a self-confidence that is not threatened, personally or socially, by the friendship. With these conditions met, the friendship can be amazing.

My first car was a 1972 bright lemon yellow, four-speed manual VW Bug, with a sunroof and booming speakers. I loved this car. Craig and I once overnighted at the end of a utility road along the NY Thruway. We dove and tumbled across the grassy median throughout the night. In the glow of their headlights, I wondered if approaching drivers mistook us for ghosts. Do they exist?

"Did you see that?"

Grandma Feeley gifted me a round-trip ticket to Alaska for graduation. Craig was in Kansas and we met in Anchorage airport and began a one (1) month camping adventure. Within 24 hours we were:

- watching bald eagles soar;
- face to face with an immense moose; and,
- passing by a black bear sitting upright, plucking wild berries from a vine.

We spent two (2) weeks hiking north to Denali, then south to Kenai Fjords. For me, the exquisite beauty of such grandeur refreshes my sensibilities to everything greater, beyond and within. My stupidity and determination blinded me one day while hiking.

We were at Kenai Fjords National Park and set off for a glacier. Instead of swinging wide and climbing gradually, we approached from underneath. At some point, I rounded a bend and was clinging face first, Spiderman style, to a crumbling barely there, non-path of glacial silt.

One hundred feet above was the glacier. 100 feet below was a creek. Tomorrow's news headline flashed: *"Foolish Hiker Dies in Tragic Accident."*

Craig soon appeared and his eyes went wide as he realized my peril. Asking, *"How the f**k did you get there?"* I replied, *"I do not need that right now. Just tell me what to do. Guide me down."* Thankfully, he did. A sliver of fear remains etched.

As we were returning to camp, a sharp rock fell and deeply sliced and scarred the back of my right hand. The park ranger tended kindly to my wound and allowed us to sleep in front of her fireplace for some rain had drowned our belongings.

One summer, Craig moved to Colorado and worked at a resort. Dan, his wife, Sandy, and their kids road tripped. We camped along the way and went white water rafting on the Colorado River.

At one point, Dan turned a clammy blue as he experienced altitude sickness. Years later, I could truly empathize.

I had fallen in love with Colorado when first visiting as a teenager. The second time did not disappoint. One day, Craig and I hiked the Rocky's tenth (10th) highest mountain – Gray's Peak (14, 278"). We started hiking at 9 a.m. as meadows of purple, red and yellow flora levitated and hallucinated amidst the summertime grandeur.

Summiting late, at 6p.m., the return trip was cold, dark and hungry. Our rations of water, a beer, an apple and a candy bar each were not enough. On descent, we spooked a family of large crows who protectively squawked and dive bombed us, a la Hitchcock's, *The Birds*. It took two (2) days of knocked-out rest to recover. It was great.

As the spring of 1982 concluded and college graduation loomed, I took another trip that mapped my near future. I interviewed for the Speech Communication programs at the University of Virginia in Charlottesville, VA and at Wake Forest University in Winston-Salem, NC.

I loved the Charlottesville campus due to its design by Thomas Jefferson and southern Virginia is gorgeous. Similarly, Wake is stunning in its design and is beautiful as well. Both schools offered tuition and a teaching assistantship. Closer to my family, I chose Wake Forest.

Wake Forest University

Founded in 1834 just outside of Raleigh, Wake Forest University (WFU) was deconstructed in 1956 and re-built, brick-by-brick in Winston-Salem, two (2) hours west. Situated on the Reynolda Estate of the RJ Reynold's tobacco family home, the WFU campus was split in two.

One half contained the buildings and campus residences while the other hosted hiking trails, the NC Museum of American Art, as well as unique shops and restaurants made from the former plantation buildings. One was an exclusive French restaurant. I was acquainted with one of the waiters, Sean, who subsequently hosted me at his apartment when I first arrived in Japan. The Wake Tavern (WT) was another.

The WT was an upscale watering hole where I waited and bartended. Years later, the salad menu resurfaced on the *Green Leaves* menu in Kathmandu, Nepal.

I enjoyed working at the WT, though it was my first, real, face to face with de facto segregation. The talented kitchen staff was almost exclusively African-American, the front of house mainly Caucasian. I enjoyed the company of all. People are beautiful in all their infinite hues. Bask in the radiant sunshine of others. It feels so very good.

One thing: One night, a colleague took me to an unfamiliar part of Winston-Salem. As their car turned down unknown streets, I sensed a change in energy. When we got out and walked bit, surrounding eyes were on me as they said, "Don't worry. He's cool."

We entered a rundown house and proceeded down a dark hallway. I paused to chat with some folks. They soon re-appeared and we returned to the WT - no harm, no foul. Looking back, I ponder on my level of naïvete. Am I still that trusting?

The WT had indoor and outdoor patio dining. One graduation Sunday, I was an outdoor waiter for a jam packed house. Someone ordered a special bottle of root beer. My tray was overflowing with two (2) dozen drinks.

As I presented the root beer, I stumbled and everything crashed to the ground. I briefly froze, composed myself and announced, *"Sorry folks that was the last root beer. What can I get you instead?"* People went joyously nuts.

Sometimes, things happen. Relax and respond positively. Don't cling and let thoughts take root. Life becomes better lived.

If any woman ever caused me to consider seriously

heterosexuality, it was my WT colleague, Nancy. There was something about her intelligence, her beauty, her kind heart and infectious laugh that gave me pause.

Over the years she worked through liquid addictions, jealousy and much suffering. During this time she would occasionally write me and I could sense the unspoken notion that perhaps things could have been different.

During the U2, *Rattle and Hum* tour, the closest performance was a five (5) hour bus trip away. A local radio station organized a four (4) bus caravan for nearly 350 people. The show was amazing. Within two (2) years, I found myself sitting in a movie theater in Auckland, New Zealand watching it as a documentary film, *Rattle and Hum*. To each one of you, thank you then and now.

One thing: I count U2's preceding album – The Joshua Tree, and, Prince's Purple Rain, as the two seminal albums of my life. Their power and capacity to touch my heart remain. For years, "I Still Haven't Found What I'm Looking For," was my personal anthem. As I write this, Prince has just tragically passed. I thank him for realizing and sharing his extraordinary talents with the world. May I one day find someone special who "Would Die for Me."

<u>Journal entry (Japan, early 90's)</u>

"U2's Joshua Tree just came on! It's been a long time, but what an album! Where are the other groups who care? Who else reflects the kind of ideas and passions that should be leading our thoughts? Question: Does music reflect society? Or, does music propel us forward?

Prior to my arrival, my parents rented a room on my behalf in the back of a garage. I shared the bathroom and there was no cooking facility. Two (2) small, ground-level windows made it very dark and unpleasant. While living there, I trained as the NPR morning news DJ.

For three (3) intense weeks, I woke up at 4:30 AM, went to the studio, and learned how to connect with the national

104

feed, sort and edit news off the wire, and fade in and out between national and local programs. Sadly, I was let go after two (2) days because listeners deemed my chirpy attitude too much for the early morning hour. I soon moved into a tiny, two (2) bedroom campus apartment.

Two things; one: If I had to choose the one thing that caused me the greatest discomfort living in the hot muggy South, it would be the invasive presence of cockroaches. Some nights I would come home late, turn on the apartment light and dozens of cockroaches scurried from the sink towards safety behind the wall. Occasionally, I would take off a shoe before entering and smash as the many as possible before they disappeared. I would spread cockroach killing powder everywhere. Nothing helped as I generated much negative karma.

Two: I experienced an identical situation when living in Sydney Australia. In this case the cockroaches were fewer but bigger and more brazen. Once, I was awakened by one crawling across my face. I really don't mind bugs, but that was too much.

My Indian roommate, Kiran, and I got along well. In the end though, our relationship was marred by my own lack of compassion and regret for my inaction. During his time at WFU, Kiran fell deeply in love with an American woman. As graduation approached, he received word from home that his marriage had been arranged and he had to return soon after his studies were completed.

Devastated, he sat one night in our kitchen and cried and cried and cried as I listened from my room. I never exited to console. I had no idea what to say. He was in love with someone and being asked to marry a stranger. I could not comprehend this. I had no words to pacify his suffering. For me, my mind touched on similar issues gay.

We graduated shortly thereafter and he departed. I do not know what has become of him and wish great happiness upon him. I send the same to all my classmates. You were an amazing group of supportive friends. Thank you all.

QtoP4: Was I ever attracted to someone who I should not have had eyes on?

QtoP5: Do I regret any love relationship I have had? Why?

QtoP6: Have I ever been emotionally unavailable to someone for whom I greatly cared?

At WFU, I was one of three (3) public speaking teaching assistants. The professor taught the main lecture to approximately 100 students who were then divided into five (5) groups of 20 for the practical application workshops, of which I taught two (2).

One of my students, Dorbin Cooley, was a straight, eclectic and innovative student who loved music. On graduation, he invited me to join him in Australia to unwind. I am so glad I accepted.

I thrived in graduate school. Immersed in the world of academia, my full time work was reading, studying, and writing. While difficult, it was always rewarding. I felt like: this is what learning is; this is how knowledge is created; this is how one critically expands one's intellect within the Western paradigm.

The overarching theme of my coursework was speech communication theory. That is, how do we create and share meaning? This focus went well with my interest in the communication required of politics and led to my graduate thesis on political sloganeering.

During the 1988 presidential race, I found my way into the press room following a candidates' debate. I asked Clinton, Gore, Jesse Jackson and the others questions relating to my thesis. Their answers were stock phrases and irrelevant to my question. I was thrilled to be there.

One thing: For those who remember these technological dinosaurs, I wrote my thesis on a WANG computer and printed it on a dot matrix printer.

With the exception of a "B" in Research Design, I achieved and "A" in each course. Some of my favorites were:

- Contemporary Rhetoric and Communications Theory: *No Sense of Place* by Joshua Meyrowitz, and Neil Portman's, *Amusing Ourselves to Death*. These works theorized on technology, news and our patterns of communication;

- Communication and Conflict: I trained as a conflict mediator; and,

- Argumentation Theory: How do we build effective arguments?

I graduated in May 1988 with my Masters in Speech Communication. I remember one classmate as a highly intelligent and organically enhanced man who had lost over 125 pounds. With his long scraggly beard and equally long hair, he sometimes walked around the Southern Baptist WFU campus in what appeared to be a very Christ-like, burlap sack. His humor, strong will and periodic rages against "*the man*" were involving.

To seek change and progress through confrontation is one method. Applying patient, focused, goal oriented persistence is another. They both have their pros and cons when igniting serious and substantial, long-term, social change.

My instructors were terrific. I still remain in contact with several of them. My second reader lived in a spacious and opulent apartment attached to the Reynolds family home. Visiting here for parties and barbecues was my first exposure to generational wealth and all of its amenities.

I attended the national and regional Speech Communication Association (SCA) conventions in Boston and Charleston, South Carolina in 1987 and '88.

Boston was my first time at such an event. I marveled at the process of publicly presenting your research and ideas for discussion, approval, and rejection. Unquestionably, my personal highlight was meeting Kenneth Burke.

Burke was a rhetorical critic who really fancied himself a poet. In the early 20th century, he hung in Europe with the dominant thought leaders of the day, including Lenin.

On analysis, he felt their work did not sufficiently account for critical aspects of the human condition and foresaw flaws in the realization of their ideology. He felt the concept of, "*From each according to their abilities, to each according to their needs,*" was unworkable.

He returned to America and spent decades researching and sharing his ideas about the interplay among words, rhetoric and motivation. He penned hundreds of thousands of words in support of his ideas, including his seminal texts, *A Grammar of Motives* and *A Rhetoric of Motives.*

In his early 90's, he appeared frail. Sitting at his feet in a Boston hotel room as he drank his favorite drink, the "*burka*" (gin and vodka) I felt blessed. He began in a somewhat rambling manner that required constant focus, and then his frailty was passionately transformed.

For nearly an hour, he enthusiastically talked and soon his points coalesced and his meaning peaked.

Three things; one: I cannot recall all of the specifics but I know he explained his desire to add "attitude" to his pentad of human motivation.

Two: I love Burke's definition of man: It is:

"Man is the symbol-using (symbol-making, symbol-misusing) animal, inventor of the negative (or moralized by the negative), separated from his natural condition by instruments of his own making, goaded by the spirit of hierarchy (or moved by the sense of order), and rotten with perfection." (Language As Symbolic Action, 1966)

108

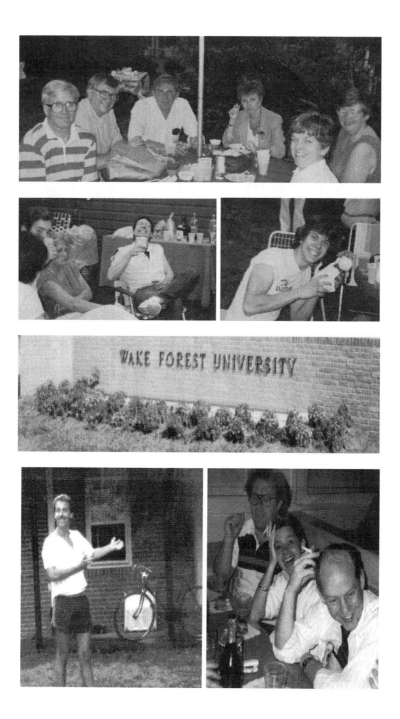

110

111

Three: Years later, the rewards for careful listening would again hold true when sitting at the feet of differing Masters.

My best memory of the Charleston convention was the Atlantic Ocean. We stopped to swim and I did what I had always done in Lake Erie. I jumped in with my eyes and mouth wide open. Oh yeah, saltwater. Lesson learned.

Having completed our studies, it was time for a party and my classmates agreed, so we rented a six (6) bedroom beach house on the Carolina coast. We had a celebratory blast. One night, we went for a midnight swim that ended quickly when I was overwhelmed by thoughts of *Jaws.*

Shortly thereafter, I took Dorbin up on his invitation and arranged to join him in Australia. He went in May and I caught up with him in June. I wrote in my journal (8/92):

(Draft of a letter to WFU instructors): "It's a general letter of update. I so often and fondly think of you, WFU, the people I met, the things I learned. Since graduation, my life has been engaging and eventful .... I am writing you offering my thanks. Judd, your Rhetorical Criticism class was truly and honestly the best, most engaging, most thoughtful class."

Australia (1988)

I both departed and permanently returned to America via Australia in 1988 and 2006. Each journey had a stop-over in Hawaii. Whether going or returning, I loved the state.

At every turn, its' beauty is breathtaking.

When going, I snorkeled for the first time in Hanauma Bay. On return, I visited my first American gay bar. Initially, I always flew United Airlines. At the time, they provided a hot, rolled towel to every passenger. I carried my knife on-board. Staff often let me sit on the floor in front of the exit door, just behind 1st class and passed me free food and beverages.

Smoking was still allowed.

It is crazy to me now, the mindset I had when packing. The things that I brought with me were extraordinary. Over the years, I have certainly learned to pack more efficiently. International flights allowed for 70 lbs of luggage. I used them all. When I first left, I carried a back pack, a large suitcase, and a suit bag; their contents included:

- A full length camel hair coat, a suit and accompanying attire;
- My Kenneth Burke texts;
- The Wake Tavern training manual; and,
- All season clothes and many other items, including a still have, Swiss Army knife gifted by Craig.

Throughout the 90's, I shed the coat and clothes, but carried my Burke texts until 2003 when I gifted them to an American, Communication scholar whom I met in Tibet.

One thing: In 2003, when I moved from Hong Kong to Australia for school, I shipped some things to myself and my parents' for storage. At the age of 39, the sum total of everything I owned weighed approximately 135 lbs.

East Coast Adventures

Arriving in Sydney, I spent five (5) months exploring the east coast, eventually arriving in Port Douglas, an hour north of Cairns.

Dorbin met me at the airport and took me to our single, two (2) twin bed and shared bath room in Kings Cross, Sydney's red light district. The differences between my Times Square in New York City experience and Kings Cross were stark.

New South Wales (one of seven Australian states) legalized commercial sex work in 1961. In Kings Cross, ladies plied their trade in open, relative safety. Australia's healthy openness to things sexual served them well when the AIDS epidemic began.

113

One thing: Whatever the image may be, commercial sex work is technically illegal in Las Vegas, Clark County.

Dorbin's father hooked him up with wonderful, local people who introduced us to many famous places, including the Taronga Zoo, Bondi Beach, and Watsons Bay where I ate fresh calamari for the first time. I found it a bit too chewy and have subsequently learned it is all in the cooking.

One night, Dorbin told me to clean up and dress up for a special party. After a long and winding taxi ride to the peak of a bluff overlooking Sydney Harbor, we arrived at a gorgeous mansion that was home to Australia's 1982 Playboy Playmate of the Year. While the party was opulent, I don't really remember much, other than being somewhat star struck by strangers and feeling out of place. A sense of, *"Who is this guy and how did he get in here?"* I do remember meeting a local television personality from my hometown of Buffalo, New York. The world is truly small.

Shortly thereafter, Dorbin and I boarded a train north to the new age community of Byron Bay. At the station, we chatted up a lady and her young son. They invited us to stay with them when we reached Brisbane and we did.

Byron Bay is home to Cape Byron – Australia's eastern most point. It is illuminated by the first light of each new day. Tenting on the beach, life felt free and limitless.

One sunrise, I joined a pod of dolphins playing near shore and they circled within three (3) feet. Another day, we boogie boarded waves that topped nearly 20 feet. They pummeled me. It was a blast.

The next day, I was 60 feet underwater hand feeding a six (6) foot shark.

Compared to the simplicity and tranquility of Byron Bay, our next stop - Surfer's Paradise - was an assault on the senses. High rises, cars, clubs and shopping dominated this major tourist destination. Interestingly, planners neglected to consider the sun's path when licensing construction. As a result, many high rises casted long shadows across the beach for much of the day.

In early 1988, Brisbane hosted the "*Leisure in the Age of Technology*" themed World's Fair. We arrived shortly after its' successful completion and the city was abuzz with energy. We stayed with the family we'd met in the train station and they could not have been friendlier. I do not recall their names. Touring the fairgrounds was amazing but visiting the Story Bridge Hotel was a highlight. The place was literally part of the bridge.

"Quietly nestled between the foundations of the Story Bridge, The Story Bridge Hotel continues to joyously feed Brisbane as the city grows up around it." (official site)

Playing off my love of design and how people organize themselves, it intrigued me to no end as cars rumbled by overhead.

Following Brisbane, Dorbin and I amicably went our separate ways. I am so grateful for our time together. May he realize all his dreams. Now alone, I stopped at Noosa Head, Fraser Island, Rockhampton and Airlie Beach.

While no particular memories or special experiences come to mind, I am sure that I enjoyed myself. From Airlie Beach came the Whitsunday Islands and access to the Great Barrier Reef (GBR). The causes and conditions for another "*Sam in the Car*" moment aligned.

One thing: I learned in my Interracial & Ethnic Communication class that travel abroad has a predictable, 3-3-3 arc of "three weeks, three months, three years."

Meaning, the first three weeks are experienced with eyes that see everything as good; life is rainbows and unicorns.

At three months, the mind realizes the fallacy of this view. We see the "not so good" in people and begin to miss home.

At three years, one truly understands that the passing of time has profoundly re-shaped, in all regards, our relationships. We have missed significant events in the lives of those we most love.

At some point during this part of my trip, I evidently held to this pattern because I called friends in America and left an f*bomb riddled message on their answering machine bemoaning how they had forgotten me. I do not actually remember this. They told me about it years later.

I was quite comfortable finding my own way – the world as my incubator. I could manifest the outgoing energy needed to meet new folks, or, retreat inwards. It was up to me. In my world, sitting at a café, reading a good book and people watching makes for an exceptional afternoon. If someone is also there to share, then it is all the better. Alone or associated, self-contentment raises our spiritual tide.

The Whitsunday Islands are a popular string of yachting destinations. I had always dreamed of seeing the GBR and Airlie provided me my first opportunity. The boat journey took two and one half (2 ½) hours during which I got motion sickness. People asked me if I was ok. I thanked them for their concern and soon found myself group tenting on the beach. "*Them*" was a group of six or seven folks, including two (2) couples. While I do not recall their names, I do recall this.

QtoP7: Who has most disappointed me in my life? Did I forgive them? If not, what is required for forgiveness?

QtoP8: Have I ever felt completely out of place? What were the circumstances? How deeply is the incident etched?

QtoP9: Am I an introvert or an extrovert? Would I like to be otherwise?

As the sun set, partying began and a bonfire blazed. Slowly, over the course of the evening, one of the coupled guys, inch by inch, nudge by nudge, moved up close and personal, space diluted by a few too many drinks. In the glow of the fire, his hands travelled. *"Hi again, Sam."*

Sure, this man was handsome but he was with his friends, one of whom was supposedly his girlfriend. What was expected of me?

On the one hand, I could act on his advances and suffer the consequences, or, I could practice avoidance and play dumb to his advances. I chose the latter. It did not matter. With the sobriety of morning, they barely said goodbye.

Two (2) days later, on the return journey, I was horny and self-loving in a bathroom stall when an old man opened my improperly locked door and got an entirely unexpected eyeful. Sorry, Sir. In time, I went further north and found myself in Port Douglas (PD), short of cash.

Port Douglas

PD is a tiny, tropical peninsular community at the base of the Daintree rainforest. Just prior to my arrival, an international corporation had built an exclusive, expensive resort. PD became the *"go to place"* for the rich and famous. They flew from Sydney, Melbourne and Adelaide to enjoy the tropical beauty and spend a lot of money.

Needing work, I wandered the town and ended up at Danny's Brasserie, an upscale dining experience within a traditional, Queensland style home. The bartender had just resigned. Seeking out the manager, Nanette, I proposed the following:

I would bartend free for a week, in exchange for two (2) meals a day and housing assistance. If you liked my work, great, if not, I would move on. She accepted. I am so glad she did. My six (6) months at Danny's were a fantastic mix of unusual people and carefree experiences, among them were:

- meeting Crocodile Dundee and chatting with Kylie Minogue while she drank Pina Coladas at the bar;

117

- introducing the Long Island Ice Tea to far north Queensland; it became wildly popular, our signature drink;
- taking a helicopter flight from Cairns to PD – rainforest to the left and reef to the right;
- enjoying the largest personal yacht in Australia after befriending the crew that included a gay captain and co-captain; and,
- visiting a coral shoal via the yacht's dinghy while blasting Motown hits.

Lodging-wise, I first lived with two (2) Aussie ladies in a tiny Airstream unit in a trailer park. I had one bed; they shared the other. It was a 20 minute bike ride, to and from. At late shift's end, the sky was drenched in stars and the Southern Cross bedazzled beyond the silhouetted, coconut palms. I can't count the number of times I nearly ran off the darkened road, gazing skyward. After one month, I moved into a house with five (5) workmates.

One thing: When missing home, I would stare at the night sky and feel better knowing that we all gazed upon the same luminous moon.

Port Douglas was a fountain of unique personalities. Our owner was a middle aged, gay man named Walter, and his mid-20's partner, Kiwanni, the crowned prince of a small, Melanesian island; he was a very talented artist and remained in Australia due to an arranged marriage with Donna, who was the partner of Johnny Mudcrab – the man who had a monopoly on the local seafood specialty, affectionately called, "*Bugs.*" The succulent, 3" x 4" tails were big, square pieces of shrimp.

Walter and Kiwanni had a tempestuous relationship. Kiwanni would come in demanding bottles of expensive champagne and Walter would ring, telling me not to serve. I would look to my boss, Nanette, for guidance.

On New Year's Eve, 1988, Kiwanni threw a full bottle of champagne across the bar because I could not accommodate his request to privately present drinks at

midnight. I remember thinking, "*Wow. I just knowingly met my first Diva!*" The second one, I soon learned, was our head chef, Edward.

He and Kiwanni engaged in some highly, entertaining smack downs that I observed in silent and astounding glee from the window of my closet. One busy night, I playfully responded to Edward's request for a cold drink with a glass full of ice, a splash of soda and lots of garnish. He went full Diva on me. I have much gratitude for Edward's presence in my life, though, for he taught me several things, including:

- Respect and acknowledge the work of others; as a professional, he appreciated the way I ran the bar and said so in meetings;

- Do not publicly tease or demean others; his diva-like ways saw him constantly telling anyone who would listen, "*Oh, Peter's got a gay boy in him. I know it.*" While true, I was not yet ready to live my life openly – my life on my terms - and he simply needed to elevate his mandible.

- I need to cultivate a greater appreciation for all the rainbowed hues of humanity; and.

- If I treated all people with a spirit of equanimity amidst celibacy, folks could gossip all they wanted. Any talk was mere speculation. Everywhere I went, life was abundant and I felt fully engaged. Equanimity reigned.

At one point, Edward's mother visited and he willfully deceived her by passing off a female as his fiancé. For two (2) weeks, everyone supported the charade. I cannot imagine his Mom believed it. Mothers always know. Mine did. She told me so. I wonder, was my avoidance actually deception?

One thing: Sixteen years later I found myself dining with an Asian and Caucasian gay couple, who lived and together.

One's mother was soon to visit and a conversation ensued about how to best explain their relationship as something fraternal in nature. The act of allowing fear to trump the travesty of denying love unsettled me. Living without personal judgments is hard.

Walter and Kiwanni lived in an extraordinary, Balinese inspired home at the base of the Daintree Rainforest, the world's second (2nd) largest after the Amazon. Their home was multi-tiered with no exterior walls. Screened, internal walls protected the bedrooms and bathroom. The jungle flowed throughout with intriguing, canvased art and eastern sculptures everywhere.

When my AU tourist visa needed renewal, I went to New Zealand (NZ) and stayed with Nanette's friend on the north island, outside of the capital, Auckland. I awoke on a sheep and deer farm on my first Thanksgiving away. My call home was forlorn and full of longing.

While visiting NZ, I joined a group of folks on a weekend visit to Whangarei Flats, north of Auckland. Accessible at low tide, and isolated at the high water mark, our three (3) days of food and beverage consisted of two (2) kegs of beer and the oysters chipped from the rocks at low tide and opened on the fire. To this day, I do not like oysters.

Shortly thereafter, back in AU, my lifetime of cold snowy Christmases ended with celebrations in a pool, on a hot humid day, with a tissue paper hat on my head, a la British tradition, followed by a swim in the Daintree Rainforest. The water was so clean and pure you could drink it while you swam.

Other characters in the PD community included a recently divorced British woman in her mid- 30s who was sleeping with Tim, the teenage kitchen helper. Justin was an accomplished photographer. Photography was soon to become my passion. Sandy was our assistant chef whose sadness saw her unsuccessfully try to end her life.

Martin was the straight, Fabio-like, hair stylist at the

local, upscale salon. One night we went out for drinks and at the end of the evening his arrogance glowed within a compliment, "*You know, Peter*," he said as he dropped me off, "*I could have gone out with anyone tonight but I choose you. I don't know why but you're interesting.*" Oh if I had had the courage to be me. He was so very handsome.

Mid-way through my time at Danny's, Walter and Kiwanni skipped town and the restaurant was bought by a wine aficionado who refurbished, restocked, and gave me a significant raise. With this extra cash, I was able to save and soon embarked for Japan. Why there? It was close and I had heard that English teaching was lucrative.

Moreover, Sean from my WT days was now living in Tokyo. My friends threw me a joyous going away party and Nanette gifted me a beautiful silver, turtle necklace that I wore non-stop for years until I lost it. A slight taste of attachment lingers. Funny that.

Asian Overview

In early March 1989, when the plane touched down in Tokyo, I did not consciously realize how much this decision would influence and alter my life. Until my return to Australia in 2003, my Asian experiences were awash in endless variations of the human condition, wondrous adventures and insightful lessons. All things were good, even when they were momentarily bad. From that initial step off the plane, I felt at home. The energies and rhythms of life in Asia suited my temperament. I felt awash in a familiarity born of lives past lived.

To a certain extent, I was and still am, a wide-eyed, innocent child, looking at the world, fresh and anew, each and every day. People are people no matter where one travels. The opportunity to gain a more profound understanding of who we are through meaningful, genuine interactions, free from attachment or clinging, is forever available. I begin with a story about my own delightful, crazy ignorance.

Japan and Korea

I arrived in Tokyo late at night and it was cold. At the airport, I made what I thought was the proper lodging choice so my 70 pounds of luggage and I boarded a nearly empty subway and rode for over an hour. Exiting and cresting the subway staircase, I beheld a vast metropolis of blinking signs, composed of thousands of indecipherable characters. It was a staggering shift in my relative reality. Where was I? What had I done?

Wandering the quiet streets, I approached doors that had *"hotel"* posted above. Time and time again, I knocked. Older Japanese women answered, stared at me, and hurriedly shut the door.

I returned to the subway and found the entrance chained shut. In a city of 30 million folks, the subway stopped running around 1am. I remember stepping into at a phone booth and unsuccessfully trying to call Sean. Meandering in circles, I continued my search. I soon looked down and realized that I no longer had my shoulder bag containing everything important, including my passport and $9,000 dollars in traveller's checks.

I eventually found a *"koban,"* or street-side, community police box staffed with two (2) officers and, without any real communication, threw my luggage at their door and re-traced frantically my steps to the phone booth where sat my untouched bag. Exhausted, I soon laid my luggage between two (2) narrow buildings, and had a cold night's sleep.

Welcome to Tokyo. The light of dawn saw more drama ensue as I became part of the rush hour. My luggage and I took up space for half a dozen. I was asparagus in a tray.

Three things; one: I once boarded a packed, rush hour train and placed by gym bag on the overhead rack. By the time my stop arrived, I had been forced to the other end.

Screaming in Japanese, folks soon realized my dilemma

and quickly body surfed my bag overhead. It was a beautiful, smile filled, sentient moment.

Two: One Halloween, an underground call went out for foreigners to meet at a particular train station, track, and time, for a loop around the city. Hundreds of us dressed up, showed up, and filled three (3) cars. Partying and carrying on, the looks on locals' faces as the doors opened at each stop were priceless. Some brave souls joined us, most waited for the next car. There was something about the rebellious energy that made it particularly satisfying.

Three: I learned to love train travel in Japan. I wish America would follow suit in such a connected, comprehensive and orderly way.

Eventually, I arrived at Sean's and he told me that I had been scouring the *"Love Hotel"* district for a room. *"Love Hotels"* are exactly as the name implies. Sean lived in a small apartment with a big dog and I felt that my place on their floor took up the only, available free space for far too long as I looked for accommodation.

Like any metropolis, Tokyo real estate was expensive. $6,900 would be required up front to move into a $1,300/ month, Western style apartment. Therefore, I opted for $400, month-by-month lodging at a *"gaijin,"* or foreigner's house.

A gaijin house was a three or four (3 or 4) story building with four (4) rooms per floor (two people per room and a bunk bed), along with a small kitchen and bathroom per floor. Shared showers were on the ground floor. The majority of residents were English teachers and ladies who worked the hostess bars - a subset of love hotels.

The hostesses would speak of work that catered to the whims of drunken salarymen, having the same frivolous conversations and fake swoon sessions, hour after hour, night after night, feigning and fulfilling a fantasy.

Ladies got money for every drink poured so they would

dump their drink into nearby plants and act drunk. The men bought more. Burn-out rates were high and the nightly take home of up to $500+ was often no longer worth it.

If sex was a factor, and in most cases it was not, rates would triple or quadruple. Once settled, I focused much of my free time on learning the language.

I studied hard how to read, write and speak Japanese. The written language uses three (3) alphabets: 1) the Chinese based, Kanji characters, blended with two additional alphabets at 56 characters each – 2) Hiragana and 3) Katakana. At my peak, I passed the level four (4), national proficiency exam.

One thing: Language is a repository of cultural values and thought patterns – to learn a language is to reflect and embrace, in part, a new way of looking at the world. By the end of my nearly four (4) years in Japan, the shift in my way thinking became apparent and bothersome and I was ready to leave.

My roommate, Derek, was a Welsh guy who dated an Italian woman, Sophia. Together with her two (2) sisters, Sophia operated *Manta Ray*, a small, exclusive resort on the pristine, remote island of Palawan, in Puerto Princessa, in the Philippines.

Surrounded by turquoise water, endless white beaches, and lush jungle, three (3) cabins and a small dining cabana, Sophia cooked me one of the best meals of my life – fresh made, Italian pasta topped with the black ink of an octopus. It was a sticky, tasty, worm-like bowl of crazy goodness.

Five (5) hours north by boat, towering marble cliffs rose from the ocean and were home to El Nido, a stunning community that was once chronicled by *National Geographic* magazine. It remains one of my favorite places ever.

127

My first job and love

In the late 80's, Japan was seen as the world's economic powerhouse and spoken English skills were prized. Teaching English took many forms, including: proper university jobs, vocational school jobs, English conversation lounges, and contractual schools.

If you were a native English speaker and had a proper, four (4) year degree in anything, you could get a work visa. The wages were terrific. Visa processing required that you do a quick turn- around trip so I spent a week in Seoul, South Korea. Three (3) experiences come to mind.

A man named Lee, befriended me on the street and invited me for dinner at his home. I accepted. On arrival, I took off my shoes. A stuttering conversation ensued as an uncertainty filled the space. In broken English, they asked me too wash my feet. I was so embarrassed. His mother made a traditional Korean meal, including kim chee, a la the stinky, smashed bottle at Digmons, and I liked it.

The next day, Lee took me to witness the on-going riots between college students and the police at the country's main college campus. In late 80's, South Korea was birthing its' new democracy amidst high tensions. I watched students advance and retreat while taunting the authorities. I got tear gassed.

We soon made our way to the woods behind the university where vendors had built make shift stalls. People were dancing, drinking and laughing. I was enjoying the chill of the cool, spring forest.

Time and time again, I smilingly refused their gestures for me to dance with our vendor, a female. Eventually, I relented. My innate hesitation was well founded as the energy shifted almost instantaneously. Lee ran to the circle, put his arm around my shoulder and said, *"We must go now fast."* Laughter turned to ugly yells as we quickly fled. My befuddlement remains.

Days later, I was strolling through a Seoul city park when I was spied by an old man wearing a illegible sandwich board, waving the Bible and screaming as if to preach. He turned. Our eyes locked, and he chased me out of the park. Why? I do not know but I could not imagine dealing with such an altercation in a culture whose ways and language I did not understand.

Back in Tokyo, my first job was with English Services International (ESI), a contractual school. It lasted nine (9) months. ESI would contract with companies for specialized English courses from one (1) week to six (6) months. My first gig was amazing. A pharmaceutical giant rented out an entire hotel at the base of Mount Fuji for three (3) months of training their 800 new sales recruits. It included two (2) weeks of intensive English training.

One thing: Japan is known for its' cultural emphasis on group over individual, as reflected by the depth, breadth and expense of this training. It built loyalty and commitment toward the company among the next generation of salarymen.

Each morning, we awoke for a run. One day, I jumped the trail to run through a field. I had shortcut through a rice paddy and trampled many sprouts. Rice is sacred in Japan and my action was flooded with serious disrespect. I was so very embarrassed and remorseful.

Soon after, I was assigned to a famous electronics firm for a six (6) month gig. Four (4) days a week, I took a train and two (2) buses to their factory -160 minutes round trip. Three (3) of the days, I taught eight (8), 55 minute private lessons.

On Saturday, I taught three (3), three (3) hour classes. It was intense and exhausting and worth it because I met my two (2) best Japanese friends, Keiji and Masayuri, the former capturing my heart.

Keiji was an only son and older brother to his two (2) sisters. Their father tragically passed at an early age.

Masayuri was married with his first child. Both were outstanding, high level students whose kindness made my time in Japan so very special.

After class one day, Keiji pulled me aside and invited me away for a hang gliding weekend. This was the start of a friendship that remains, albeit with a sad heart for I surely fell in love.

What I know now and failed to understand then is that, as the only son in a fatherless family, he had to get married, pass on the name and provide grandchildren. Whatever he may have felt for me, and we had many powerful moments of longing, our future was my fantasy. At the start of our last vacation, I told him that I loved him and we spent a week in silence. I am sure he is an amazing father. I am better for us having met.

That first weekend, and for three (3) years following, twice monthly from May to November, we drove west to the mountains for hang gliding and parasailing fun. He picked me up Friday evening and we returned to Tokyo late Sunday night. In between, I flew among low hills and he soared at 2,000 feet. He was very accomplished. His friends were kind and welcoming.

One thing: It is amazing how jealousy creeps into your mind. At one point, our trips included a lovely young lady. Over time, after always sitting in the back seat, she asked to swap and sit up front. Of course he agreed and we subsequently alternated. I found myself so conflicted and angry; I was jealous and it felt almost uncontrollable. It sounds so silly and childish now but it was a new reality for me. Later, in Hong Kong, I became the target of this corrosive emotion.

Beyond these weekends, Keiji and I traveled extensively throughout Japan, twice to the Philippines and Thailand. Later, he visited me in both Nepal and Hong Kong. The last time we were in contact, he wrote, *"You are so lucky. You get to live the life you want."* Our many adventures included:

- Summiting Mt. Fuji;
- Visiting Nagasaki and Hiroshima;
- Weekends at his family's beach condo; Snowboarding the Japanese Alps;
- Road tripping Hokkaido on a hot spring tour;
- Hiking Mt. Aso - Japan's largest, active volcano;

- Scuba diving in El Nido, and getting our licenses;
- Night scuba diving and food markets in Thailand;
- Attending the Log Riding (Onabashira) Festival;

- Overnighting on a fishing boat and netting a rare fugu fish. Improperly prepared, fugu kills; and,
- So much more. Love.

One thing: The following journal entry was written while on Christmas holiday, shortly before leaving Japan. The repressed and frustrated angst revealed makes me wince and wonder and be grateful for who I have become. We all survive in some fashion until we don't.

***

"It's Christmas Eve and I am lost. Where am I? Why? Too introspective. Cut the shit. The answers lie before you and between her legs. Just take them. Enjoy. Fulfill desires. Experience pain. Then, die. How bloody boring! Is that all? Just tell me why? So simple a question, and yet, never seemingly answered to one's satisfaction. But, what if I were to tell you that I have the answer? That I possess the definitive response to its' asking? What would you give me? how much would you pay? Is there a way to make the world right? A way in which the starving can eat, the sick can be healed, the lost can be found? God, where are you? Just tell me that you love me. Please. I am going nowhere slow."

***

Masayuri and his wife were wonderful friends and cultural educators. They taught me that serving different foods on the same plate evoked frowns. I taught them that one gifts

131

corked wine rather than a screw top. Together we learned that moments of silence amidst conversation were good.

Three (3) highlights of our time together were:

- the annual "*Hanami*," or Cherry Blossom festivals;
- a trip to a volcanic "*onsen*," or hot springs where monkeys playfully scooped hot water onto fellow furry loved ones; and,
- a New Year's trip to Mama Masayuri's house in Akita, in northern Japan. I was the first foreigner she had ever met.

As Japan's biggest holiday, I am grateful to have celebrated in such an authentic and genuine way, including eating "*mochi*."

Mochi is a sticky, taffy-like square of goopy rice. Eating it on New Year's Day is said to bring good luck. Sadly, dozens of older folks annually choke to death on the sticky mix.

> *QtoP10: What is gossip? Am I an active gossip? To what extent do I consciously monitor my words?*

> *QtoP11: How much do I believe in stereotypes? Do I have any negative tendencies towards anyone?*

> *QtoP12: Have I ever experienced extreme jealously? What did I do? How did I deal with the feelings?*

Mainland China

In December 1989, I visited mainland China where only six (6) months earlier, the government had brutally cracked down on democratic advocates in Tiananmen Square, killing over 200 and arresting thousands.

Years later, the most memorable dinner of my life revolved around this stain on China's history for I dined with Duang Yang, a main protest speaker. He was living in Hong Kong and advocating for workers' rights into southern China via radio.

He shared that after speaking, he boarded a train home and halfway there, he saw his face on television. The government had declared him a wanted man for subversion against the state. Feeling he had done nothing wrong, he returned to police headquarters in Beijing. On presenting himself, a policeman just outside the station told him to turn around and run. He didn't.

Story short, he was imprisoned and placed in the Tuberculosis ward where he contracted the disease. Rescued by an international human rights group, half of his right lung was removed and he was then well. He had the calm, compassionate composure of a man living a realized life of purpose.

Heading to China, I took the bullet train south, from Tokyo to Kobe, and boarded an old cruise ship for a three day, two night (3D/2N) journey to Shanghai. Now a revived city, in 1989, Shanghai was a gloomy, stark reminder of the vastly different ways people lived their lives.

Journal entry (12/89)

"The boat? Not bad. A bit old and tattered... restaurant – cheap, bar – also cheap, dance hall. In all, a nice experience.... There were only about 70 passengers of which six, myself included, were Westerners: two Germans, two Yanks, and a Canuck (we all bonded.)"

"Until today, I just didn't realize exactly what Tokyo takes out of you. I am tired. Shit. I certainly have a greater understanding for the Japanese."

"Met a Chinese doctor on board – Dr. G – who insisted on getting us a place to stay, transportation and sightseeing. Really nice, but done in such a high strung, high powered, railroading type of way that we all agreed that we felt a little nervous and pressured. Oh well, Life could be worse. Right? ....So, after unboarding and doing the customs thing (no one asked me a thing; no one looked at my stuff), Dr. G arranged an ambulance from his hospital to deliver us to

136

our hotel. Crazy! 'The unexpected ventures of travel have begun' was my thought."

"On wandering the streets, the real genuine flavor and feel of China started to hit home. Being foreigners is a hoot! If we stop for one brief instant, a crowd gathers. No one really speaks, they just look, gawk.... In many places, employee name tags are numbers...Would you want to be a number?"

And on it went throughout the city and surrounding areas. After a week, I boarded a plane to Kunming, the largest city in the southwest, and then bussed to Dali. My travel guide praised the area's incredible, rural beauty.

My two (2) greatest memories here relate to the Shapin Market and fishing; fishing not with nets or hooks, but with Cormorant, a type of bird. Fishermen placed a ring around the bird's long neck so it could swallow but not ingest when it dove for a fish. Hitting the boat's edge with a paddle, the bird returned to the sound. Reaching down, they grabbed the bird by its' feet and shook it until the fish fell out, then threw it back into Lake Erhai for another round. The poor cormorant, it's endlessly eating and perpetually hungry. Ornithologic karma.

Here is a sampling of journal entries:

"Off to explore Dali. What a place! I think I am in love. Everything I've ever dreamed about / imagined concerning a small, mountain bounded Asian town is fulfilled by Dali – quaint, frantic, exotic, and serene."

"The Shapin market was brilliant. Brimming with colorful vendors, unusual goods, and fantasty-filled scenes ... returned to a marvelous bath and massage."

"What a vile trip to the public lavatory. 20 gallon drums, some overflowing, into which you pissed. Large cavernous cement holes into which you shit. Gross. China at its sanitary best!"

"Their questions are direct and pointed concerning America,

freedom, democracy and the lot.... These people don't even know who the Beatles are! But, they know Michael Jackson."

"Had a convo with an American couple here teaching 'Medical English.'... concerning the Cultural Revolution's impact on medicine ... detailing practices of plumbers and bricklayers being re-assigned to health care – no knowledge whatsoever – because they were 'pure' in their thoughts."

"Oh how the night can fulfill fantasies of exotic smoke filled bars, music and conversation. Smoke of a substance wantonly unlawful at home – clouds of hash and marijuana lazily linger as people of the world enjoy the time which is being offered them. Here's to Jim's Peace Café"

One thing: I resonated with Jim immediately. I described him as follows: *"Jim himself is one sharp guy. Taught himself English and must contend with a government that threatens to close his restaurant if he is TOO successful... Two undercover Beijing police visited last week. I guess Jim played quite the diplomat in their presence."*

"As I pass them (Chinese) on the street, they look with caution and wonder; their faces read of questions. When I flash a smile coupled with "Ni Hao", 99% of the people radiate smiles of warmth. A smile goes a very far and the response it elicits is warming to the soul."

"Headed to the Three Pagoda Temple" but were turned back by the Police with the utterance of one word – out! Ok, no problem, Buddy."

"I feel solemnly reflective about my time in Dali. Content. Pleased. It really serves to lend perspective and offer calming thoughts about what is genuinely important in the throes of hectic activities.... The peoples' happiness provided by the toils required for basic survival can be seen in their faces – self-satisfaction at self-preservation, though, they know little else by which to compare and contrast ...

I am really looking forward to my return to Japan..."

My Second Job and Home Life

Shortly after returning to Tokyo, I joined Derek at TFLC and moved into a traditional Japanese style apartment. TFLC was an English language vocational school. Our top female students joined the prestigious Japan Airlines (JAL). Mid-level students filled various, service industry positions. In Japan, getting into college is the challenge. Once enrolled, graduation is essentially guaranteed. Unfortunately, this perspective conflicted with Western notions of how education should operate and caused much friction among teaching staff and management.

In the early and mid-80's, TFLC had approximately 400 students, by 1990, nearly 4,000. The pains of this explosive growth were evident on my joining. The 150 foreign instructors had aligned with the Japanese teachers and formed the largest foreign workers union in Japan. Wages exploded. Certain practices were abolished, i.e., kneeling and bowing to the owner when receiving one's yearly bonus check. Staff/ management tension ran high.

At one point, we actually did the unthinkable and went on strike. In a land where conformity and saving face were paramount, the atmosphere was nearly unimaginable. As police escorted us on our march through the streets of Tokyo, nearby workers hung out windows and cheered us on. They had rarely, if ever, seen anything like it.

One thing: I will never forget my despondent feeling the morning the office radio proclaimed that the first shots of the 1991, Desert Storm Gulf War were fired. Some folks cheered. Others, like me, remained silent and so very sad. Little did I know then, that the repercussions of this Iraq war paled in comparison to what would follow.

Stories of staff craziness abounded. Everyone had huge classes of up to 52 students in cramped quarters. The retractable walls were porous. Everybody could hear everything. I taught reading, writing, and conversation to various levels. We had school wide sports days and rented a 2,000 seat auditorium for a class talent show. I was joint emcee. Overall, I found the work fun and intellectually satisfying. The tax free money and three (3) months of holiday per year were welcomed bonuses.

My colleagues were an eclectic mix of personalities and our tight office space was always abuzz with a powerful energy - sometimes good, sometimes not. Seated at an adjoining desk, Ray became a good friend. He was smart, driven and often dominating. Shortly after he and his wife, Debbie arrived, she got pregnant. I shared in their journey to parenthood and the infant years of their beautiful, little girl. I enjoyed it very much since I missed my niece, Trisha, greatly. Plus, by this point, I had gained another niece, Kim, and a nephew, Tom.

One thing: Throughout my time abroad, not being there for Trisha, Kim and Tom is my one regret – to not be their Uncle and see them grow up. Further, I failed utterly in my "name only" role as Kim's godfather.

Part of Ray's dominating nature included a hot temper that scared when it flared. One night we were at his place discussing something and things got heated. He started yelling and berating my position. Given the calm nature of my upbringing, I sat bewildered at his behavior. My insides churned; it hurt. *"Why are you screaming?"* I thought, *"Why?"*

One thing: I have only seen my Dad angry three (3) times in my life. To this day, I struggle with anger – how to both deal with, and express, it. As an emotion, it does not make sense to me. In the end, it seems only to disturb and disrupt my own happiness and inner peace.

Debbie, having unavoidably been listening from another room, came in and screamed at him, *"Ray! What is your problem? Do you want to lose another friend?"* Wow! What a question - loaded with a backstory about which I have never asked, nor ever care to hear.

Silence ensued and a meek apology was forthcoming. In the late 90's, a similar situation arose when he visited

Nepal. The incident was again re-imagined, and better understood, years later in Hong Kong.

For a while, I worked with another TFLC colleague, Mark, who was spearheading a non-profit group that supported women weavers in rural Thailand by selling their goods in Tokyo. I joined him once on a site inspection and product pick-up trip. While in Bangkok, we got locked inside a strip club. The staff tried to extort money for drinks and a show. We were fortunate that Mark spoke enough Thai to ensure our safe departure.

Yes, women shot ping pong balls via their nether regions, a la, *Priscilla: Queen of the Desert*. It had an entertaining quality, I admit. But, the drug glazed eyes that held my gaze, asking me, "*Are you enjoying this?*" as she pulled a string of razor blades from her vagina, were awful. Her stare is still upon me - complicit guilt.

I lived in Nakano, one (1) train stop from work in Shinjuku. Life below the tracks was a labyrinth of lanes, tiny sliding shop doors, hanging flags and colorful paper lanterns. I found and hung out in places that looked like scenes from childhood movies. A magical, mysterious, and mesmerizing quality was afoot. Sometimes after work, I would pass my station for a longer walk home. With narrow streets and a rickety house, my neighborhood and living quarters, much like my life, were leaning heavily Japanese.

I had my first experience of an interconnected world along these streets. I had gotten a new Visa card and tried unsuccessfully to use it. I dialed the 800 help number in America and the assistant told me, "*Let's see. You just tried to buy some socks in ...*" It was astonished. It was the early 90's.

I became a friendly regular with the owners of a corner "*yakitori*" shop, attached to the laundromat I used. "*Yaki*" means "to burn." "*Tori*" means bird. Together with sake (Japanese rice wine), yakitori shops served little skewers of assorted meats and cooked them on a tiny, counter-sized, charcoal grill. The chicken and liver were my favorites. I love the fresh and healthy nature Japanese food. It is one of my favorite cuisines. Keiji and I got our scuba diving licenses in Dumagette, Phillipines because the owner of this yakitori shop had a school there.

One political season, a candidate claiming spiritual powers ran in my district, or *"ku."* His supporters costumed up in masks and creepy outfits to look like him. They were everywhere. He lost and shortly thereafter, launched a sarin gas attack on the subway killing 12. He and 13 disciples remain jailed and awaiting execution.

Five (5) minutes from my apartment was an extraordinarily, eclectic coffee shop. Though my words fail to fully suffice, I try - The Classic Coffee House in Nakano, Japan.

- *Hunched over to enter;*
- *A tiny, dark wooden lobby with card catalog type, library drawers along one wall;*
- *The sound of scratchy, skipping records wafting;*
- *A perpetually grim looking lady, always dressed in black, greeted you;*
- *A small staircase led to an attic-like second floor that creaked with every step;*

- *Everything was wood;*
- *Old, dusty instruments and bizarre, Dali-like portraits hung from the ceiling and various, Asian themed sculptures sat dusty and undisturbed;*
- *The ripped seats of old train benches adjoined slightly tilting tables; People slept in hidden corners and talked in whispers;*
- *Coffee was served in stained white cups on old, chipped saucers with sugar cubes stacked. If you didn't use your cubes, they were collected by a white gloved server and shared with others;*

- *Screw top medicine caps, old and still white, contained your creamer; and,*
- *Cigarette smoke lingered.*

142

143

My apartment was at the end of a tiny street in an old, primarily bamboo home with two (2) residences below and above. Mine was above and to the left. I paid $480US a month.

Two, six (6) tatami mat rooms were separated by sliding "*shoji*," or rice paper doors. One tatami is a thickly woven bamboo mat roughly 6' x 2' 8" in size; it is their traditional measure of floor space. The front room had a squat toilet, no shower, and a kitchen area with a two-burner gas grill.

The back room had a small storage area where you kept your clothing and "futon," or mattress. A window overlooked a garden. Soundproofing was non-existent. If I did not feel like sponge bathing, I paid $2 to enter a traditional, neighborhood "*sento*," or public bathhouse.

Sentos once dotted all neighborhoods and were a regular part of collective life. The advent of Western style, in-home showers has signaled their unfortunate decline. The various herbal baths and steam rooms were incredibly relaxing. Each sento had rows of squat showers. You sat on plastic stool in front of a mirror with a shower nozzle on a flexible hose. Washing thoroughly was mandatory.

The rows of mirrors meant that you could look into A to see the reflection in B to see C. The presence of any foreigner triggered intense curiosity. It was funny to watch their obvious mirrored attempts at subtle gawking. Sentos were unisex until post-WWII, when American occupation officials enforced gender separation.

Commonly, Japanese are seen as a reserved people. When it comes to public nudity, their sense of community and cohesiveness can be taken as relaxed.

Once, my TFLC colleagues and I road tripped to the mountains. By chance, we came upon an "*onsen*" village nestled among the mountains along a small section of hot river. Many folks, from babies to grandparents, were soaking, eating and drinking, and playing in the nude, a genuine communion in the beauty of natural hot baths.

145

Early in my Japanese experience, one student took me to something vastly different from a sento. We entered an old home and sat briefly in a small waiting room. Called separately, a kimono clad woman led me to a small, private room. It had a bed and breakfast feel with a small mattress, a dresser and mirror. A tiled area had a small squat shower and a large drum-like seat, pressed with a plastic trough. I was left briefly alone and hosed down.

An older woman dressed in white, several decades a cougar, soon entered. She went behind me and lathered my nether regions via the trough. When done, she directed me to the bed where she jerked me off and left. It took about fifteen minutes. I have no idea how much it cost and I am still not exactly sure how I feel about it. I do know that I lied when I told my friend it was great.

Beyond the food and language, I got certified in *"Shiatsu,"* a traditional, Japanese style massage. I learned Thai and Balinese massages in their respective countries and visited many Zen Buddhist temples. Their impact on my spirit, though reverent, paled in comparison to my palpable, visceral reaction when later visiting Tibetan Buddhist temples in Nepal.

Joining a western style gym was the only predominantly Western thing I did. I did a lot of aerobics. Two (2) of my teachers were the National Pairs champions. When leaving for Nepal, they offered to take me for a secretive and illegal dining experience – raw monkey brain, a la *Indian Ford and the Temple of Doom*. I declined. Even now, the thought of it makes me queasy.

By 1992, I found the Tokyo grind tiring and felt stifled by the impact of studying Japanese with such zeal. The language is filled with numerous self- deprecating features that foster self-doubt. For example, you constantly end statements with the word, *"maybe,"* or, *"I think."*

This ingratiates you to the listener as they confirm your thought, re-affirming the "we" between the speakers. Over time, the "I" of one's confidence wanes.

146

One 1992 journal entry reads: *"I need to re-enter the world from the cocoon known as Japan. Hatch. Stretch. Awaken. Fly. Get out of this place. It is eating my spirit."*

Related to my language studies, I became enamored by the English translations of Yukio Mishima's books. He is one of Japan's best 20th century authors and was considered for the Nobel Prize in Literature three (3) times. Much like the mind games played by the language, his books are tightly wound reflections of his perceived demons (see *Forbidden Colors* and *Confession of a Mask*).

In real life, he was allowed to lord over a personal army of 100 men who camped at the base of Mount Fuji. In 1970, he and four (4) of his men invaded their Ministry of Self-Defense and committed *"seppuku,"* or ritualistic suicide, on the roof; he had hoped to incite a coup. Also on this day, he submitted his *Sea of Finality* tetralogy, printed posthumously. I read all of his books, sequentially, cover to cover. In the end, they messed with my mind.

Thankfully, Haruki Murakami's works were redemptive. Sample *A Wild Sheep Chase,* and so many others.

Down the street from my house was an old school, Superman style phone booth. One night, lonely, drunk and wanting to hear my parents' voices, I rang. Talking about this and that, my sporadic, giggle filled chatter caused my Mom to sternly ask, *"Peter, are you with a girl? Are you sleeping with a woman?"* I was forlorned and surprised. In time, I got a land line and it rang one day with a haunting call from home – a moment that instantly chiseled deep.

On answering, I immediately sensed something was awry. Despite a physical distance of nearly 6,500 miles, the pain was immediate, real.

"Peter," Dad said, *"your brother Adam is in the hospital."*

"What happened?" I asked.

"He... he... he," my Mom stuttered, *"tried to kill himself by overdosing on some pills." "When?"* I muttered. *"Three and a half weeks ago, but thankfully he's ok now,"* they said.

In that moment, space refracted.

The floor shrunk as the walls collapsed. Questions present and patterns past flooded my mind. A stark brittleness overwhelmed my heart. My body became cold.

Present questions
- How? When? Where? Why?
- How are you, Adam?
- How are Kat, Trisha, Kim and Tom?
- How is everyone?
- Really? You could not tell me sooner? He has been lying there without contact from me as if I do not care?

Patterns past
- Like Charlie's death;
- Like Grandma's passing;
- Like talking not of certain things; better he not know, protect.

Brothers loved, what happened to us all?

My wonderful parents' compassionate hearts encountered, endured, and overcame. Love has always been present, never lacking, in our home; neither now, nor all those years ago. As I write, we all remain blessedly.

These were tales of my 20's.

***

I encourage all groups to begin chapter discussions with the following three (3) questions, then reflect and share.

What is my overall impression of the chapter?
Which story did I most prefer? Least?
What is a theme of the chapter?

Reflect and Share: My 20's

A suggested way to proceed: *Someone call out a letter (A-Z). Read aloud that question and answer it until conversation is exhausted, then, continue with another letter. Enjoy.*

a) What is your reaction to this statement? (pg. 91)

> "*Once unbound from the rules and regulations that guide and shape our youth, we must face adulthood, knowing that we alone are responsible for scripting our future, that the boundaries and limits which newly bind are of our own making.*"

b) At what age did you move out? What were the circumstances? Describe your first apartment in three (3) words; the neighborhood?

c) What live concerts or shows have you seen? What was your first? Best? Worst?

d) What is politics? Are you political by nature?

e) How active was your dating life? Who and what do you most recall?

f) Are we (pg. 93) "*infinitely more alike, than not.*"?

g) Did you attend college? If yes, what did you study? If no, what did you do? What path did your life take?

h) On page 95, I share a story of a woman with a "*mirror and a gynecological tool*" and ask, "*What exactly was the offense?*" How would you reply?

i) What is your opinion of public breastfeeding?

j) Did you have a "*Chad*" in your life? (pg. 99)

k) What was your first car? What do you most remember about it? What is your dream car?

l)   Have you ever lost something that you wish you could get back? What? Why?

m)   Growing up, were you aware of racial segregation? When? Where? What were the surrounding circumstances? How did you react?

n)   Name the top three (3) influential albums of your life. Why are they so special? What do they teach you?

o)   What do you think of Burke's definition of man (pg. 108)? *"Man is the symbol-using (symbol-making, symbol-misusing) animal, inventor of the negative (or moralized by the negative), separated from his natural condition by instruments of his own making, goaded by the spirit of hierarchy (or moved by the sense of order), and rotten with perfection."*

p)   Do you do any extreme sport? What is the most dangerous thing you have ever done?

q)   What type of social environment do you most/ least enjoy? What makes you most comfortable? Awkward?

r)   Do you have an affinity for a particular animal? Which one? Why?

s)   What is a hero? Is Duang Yang a hero? (pg. 132) Why or why not? Who is your hero?

t)   What is your opinion of commercial sex work?

u)   What is your greatest curiosity?

v)   Where was your first Thanksgiving? Christmas? Birthday? away from home. What were the causes and conditions that put you there? How was it?

w)   On describing my initial reaction to Asia, I write (pg. 124): *"From that initial step off the plane, I felt at home.... The energies and rhythms of life in Asia suited my temperament. I felt enveloped in familiarity."*

Have you ever experienced such a reaction to a particular place or person? If yes, when? Where?

x) Do you agree or disagree? (pg. 127) *"Language is a repository of cultural values and thought patterns – to learn a language is to reflect and embrace, in part, a new way of looking at the world."*

y) Do you struggle with any particular emotion? If yes, which one? How do you adapt?

z) What three (3) adjectives best describe your 20's? Why?

Amusing Journal Entries

Reviewing my journals, I came across many wonderful descriptions, stories and memories that did not find their way into my tale so I share them here for your amusement. Please enjoy.

From My 20s

Singapore, Malaysia and Thailand, 8/91

1) *"I boarded a Singapore bus this morning, bound for Malaysia, and smacked a lady in the face with my left elbow. Ooops.... The bus into Malaysia proved to be a drive from order into chaos. The border checks, luggage, etc... were virtually non-existent. And, what did transpire occurred within rundown quarters, carried out by rundown looking people."*

2) *"The spider of doubt weaved a heavy web. Lingering thoughts weighed forcefully on my mind. Where had I gone wrong?"*

3) *"As the sun slowly descended into a serene*

peaceful sea, giving off radiant hues of yellows, reds and oranges, an old man sat looking reflectively."

4) "I've got the shits (cleans me out, right? The good side. Always the optimist.)"

5) "On my way here, came through a palm tree plantation. Raised for oil, they harvest the red/orange hued seeds from a large honeycomb, like pod. So interesting. And, the trees lend themselves to an incredibly soft, lush underbrush. Would be great for camping."

6) "A rather plump lady drinks too much beer. Soon swiping at unseen creatures, her husband looks on, helplessly, listlessly, lovingly."

7) "Have shacked up at a tiny, local village.... The people are said to be of the Orang Asli tribe.... I met an Indian man who's been here for years helping them preserve and promote their unique, nomadic heritage and customs. He gives them 10 years before it is gone." Comment: The government was trying to assimilate them into the dominant Malay culture. This tribe hunted with blow guns. So cool.

8) "Rajan (hostel owner) just informed me, when asked about health care, that the village has two witchdoctors. Yes, genuine, authentic, cast out the evil spirit witchdoctors. Evidently, the ceremonies are public events.... He also said the only form of acceptable, government provided health care is vaccinations. Why? Because they are accompanied by pain and that signals something is being done right. Any Western tablets or liquids are gratefully accepted then disgarded."

Comment: Hiking for over an hour through a thick jungle, we arrived at a small hut where I witnessed a healing ceremony, complete with drums, incense, lots of chanting, and the occasional appearance of

152

something bloody – supposedly pulled from the ailing patient, now said to be healing.

9) *"Last night's witchdoctor ceremony was simply astounding. My writing is sorely inadequate in capturing my feelings about being witness to the entire event."*

10) *"The locals have recently seen a tiger in the area; they're being driven from the mountain by construction and logging.... The locals are very afraid. And, there I am walking around like Joe Cool. Is ignorance truly bliss? Perhaps. But, it can lead to serious bodily damage or even death."*

11) *"There is a village lady who went for her morning constitutional squat, a baby came out. Big news!*

12) *"Fleeting slivers of electricity pierce a sky that yields no rain. The ground is parched; the plants withered. People starve and cry in unheard pain. The world is being cruel. Again."*

13) *"The coffee here, served with sweetened condensed milk, is truly a dessert in a glass." Comment: In Vietnam, I enjoyed these all day. They were tasty, hot or cold, and cheap.*

14) *"The West will never be able to recapture the simplicity and wonder of life which provides the necessary balance for peaceful co-existence. Are we therefore doomed? Doomed to What? Perhaps the horrific visions of walled cities and perpetually patrolled streets to secure our safety? And, we're doing this to the rest of the world!*

Thailand, 8/93

15) *"A guy gave us a ride. The, on dropping off, I left my wallet in his back seat. He came back two minutes later and returned it! Unbelievable!"*

16) *"Dogs. Dogs. Dogs. They are fornicating all over the place!"*

17) *"The Kota Bharu Market was beautiful. It was covered in yellow tinted glass that cast a luminous glow over everything. The fruits and veggies looked amazing!"* Comment: *My most favorite market ever!*

18) *"Morning. Morning. Morning. A various assortment of ritualistic greetings echo through the halls of the guest house. None of them really imbued with meaning, but all of them greasing the cogs of the collective mechanism we refer to as society."*

19) *"Boy do I want to get back into a real classroom. I envision myself in front 300 UB students, rambling on as only I can, in my own way. Feeding some minds, disturbing notions of the world and its' ways, aiming to shatter the mindsets which breed prejudice and stereotype. Anyways, a bit heavy handed for this early morning hour."*

20) *"Wow. What a day! Ate my first mushroom omelet and floated in the turquoise sea with Jim and Annette – a Canadian couple, looked after me. MAGICAL!"*

21) *"Giving strong thought to tossing it all in May and travelling for one year to Africa then teaching. Life only changes when we make it so...."*

22) *"Coconut maroon cake smeared all over your body, then tastefully consumed with delicate gestures."*

23) *"I ended up drinking with some Thai guys. They were off their faces and one of them started massaging my ankle. A nearby waitress poured beer on him. He was shocked and stopped. They left shortly afterwards."*

24) *"Her petite 5'2" build was traditionally Asian. Long, black, silk-like hair and subtle curves accentuating*

her breasts and bottom, she sparkled with a sense of eternal youth that seems to characterize the Western image of Eastern ladies..., She radiated a sense of westernization in her wearing of tattered Levis and multi-buckle boots. Intriguing. Alluring. Perhaps dangerous. She was a prostitute and I paid for an hour of embarrassment and performance anxiety. I tried. I know. Sigh."

25) *"Rode an elephant today. Got motion sickness."*

26) *"Mr. O, our guide, declared, the cleansing nature of a tropical Thai rain energizes the soul and refreshes the spirit. It is a righteous rain."*

27) *"I could barely walk as I left the place. It wasn't the walking process itself that gave me problems. Rather, it was the uncertainty I had as to whether or not the ground would be present to meet my feet."*

28) *"Her head was bound by a beautiful, yet soiled, blue and red kerchief and topped with a wide-brimmed, finely woven straw hat. Her teeth, visible only when hawking, were in desperate need of repair. They needed the attention of an ambitious dental assistant,"*

29) *"I am a rather innocuous, quirky kind of man, filled with ideas and ambitions that await their chance at fruition."*

Chapter Four: My 30's Nepal

Introduction

Nestled between Tibet and India, Nepal's borders embrace the stunning grandeur of the Himalayan range and give rise to the world's tallest mountain - Sagarmatha, or Mount Everest. Soaring, snow-capped peaks and lush, green valleys extend east to west more than 1,500 miles. The foothills unfold southward in an expansive and undulating plain, the Terai, onwards to India.

The region's breathtaking beauty has long been a source of profound spiritual inspiration, birthing numerous paradigms including Hinduism, Buddhism, Jainism and Sikhism.

The beauty of the Himalayan region infused my life with growth and joyful tears. It created the ground to enhance my understanding of certain universal truths– the kind of understanding you *feel* to be true, beyond the conscious act of *knowing.*

While visiting Nepal in July, 1992, an off-handed comment saw me depart Tokyo for Kathmandu seven (7) months later. A new English teaching job, a trekking agency, a restaurant, and as a Principal awaited. Friends, travel and many wondrous opportunities overflowed.

Signs of an ancient culture steeped in spirituality were everywhere. Special folks lived their lives according to a philosophy grounded in teachings perpetually renewed, refreshed and refined, shared forever forward. They allowed me into their lives, homes and hearts.

From work to travel to friends, I laughed. I cried. I learned to appreciate less was more, and that we required far fewer things for happiness than we were commonly taught.

These are tales of my 30's in Nepal.
***

<u>Journal entry (5/01/94, Annapurna Circuit)</u>

"The first thing to write are words of release, release for the anger... Shake my mind free of its attaching nature. Clarity, resolution and deep contentment, empty wholeness. I speak my heart and feel such pain. I speak to years which choose not to listen and I am torn by the right of not hearing. I have the freedom to speak and the freedom to listen not, nor respond. Sullen forces of pained intensity...caring eyes with pure intent. Was it a cultural misunderstanding or a backspace thought - something which transcends the binds in which we now find ourselves entwined?"

***

On December 31, 1992, I flew from Tokyo to Kathmandu (KTM) to a new sense of truth and random knowingness.

***

"I have a habit of walking aimlessly with some semblance of fuzzy direction throughout the streets of an unknown town. Because, I keep seeing people who I think I recognize. He walked out the door with marked mixed emotions... why is it that we are truly hurt the ones we love? ....

A breakfast of toast and porridge... Eleven cool shades of morning. What to do with anguish and pain? Where have they come from, and, where and how are they to go?.... Security checked hands clasped behind her back, she screams and seems to scowl at those in waiting.

I used to believe that good things come to those who wait, and while I still find this generally true, what of its inverse? Bad things come to those who take?....

Lazy days and wilted spirits. Watery laughter and empty smiles. "

Over two (2) years had passed since my arrival in Nepal and the penning of those journal entries. That day in the

157

rhododendron forest, when my guide suggested I contact his former English teacher for a job, was life re-returning.

Two things; one: That was also the day I stopped and found over 30 leeches on my body – not the large, date-sized type, but the tiny, stand up, wiggling worm version. They dropped from the trees and got all up in your stuff. I flamed and salted myself leech free.

Two: I once hiked with a monk who allowed a leech to gorge on, balloon up and fall off, his foot. He explained, "They eat then sleep for six (6) months before needing another meal. I am so happy I could help him."

<u>Around the Kathmandu Valley</u>

Kathmandu is a bustling city of jarring contrasts. Its' spiritual underpinnings are pervasive amidst the wealth of smiles and squalor of poverty. Together with Patan and Bhaktapur, these three (3) sprawling cities increasingly congest the Kathmandu Valley. I arrived at a pivotal moment in Nepalese history. The King had just abdicated his royal powers in lieu of democratic ways. He had become a titular head, much like Queen Elizabeth of England. Politicians were vying and shifting newly for control.

"*Bhandas,*" or public strikes, were a common form of political protest. Angry crowds forced all businesses to close as protestors marched. I once sat atop a hotel and peered down as the police and protestors played a game of cat and mouse, tear gas vs. rocks. While isolated to a few blocks, American television news portrayed the uprising as all enveloping and my parents called, worried for my safety.

I was fortunate to befriend, Sunila, a main student agitator for change in Nepal. She gave speeches advocating for democracy and was jailed. Once free, she and her boyfriend turned towards change through spiritual advancement by opening a yoga farm at the valley's foothills. Here, I was introduced to "*Ayurveda.*"

1000 years older than its' Chinese counterpart, Indian Medicine became my primary source of health care.

Walking the narrow streets of KTM's traditional shopping areas, history and spirituality were palpable. Statues and temples, Hindu or Buddhist were everywhere. Behind every building was another path or courtyard to explore - places where food was prepared, animals were slaughtered, and well water was pumped into large brass jugs that women and young girls carried on their hip or head.

Cows are sacred in Hinduism. They roam freely without repercussion and often lie down in the road and stop traffic. Drivers simply wait or go around. Any beef for sale has been slaughtered by non-Hindus in India. My first week in town, a new friend was touring me through a market. Ahead was an older woman and beyond her a cow. The cow stopped to pee and the woman quickly doused her hand in the urine stream, then blessed herself and moved on.

Cooking briquettes were made by sun-drying a patty of water buffalo dung and straw. A common chore for young boys was dung collection. Once, while walking along the Ganges River in Varanasi, India, a water buffalo stopped in front of me to poop. Clearly on a mission, a boy quickly skirted by and caught the dropping mid-air, screaming to his friends, *"It is mine!"*

In 2016, the Kathmandu region was rocked by a devastating earthquake. May compassion prevail for the thousands who died and for the multitudes whose lives were impacted. Many ancient and precious temples crumbled, including those found in the city center – Durbar Marg - where an indelible lesson on dying and death was etched.

Dasain is to the Nepalese, as Christmas is to many Americans. During this month long, October holiday, each family had to sacrifice an animal. The less fortunate offered chickens, sheep and goats while the well-off provided water buffalos. Weeks prior to the holiday, shepherds guided their flocks and herds into the city. Surrounding trails were often impassable. You could round a corner and be face-to-face with hundreds of paint dappled goats. The neon colors identified owners.

The government annually honored Dasain by sponsoring a massive sacrifice in Durbar Marg with the resulting meat consumed by soldiers. The accompanying pictures speak infinitely more about this experience than my words can ever conjure. The rituals and constant stream of death were at times, overwhelming. Its primal energy was palpable, repulsive, and utterly enthralling. *You have been alerted.*

One thing: The sufferings of birth, aging, sickness and death apply universally. Reflecting regularly upon this truth cultivates a more grounded and balanced perspective on life. In turn, a greater sense of equanimity and effortless compassion arise, positively transforming the negative habits of our mind.

Pashupatinath Temple is one of four (4) sacred sites all good Hindus should visit at least once in this life, much like Muslims visiting Mecca. Annually, during January revelry, devout Hindus celebrate *Shiva Ratri,* or *"night of Shiva's birth."* Shiva is a Hindu god.

All through December, hundreds of Hindu *"sadhus,"* or holy people, walked north from India for three (3) days of celebrating. They often marked it by smoking bowls of fresh and tasty hashish. Many sadhus had a particular spiritual practice in this lifetime.

One devotee never lowered his left arm; his fingernails had curled into a roller coaster of extraordinary length. Another drank only water and inhaled necessary nutrients from the all-pervasive *"prana,"* or life-force, that surrounds. He was not at all emaciated like you might well imagine. A third hopped continually on one leg.

Regardless their practice, each was seeking enlightenment

by overcoming the cycle of suffering that is perpetuated by our ignorance, our monkey minds.

One thing: I often visited Pashupatinath and meditated on cremating bodies. Amidst the radiating heat of crackling flames and the dulling haze of an acrid smoke, the inherent truth of our impermanent nature was beyond reproach.

Swayambunath (*Swyambu*) or the "*Monkey Temple,*" is a main Tibetan Buddhist temples in the Valley. Sitting atop a high hill, it is surrounded by jungle where monkeys roam freely and swing and swoop and steal your things.

A local wedding custom has men seated on long, narrow rolls of woven bamboo while drinking a crude rice wine poured high from a silver pitcher, splashing down into small clay cups. Once, I witnessed a large, elder monkey sitting at row's end and drinking as if human. He shook his cup when empty and grunted when re-fill time was slow.

QtoP1: Am I an indoor or outdoor person? Where do I most/ least enjoy spending my free time?

QtoP2: Have I ever seriously, physically injured someone? Emotionally?

QtoP3: What do I find sacred? Profane? What inspires me to goodness?

Nagarjun, or the Queen's Forest, was my go to hiking place in the Valley. Pristine and virginal, the lower half was a shadowy jungle, drenched in a compost-like smell. In rainy season, I slathered my legs with bar soap to prevent the leeches from grabbing hold, then ran to the exposed top and looked down on the city. It was gorgeous.

I loved the road. It edged right for six (6) miles, rising around the forest and out of the valley. One year, engine off, I silently surfed my motorcycle down and back to town on the deafening wave of chirping beetles in search of a mate. The cicadas had hatched.

161

They live for 30-45 days, lay their eggs and die. The offspring, like parents like children, hatch 17 years later and the cycle repeats.

The back side of Nagarjun abutted an Osho spiritual center where I once stayed while engaging in a bout of *"spiritual shopping,"* a term one Master coined to describe the influx and motivation of many Western visitors. Osho was not for me, though the accompanying vegetarian restaurant was one of my favorites.

Thamel is KTM's main tourist area. Visitors flocked here for food, fun, shopping, and organizing their trekking or river rafting adventures. I spent much time here with my friends – my *"sathi"* - Ram, Kiran, Arjun and Badri. Their kindness and good hearted ways made my life in Nepal exceptional and rewarding.

I joined in family holidays and was blessed with gifts on my birthday. They once took me to a wedding reception with over 1,200 guests. Two (2) huge boars were roasting on spits as I met the Prime Minister of Nepal. They sent a truck to my rescue when my motorcycle snapped in two. They cared and looked after me with the utmost fraternal love and energy. I am so very, very blessed and grateful.

Much like Japan, my free time was mainly spent with local people, learning their ways and language. With the help of English phonetics, Nepalese is a relatively simple language to master. Writing wise, it is a Sanskrit based alphabet of many characters (for example, फेंड, meaning sathi). I never attempted literacy.

For six (6) years, I worked with them on numerous projects and took many treks. Everything I did came from my heart and was rewarded with priceless experiences.

Habits established with Keiji, however, carried over as I fell forlornly in love with yet another man who I could, and would, not ever have - real and unrequited due to fear and cultural expectation. He too, is now married and a father.

"I get so frustrated. I am so frustrated. I'm in a no-win situation whereby my happiness has become predicated on another, impacting on all my friendships. I don't know what to do. There is but one answer which will satisfy me, and in that event, change my life. I am causing such pain in others and want it to stop. Mine and theirs. Have I run things to the limits whereby returning to good times and love are impossible? ... Let me know what you think and where I should stand. I know no other way... Shutting down and turning off only aggravates and perpetuates."

Projects

Our many projects included: drafting business marketing materials, publishing a quarterly environmental journal, *Everest Voice,* raising money for school sponsorship, and opening a restaurant - Green Leaves.

Green Leaves was wildly popular. It was in the heart of Thamel, in an old, residential compound with indoor and outdoor dining. A huge tree shaded everything and the kitchen had a unique glass window feature whereby folks could watch their food prepared.

Western people love salads, especially after weeks of trekking. Nepali people view raw greens as animal fodder – everything must be cooked. Our exclusive salads were based on the Wake Tavern (WT) menu from years prior. The greens were extraordinary.

Each morning at sunrise, two (2) pounds of mixed lettuces, herbs and edible flowers were hand- plucked and delivered fresh. Every bite and chew erupted in a burst of life affirming flavor and freshness. An American woman had established an non-profit farm to re-introduce traditional, organic farming methods to farmers.

Green Leaves hosted free, nightly concerts with traditional Nepali music. The energy and environment was fantastic. I

163

loved playing the host and mingling among guests. Two (2) ladies once returned from a trek with an abandoned puppy. They could not take it home so I got Norbu, a Tibetan mixed mutt Mastiff. He served as guard dog at Green Leaves, and later at my teacher's K-10 school – Trungram International Academy (TIA) - where I served as the Academic Advisor and interim Principal.

One thing: Once, while joining a family for their post-trek meal at Green Leaves, I mentioned in conversation that their guide's children were lovely. A hesitant quiet ensued and they asked me to repeat myself. I did. Sorry. For whatever reason, their guide had told them he was single. Throughout my life, I have been prone to such truthful blunders, sometimes blind to the underlying social dynamics at play.

Trekking: Everest and Annapurna

Trekking entailed putting on a backpack and walking. It was abundant and wide ranging across the foothills of the Himalayan range and into the southern plains, as well as eastern and northern India. Highlights on the Nepalese side included: treks around the most popular circuits: Everest, Annapurna Circuit, Annapurna Sanctuary, and Langtang, as well as numerous, "*off-the-beaten-path*" trips to the home villages of local friends.

Villages dotted the trails, offering basic accommodation in wood slatted lodges. Some had private rooms while others had communal rooms with rows of bunk beds, dependent on location and demand. All offered a basic meal of Nepalese "*dal bhat*" – rice, lentils, boiled spinach (if available), seasoned potatoes and a meat, usually chicken, goat or buffalo. Traditionally, this was eaten twice a day, at 10am and 7pm. Accommodation and a heaping plate of dal bhat cost approximately $10 a night.

Early sunrise sustenance was often a cup of chai tea with fried eggs wrapped in a "*jhapati,*" or pita-like bread. The most popular trails catered to Western tastes and served pancakes, spaghetti, beer, and even deep fried Snickers.

167

<u>Journal Entry (8/95)</u>

"Sitting atop the mountain that overlooks the final village along the Everest trail, the highest elevation I have attained is nearly 18,000 feet. The partially clouded view is stunning as the scraping sound of a slowly creeping glacier splinters and echoes from below."

I trekked Everest three (3) times. Access via Tibet was a half day, 4wd journey to 15,000 feet. When visiting, I hitched a ride in the back of a cargo truck, bouncing and vomiting much of the way.

I trekked Everest twice from the Nepal side. Done in its' entirety, it was a three (3) week test of strength and endurance, a pilgrimage. It can be shortened by flying into Lukhla and walking for 10 days. I did it both ways.

One thing: At 9,200 feet, the flight into Lukhla cuts the air amidst soaring peaks and the world's steepest valleys. Final ascent feels as if you are running smack into a mountain. According to Wikipedia, "A program titled Most Extreme Airports, broadcast on The History Channel in 2010, rated the airport as the most dangerous airport in the world."

Both my Nepal-side treks occurred during the July rainy season when it was quiet and uncongested. One lodge remained open in each village.

Fields of wild flowers swaying purple, white and yellow painted the lush green landscape and contrasted starkly with the jagged, gravely and gray peaks. At lower altitudes, I awoke with the sun and walked eight to ten (8 to 10) hours a day. Up 1,000 feet then down the same, only to ascend yet again before stopping with the setting sun.

Because of perfect growing conditions, apple orchards speckle the lower elevations. Seasonally, everything apple is available, including pancakes, pies, and brandy. Journal entry: *"This side of the trail is exceptionally tasty."*

Due to the perils of altitude sickness, higher elevations (over 5,000 feet) required a slower ascent so day long walks were discouraged. Like Dan in Colorado, I once learned this the hard way.

At 11,000 feet, I suffered through severe nausea and a mind splitting headache, as if my head was trapped in an ever tightening vice. Thankfully, I had the proper medicine (Diamox). At least 10 uninformed trekkers die of altitude sickness annually.

Prior to any trek, I got a free medical kit from the US Embassy medical compound (a job perk). It was prepared to address commonly encountered emergencies. Unused items were simply returned and re-distributed.

Besides self-care, I also used the kit tending to locals. In such cases, one must face ethical issues and realize the limits of one's knowledge and ability to assist. Two (2) particular situations resonate.

I was circling Annapurna. After settling in for the night, word of my arrival spread and a lady brought in her ailing husband, hunched over in moaning agony. He had a boil the size of a half dollar in the center of his stomach. Per the kit's first aid book, a travelling nurse and I first dabbed it with a hot towel. After several applications, a white peak erupted so we sterilized a needle, lanced and drained the boil. We applied an antibiotic cream, then bandaged it accordingly. I left the next morning and trust that he was ok.

Another time, I visited a friend's remote village in the rarely trekked, Ganesh Himal region. It took five (5) days of intense walking to arrive at a place few travellers have ever seen. While there, a man who had recently put an axe through the top of his foot appeared at the doorstep seeking help. Per local custom, he had packed the wound in water buffalo dung.

A foot soak and good clean revealed a deep, gnawing gash and bone. I applied antibiotic creams and wrapped it in sterile gauze, then provided some antibiotic pills. Whether or not my instructions for dosage were applied, I will never know. As he left, I watched him trudge through a muddy field just outside the door. The bandage was clean no more than two (2) minutes. Act with a pure, well intentioned mind and open heart, dedicate, and be.

QtoP4: Have I ever actively questioned my religious upbringing?

QtoP5: Do I feel whole as a person or do I need someone to complete me?

QtoP6: What is the most difficult ethical dilemma I have ever faced? What did I do?

Amidst the breathtaking beauty, my time in the Everest region is marked by three, deeply etched experiences. The first dealt with my hands and an unexpected meeting, the second books and the third a sacred festival.

I have suffered from eczema since childhood. It first appeared on my legs, later mainly my hands. One year in Nepal, a de-habilitating bout erupted, such that, each finger was cracking, itching, dressed in gauze, and oozing me to tears. I tried all manners of Western treatments, as well as Indian, or Ayurvedic ones, but to no avail. The latter included collecting my urine in a jar and pouring it over my hands. While bringing much relief, it did not heal.

Frustrated, I went trekking, hoping that that the fresh air would do me good. It did. Within three (3) weeks, my hands were better. And, while memorable, the main point of my story is this: due to my hands, I went to Everest.

Because of this, I had an extraordinary encounter.

Arriving in a village famous as the birthplace of a contemporary Tibetan master, Lama Zopa, I visited his childhood monastery. Here, I was greeted by a sentient being who was ageless in the two (2) primary roots of Tibetan Buddhist philosophy - wisdom and compassion.

170

Though only four (4) years old and a child by convention, he spoke fluent Nepalese, Tibetan and passable English. Welcoming me as if life-long friends, he took my hand and led me to the main chant room. He then conducted a healing puja, or prayer ritual. Complete with bells, drums and incense, he his power and clarity enveloped me in soothing warmth and lasting inspiration.

Returning home from the trek, I immediately found the cause of my eczema on opening the door – mold, oh the smell of it. My eyes and nose immediately ran. Checking my closet, much of my clothing was ruined. Cutting open my pillow and mattress, all were drenched. I had been breathing this toxic mess nightly. I spent the next two (2) days cleaning and disinfecting. To this day, I react at the slightest hint of mold.

Months later, I heard that the young Master was in KTM and I sought an audience. In a tremendous act of disrespect, I smoked some hash prior to arrival. As soon as we met, his smile turned to a questioning glance. He sensed the high about me and was cordial and quick in dismissal. I was, and still am, deeply regretful for this and other similar experiences. Lessons are still being learned.

Akin to my fascination with Yukio Mishima's work, another author's books crossed my path many times throughout my travels. I would by chance, find them on a bookshelf in an empty lodge, trade for them at a book exchange, or be gifted them when the time was right. I loved them all.

From *Don't Fall Off the Mountain*, about her adventures in Bhutan through to her recounting of the El Camino trail in Europe, *The Camino: A Journey of the Spirit*, Shirley MacLaine has enthralled and inspired me for years. In my dreams, we once shared a meal while sitting on a couch and careening down Kathmandu's main street as traffic parted like the Red Sea before Moses.

For years, I had heard about Everest's Mani Rimdu festival. Held annually at Chiwong Monastery in Autumn, it celebrates the establishment of Buddhism in Tibet. Grain by grain, over the course of many days, monks created a giant sand mandala symbolizing their God of Compassion. A series of elaborate dances depicted the clash of positive forces against unruly chaos, ultimately raining blessings on all who attend.

The colors, the pomp and circumstance, the noises and happy joy of attendees – ultimately, the manifesting of compassion – resonate freshly still within my mind and spirit.

Journal Entries (10 & 11/96)

"In the distance, high on a ridge, was a large complex I was soon to learn is Chiwong Gumpa where "Mani Rimdu" will be in less than a few days…. The walk here was gorgeous as the trail meandered around trees, rocks and streams, soon rising up a hillside to the monastery. Very Tibetan in feel and style, monks, nuns, and lay people are all abuzz with activity….

Then, at 7:30pm, in an adjoining mud walled, tin roofed, wood planked room, the drums pounded, cymbals crashed, and the show began. Over the course of an hour, a snow lion danced, yaks pranced, and rainbow colored, silk clad Tibetans sang and foot stomped their way through a traditional opera… At the end, on exiting, we found a dozen monks pressed against two small windows, peering in to see. As they dispersed, we chatted and laughed about this and that. Then, I soundly slept.....

Tonight I stood, watching the full moon rising beyond the distant, pine topped ridge. As a grey-white glow bathed the trees in a soft warm light that fused effortlessly with the darkened night, a cool wind from the valley floor below rippled thru the forest causing me to shiver slightly and pull my jacket up and tight.

A dog barked.
A child cried. Families gathered for their evening meals.

172

I walked slowly through town, hands clasped for warmth, and tried to imagine a world in which our ignorance and suffering is cleared away, revealing a clarity and peace of mind as serene and natural as the moonlight."

Annapurna

Annapurna treks launch eight (8) hours west of Kathmandu, from Pokhara. The Circuit, takes you go around the Annapurna mountains (South, 1, 2, 3 & 4, and Macchapuchare). The Sanctuary trek takes you up the central valley.

In 1994, Ray from TFLC joined me on a two (2) week trek around the Annapurna Circuit. Reaching 17,769 feet at Thorong Las Pass, the trail was filled with hot springs, sacred spots and boundless inspiration.

Journal Entry (10/94)

"The vast sacredness of this land seems to be pervading his (Ray's) reality. It is a special, special place and its' impact is just making itself known… if one allows as such."

My journal entries indicate that things were going well between us. I wrote, *"My trepidations about his angst have proven false and we're having a good time."* Though, intestinal disruptions seemed abundant – *"my 'illness' has kept me tempered in action,"* and, *"Ray's stomach seems somewhat tumultuous,"* these too passed. Ray's searing anger, however, re-surfaced at Thorong-La.

October 7th, we awoke at 3am to begin a sunrise summit of Thorong La Pass. A cold snap lingered and the air was thick with a chilling fog. The discussion about delaying our ascent quickly became a Ray-filled scream fest. With thin wood walls, his full-throttled, f***bomb laden defense of staying surely woke everyone. I could not believe it; I was embarrassed and appalled. You have to disturb everyone else because we are at odds? I stood, numb in mind, my gut twisting in pain. I stared and wondered,

"Why are you like this?" I simply could not be bothered and left. He stayed. Subsequent journal entries read:

10/8 (Muktinath);
10/9 Same;
10/10 (Kagbeni): What happened? Perhaps later;
10/11 (Marpha): Hello.Hello. What's up?

We re-connected somewhere on the other side. I do not really remember if our feelings were laid bare and resolved, or simply dissipated into an energy of whatever. I do know that we are no longer in contact.

One thing: I received my first Buddhist teaching from a Buddhist nun (an "Ani"), an ordained American woman. Her message focused on being compassionate while not being a doormat for the issues of others." I found this applicable to Ray and me, and, still grapple with the truth of her teaching as it resonates in my life. At times, the desire to "people please" is an undertow to maintaining a more helpful, balanced perspective.

My journal on the 11th continues:

"After coming over the Pass, I stopped in Muktinath for a rest day. Sitting atop the hotel amidst such resounding beauty and tranquility, I greeted people as they filtered in.... The following morning I arose early to cross over to the villages opposite – Jhong and Patar (?)...

Aqueducts. Fall leaves. Yellows. Oranges. Smells. Shadows. Shade. Horses. Goats. Kids. Monastery grand. No monks. Vistas. Fields and thrashing wheat. Sunshine.

Narrow paths of stone. Prayer wheels. Bells. Tiny passageways. Weathered faces digging dirt. Smiles. Songs. Horses black and white. Dung patties drying on roofs."

Tourism is Nepal's number one industry. In efforts at limiting cultural and environmental impact, access to much of the country has been regulated.

174

In the early 90's, the 110 mile circuit around Mt. Manaslu was opened and I was fortunate enough to join four (4) European gentleman and the daughter on a three (3) week adventure filled with so many, many experiences.

One porter's sole job was carrying the bamboo basket containing various homemade, Austrian schnapps. The tastes were incredible, the nature pristine.

While cooking dinner one night, the cook startled me by slicing a goat's neck without warning and laughing somewhat maniacally. I should have seen it coming. Watching the Nepalese staff try to catch the daughter's eye was endlessly entertaining. I felt so blessed.

> QtoP7: Have I ever seriously disrespected someone?
> How so? Why?
> Would I change my behaviors in a do-over?

> QtoP8: Am I highly self-motivated? Am I ever lazy?

> QtoP9: How do I capture someone's attention?
> Their heart?

The American Language Center (ALC)

Meandering your way through the congested and sometimes squalid backstreets of KTM, you might have come upon a clean brick wall and well-kept iron fence. It opened to the American Language Center (ALC).

Government supported, the Director had created an exceptional, teacher friendly, state of the art, school. Seven (7) out of eight (8) teachers held Master's degrees. Team teaching and back office discussions about methodology and success were engaging.

Course-wise, I taught all levels of conversation, Public Speaking, and English proficiency test preparation. For six (6) years, my schedule was six to eight (6 to 8) weeks on, then two to five (2 to 5) weeks off.

175

Over the course of my tenure, our pay ranged from $7-11 per hour.This wage afforded a comfortable lifestyle that allowed me to both travel and save. I had a housekeeper that came twice a week to clean and cook; she always left my fridge full of meals that included lots of tofu, beans and vegetables with lentils. I ate some meat, mostly chicken, and occasionally Indian beef though this consumption dwindled as time passed.

Among the lessons learned, I benefitted greatly from better understanding my *"needs vs. wants."* How much, and what do we *really* need, to survive?

ALC's student body was a mix of well-off Nepalese, and a range of embassy employees, e.g., French, Chinese, and German. It was a tremendous educational value with a floating fee of $3-6US per hour for students.

I am not sure how it started, but I began ending each class with the phrase, *"Be happy. Be healthy. Peace."* One day, I forgot to say it and I left the room; the students did not move. I returned and asked what had happened. They replied, *"Mr. Peter, you need to say "be happy be healthy peace" before we can go."* Fast forward, 20 years, and this simple, heartfelt phrase had the same impact on my American students. Ah, the power of well-intentioned words.

Russian history at the end of the 80's and early 90's was marked by Mikhael Gorbachav's transformative social policy of Glasnost, or opening. This impacted my immediate world. Embassy staff and families rapidly appeared everywhere, including the American Language Center. I found them a boisterous and educated people who enlivened our classrooms with their outgoing natures.

They opened restaurants and shared their cuisine and music. They befriended and benefitted us through genuine interactions. I enjoyed their company and the transparency of our common humanity. For too long, our countries had been stuck in the muddied shores of fear and hate. Sadly, this seems again arising.

A colleague and I once attended dinner at a private residence within the Russian embassy compound. Serghey, an alternative doctor, and his wife had invited us for a lovely evening of fine food and engaging conversation.

Towards the end, a knock was heard and answered. Serghey welcomed and introduced us to an overly friendly man who politely peppered us with a litany of questions, then left. Later, we learned that he was KGB.

Friends and Travel and the ALC

ALC being the source, life cascaded into waterfalls of loving friendships, precious and precarious experiences, profound spiritual connections and death in a manner never imagined.

Weekly, I enjoyed the company of good friends in a Buddhist reading group hosted by a Nepalese /American couple, Ramesh and Jessica. Our book club was fortunate to host His Eminence, Sogyal Rinpoche for several public teachings based on his world-wide, bestselling text, *The Tibetan Book of Living and Dying.*

With over two (2) million copies sold and 32 language translations, this contemporary classic shares extraordinary wisdom for the ever present ages.

Kiki, a Tibetan friend and former student, introduced me to the Tibetan community in Boudhanath, another sacred Buddhist space where for years I attended weekly, Saturday morning teachings by Chokynima Rinpoche My gratitude for his wisdom shared. His brother, Tsokyni Rinpoche, conducted a powerful five (5) day, silent meditation retreat atop Shivapuri at Nagi Gumpa, the monastery of their realized father, Tulku Urgen Rinpoche.

Two things; one: Anyone who knows me, appreciates how hard these five (5) days were, non-speaking wise. The space my mind momentarily attained was an inspiring tease.

177

179

180

Two: My birthday was the last day of the retreat so that night I went out for dinner. Friends had left and I was warming myself by an outdoor fire when Tsoknyi Rinpoche and his entourage appeared. They sat with me and he asked, "What are you drinking?" A margarita. "I'll try one," he said, "One, Peter," he added, "one is ok." I sometimes fail to heed this teaching.

I joined Kiki's family for annual Tibetan New Year's celebrations (usually in February). These included his mother waking us up at 3am and pouring milk over our heads to signify cleansing and eating special prize, filled foods.

Kiki and I once traveled east through India to Darjeeling *(yes, the tea)*, Sikkim and Gangtok. In Darjeeling, I surprised myself with a twinge of jealousy as Kiki pursued a local lass.

In Sikkim, we white water rafted the Teesta River and I got car sick as we zipped and zagged the curvy road. In time, he moved and married a Hong Kong woman. Our friendship re-ignited when I re-located to HK in 1999.

My friendship with Amelia, an ALC teaching colleague, continued a life pattern that started with Caliste in Australia and remains to this day – befriending, successful, confident women whose lives re-define the boundaries of female expectation. Angela, Nikki, Judi and Penelope followed. When I finally meet a man who *"gets me"* like these ladies do, he is the one.

In Nepal, Amelia and I enjoyed many treks together, including Annapurna Sanctuary, as well as trips to the Terai – the wholly wondrous yet vastly different landscape that is south central Nepal. Its' gentle rivers, sweeping plains, temperate climate and dry jungle are filled with tigers, elephants and rhinoceroses.

The Terai is home to Lumbini, the birthplace of Siddhartha Gautam, the historical Buddha. It hosts Chitwan and Royal Bardia National Parks where, one morning, a Royal Bengal tiger quickly crossed my path not 150 feet ahead. I stopped a little scared and disbelieving, engulfed with adrenaline.

One thing: Honoring the holy and profound significance of Lumbini – Buddhism's Bethlehem – Trungram Gyaltrul Rinpoche (dharmakaya.org) has established the World Center for Peace and Unity in 2011. May we all one day visit for calming inspiration and insights.

I visited India four (4) times with the last being a blessing of ceaseless benefit. Each visit was an extraordinary test of patience, endurance, and an overwhelming assault on my senses. The sights, sounds and smells must be experienced first-hand to truly be believed.

Home to over one (1) billion people, India, much like mainland China, hovers on the edge of uncontrolled chaos and somehow still strives, survives and thrives. Its' rich history and overt displays of wealth and opulence, contrast sharply with the pervasive poverty that consumes the less fortunate.

"Toto, I don't think we are in Nepal anymore."

Journal Entries (2/94)

"The border town, India-side, is a maze of dusty streets. Beneath my bus window, a white puppy lies dead; a puddle of blood streaming from its mouth. A brownish-black dog, utter hanging low, is licking it while another dog is prodding the puppy with its' paw. The parents? Surely they grieve.

A scam ensues as luggage is placed up top and a fee is demanded. Why should I pay? Where the charge written?... Sputtering mopeds are driven by turban wearing gents, so prim, so proper. Are people really good?

A man enters the bus carrying a basket wrapped in a soiled cloth. Its contents include a small brass container, a matching bowl and some change. The container is filled

182

with water that a man proceeds to splash on the deity placed in the front of the bus. A few words are uttered and he then proceeds down the aisle, blessing people as he goes by. He places a tikka (colored powder) smudge on my forehead and I give him two rupees."

***

My first visit to India included Varanasi, and Agra, home to the Taj Mahal and the equally impressive Red Fort. The architecture of these majestic buildings reflects India's rich history of intellect and accomplishment throughout their expansive borders, including the far west, a land of walled cities, draped in the cloth and colors of Aladdin and inhabited by camels.

> *QtoP10: At what point do I consider myself successful? Wealthy? Content?*

> *QtoP11: Do I defy people's expectations? How so? Am I better than most people I meet?*

> *QtoP12: Do I view people as fundamentally good, neutral, or bad?*

Situated along the sacred Ganges River, Varanasi is one of the world's oldest cities and the spiritual capital of India. It is reverent to Hindus, Jains, and Buddhists, alike. On attaining enlightenment, Buddha gave his first teaching, *"The Four Noble Truths,"* at nearby Saranath. They are:

- The truth of suffering;
- The truth of the causes of suffering;
- The truth of cessation; and,
- The truth of the path.

Journal Entries (9/95)

"Took a rickshaw ride to Saranath to see the site of Buddha's first teaching. A lovely, tranquil, serene spot with many archeological ruins and immense brick stupas, similar to Lumbini's but larger. There's also a nice museum

183

filled with 1ˢᵗ-6ᵗʰ century artifacts. So old. Do we produce anything these days (besides nuclear waste) that will remain 1,000 years?"

Relating to Varanasi, my entries continue.

"Backstreets, no wider than a meter, crisscross in seemingly endless mazes. Shop windows, no higher than my knees, open from the footpath selling goods with unknown names. People. Smiles.... Everyone calls me their brother, their friend, who and what constitute each? In front of me a coffee and a Coke. Below, throngs of people move like ants. Beep Beep. A Vespa goes by.... My coffee spoon is square! Really! To posterity."

"Which part of me is real? Which part of me to bury? To reveal?.... Night brings quiet. With it, a quiet restlessness and a wish for morning to quickly come."

"Today, amidst these narrows streets, I turned a corner and found a newly birthed calf, kicking and squirming in the viscous red fluid of afterbirth. The mother lay still, looking on, clearly exhausted."

To complement the chaos, the city's high powered *"Bhang Lassis"* – a weed filled yogurt drink - floated the mind as the vibrant, somber, and energetic interplay between life and death focused riverside, the site of constant cremations.

Journal Entries (2/95)

"Wrapped in cloths of gold and orange, carried on a bed of bamboo and angled down stairs w/feet in the river, people scoop up holy water and pour it in the mouth, on the face, of the deceased. Boats filled with wood. Cows and buffaloes. Charred skeletons. The smell of flesh and wood mingle as they waft up and away. Long sticks prod and reposition the burning body. It takes about 3hrs to burn. The bones are collected by the family, only men, and are offered to the Ganges. All day and all night they burn.... An

184

electric crematorium. Only five minutes to burn. The times they are a changin'!"

"The five elements of life: air, space, water, earth and fire, are all symbolized in ancient ritual.... I sit and feel apart. Pyers alight. A cow chews the hemp rope which binds the bamboo frame used to carry a body. Time to go. Respect."

Leaving Varanasi, I boarded a train heading for the far western state of Rajasthan and the cities of Jaipur, Jodhpur, and the magical, Jaisalmer. At every turn, locals amused and confounded me by engaging in political debate.

Journal Entries (3/94)

"An interesting gentleman with a round face, moustache, glasses, and a distinguished yet receding head of well-tended to, grey hair spoke in a slow, methodical lull, stopping to slurp and breathe with noticeable frequency. His lead question was: 'Do you like peace or war?' All the while, he ate an amber colored powder from a small foil pack."

***

Composed of pink sand dug from the surrounding hills, Jaipur is known as the "*Pink City*." With its' rich history of art and culture and extensive architecture, it is also referred to as the "*Paris of India.*" A rickshaw tour revealed the deserving nature of these accolades, although, my first journal entry begged to differ.

"The city really waffs of urine. Noticeable to the nose. People pee wherever... What a beautiful city. Being pedaled around is a great way to see it. Started off at Bilabandi Temple. It is a magnificent marble structure surrounded by manicured gardens and overlooked by an ancient fort. The marble is inlaid with stones and stained glass windows depict different stories from Krishna's (a main Hindu God) life. Rivals the European cathedrals, though I have never seen them..."

185

"Visited a museum built by a 19ᵗʰ century British King, I don't know, one of them. The place is a musty catacomb of artifacts and relics past. X (cross) sections of human positions abound...... My driver's English is poor and I find myself short. Best to calm, calm, calm down. Tea has arrived."

"Jodhpur is a city of white, brownish brick, households (the highest caste). The overlooking fort? Simply phenomenal. Such grandeur. An architectural triumph? What do I know? Only that I like it! It is buttressed by 10 meter walls of sandstone blocks. The inner walls are red and carved in fine mesh 'fencing,' with window frames of ornate design."

"The light of lanterns and fires dot the blackened landscape ... Yesterday, I got a really good belly laugh when I queried an older rickshaw driver the price to Delhi (372 miles). His reaction was one of jovial pronouncement to the many people within earshot. Several cat calls were made and lots laughed..."

***

The following journal entry jumped off the page. What a momentary mess of beautiful humanity laid glistening and bare. The frantic energy of my closeted, mis-placed, and judgmental suffering resonates:

"I want to fly and be free. Shimmer, shake and ****. I want to engage some young lass in a round of banter, then have her **** ** ****. Red-lipped lady sitting close, why do you don such a makeuped mask while travelling? Does it enhance your sense of self? Give definition to who you think you are? If so, then look inward....

For these things cannot be bought or worn externally; they must weave their way through everything you say and do in your life without realization of the process. Process? It implies a beginning & end, to which I wrongly transmit meaning....Disparate energies collide within my head in silent clamor. They all go at some point."

186

Jaisalmer, the farthest and last stop on this journey was other worldly in landscape and construction. Elevated and walled, it would have been impenetrable in earlier times of war. Cloth colors abounded. During a 3D/2N camel safari *("Not too uncomfortable. Much better that an elephant.")*, I walked amidst the ancient structures of a sand swept city long ago abandoned. Unfortunately, my main take away from Jaisalmer still haunts my heart and mind. Etched deeply like the piercing stare of the woman from the sex show in Bangkok, my journal reads:

"Things get weirder by the minute. I was just downstairs watching TV. Inderet, the lodge keeper, had returned home and invited me down, and I felt obliged given our earlier encounter of a nasty sort (I do not remember to what I was referring; it is not written down*).*

Khamuldin came home. He is a young boy working here; we'd met earlier when he served me tea.... He arrived happily, telling me he had been to the movies. We talked a little while. I asked him about school – he does not go – and his family, 'I have no mother or father.' All the while Inderet was up and milling about. He returned and they ate a meal.... After eating, attentions fixed on the tv for a short time, Inderet asks, 'Do you ever fuck boy?' I say, 'No. I haven't. It is not my thing.' He says, 'What you think? You wanna fuck a little boy?'

I was silent. He says no more and it is over. The moment come and gone. A question whose blunt audacity I had never ever heard. A question whose presumption I well observe. But, a question based on me purchasing some young child for my sexual pleasure – boy or girl, regardless, neither. It is repulsive and immoral and heart renderingly sad. I must calm at the thought. Worse, I am not stupid enough to think that there are not some individuals who would take advantage of the offer....

We live in a sick world."

189

I locked myself in my room, barely slept, and left the next morning after complaining to the boss.

QtoP13: What is the greatest physical pain I have experienced? Mental or emotional?

QtoP14: Do I support the death penalty? Why/ not?

QtoP15: Am I a happy person? How do I gauge my level of happiness?

In 1999, Amelia and I visited of our mutual friend, Sandra, and her now husband, Thundoup, in Bhutan. We gratefully accepted. From beginning to end, including a trip to the stunning, Taktsang Palphug, or "*Tiger's Nest*" Monastery, it was Shangri-La incarnate.

At the time, Bhutan was the last remaining Buddhist kingdom on Earth. In 2008, it transitioned into a two-party political system with the monarchy remaining as the titular head. Tiny in size and population (less than one (1) million), it is nestled among China, India and Bangladesh. The government regulates outside influences by limiting tourism to 10,000 visitors per year and charging a minimum of $250 per day, per visitor, plus, a mandatory government guide wherever you travel.

As Sandra's invited guests, these rules were waived and we experienced the local side of Bhutanese life. At night, under the star drenched sky, we fired boulders to glowing red then dropped them into a water-filled, coffin sized hole in the ground to create a hissing, bubbling hot tub.

One thing: In America, we use the GDP (Gross Domestic Product) as a measure of progress. In Bhutan, they have the same, combined with the GNH, or, Gross National Happiness. Each year, the government interviews and derives a figure to reflect the general level of happiness among the populace, then adapts its' programs accordingly.

Now living close in California, Amelia and I remain in contact; her wonderful, inquisitive spirit still shines.

191

Meeting my Teacher

One day, the ALC gate opened and in drove my teacher, my *"root guru,"* first teaching as my student. Trungram Gyaltrul Rinpoche had enrolled in the ALC Public Speaking class. For 10 weeks, he graced and blessed us with his calm and abiding presence.

From immediate greeting, his radiant qualities of kindness and compassion filled the space. I will never forget the class where I showed a clip from Martin Luther King's *"I Have a Dream"* speech.

When Dr. King's truthful voice declared, *"I have a dream that my four little children will one day live in a nation where they will not be judged by the color of their skin, but by the content of their character."* I cried in front of the class.

The confluence, whereby a Tibetan Buddhist Master sits in a classroom with numerous foreign nationals, listening to the wisdom and compassion of an African-American Master now passed, speaks volumes about the righteous power of words and ideas to transcend time, peoples and places.

Conversely, the most contentious classroom moment I ever had was in my ALC Public Speaking class. A Nepalese student gave a blisteringly critical speech about atrocities in Tibet, fair enough, except, the Chinese ambassador's wife was also a student. The uproar was huge and shifted the dynamic of the class for the remainder of the term.

Simply put, Rinpoche resides within my heart and mind and is my teacher. Over the years, he has blessed me with so very much.

From ground breaking to initial graduation, I served for 14 months in numerous ways at Rinpoche's school. Later in Hong Kong I attended his teachings. And over a decade later, I held weekly, meditation sessions and helped organize public teachings during his Vegas visits. I was also blessed to host his teacher, Kenchen Rinpoche. May his long life and wisdom be realized. Lama Phurba is.

TIA evokes so many wonderful memories, including:

- The wonderful staff of monks and lay people, alike;
- talent shows, sports competitions, and walks in the surrounding rice paddies;
- picnics atop a hill overlooking the Valley;
- working with overseas volunteers who taught art, music and more; thank you all;
- finding Norbu on school grounds gnawing at the rib cage of a slaughtered water buffalo;
- ushering out animals trapped in classrooms (a six (6) foot snake and small mountain lion); and,
- watching students learn and grow.

Rinpoche's monastery, Shanku, was a 16 mile motorcycle ride from my home; the last two (2) miles were an off-road, uphill challenge. I visited often for practice and peace. One time, I arrived and found a tiny, mange riddled puppy suffering from malnourishment. It had a spinal deformity such that it was pooping all over itself.

According to the monks, Norbu and Ginger, Rinpoche's dog, had had some fun. Shortly after birth, she accidentally swiped at her sole puppy and broke some lower vertebrae. The look on this dying puppy's face was heartbreaking. No bigger than a tiny butternut squash, I put it in my small backpack and headed home. Ginger barked and followed for over two (2) downhill miles.

I tended to the puppy for three (3) weeks, including special shampoos, worm medicine, and five (5) electrified acupuncture sessions in her hip area to re-activate the muscles. Nightly, she slept in a box next to my bed wherein I dangled my hand. If I rolled over and removed it, she barked until it returned.

By week four (4), I returned to Shanku with a gorgeous, healthy, happy, non-soiling puppy. Mother to child, Ginger's ecstatic re-acquaintance was a love to witness.

The puppy though, had one, lasting concern.

Given her right twisted spine, she forever circled that direction when moving forward. It was adorable to see on greeting. She hopped with such joy. Forever running in circles, I named her, Mani.

"*Mani*" is a chant, practiced when walking clockwise around stupas like Boudhanath and Swyambunath. It comes from the Tibetan, six (6) syllable chant, "*Oh Mani Peme Hung.*"

This chant cleanses and purifies the mind of the six (6) negative emotions of: *pride, jealousy, desire, ignorance, greed, anger.*

Mani lived and brought joy for two (2) wonderful years before a mountain lion found her an easy meal.

Looking back, my kaleidescoping karma seemed to clash, causing me to wobble, learn and grow - to see how patience and meditative, spiritual practice is applied to real world situations. Rinpoche shares:

"*Many Buddhist teachings provide a way to live in the world more fully, more positively, more peacefully. While mediation and other clearly defined practices clarify our understanding and strengthen our intent—the mindful equivalent of muscle memory—in truth every aspect of our lives provides an opportunity to put these teachings into practice. By integrating them this way, we can, indeed, live better.*" (**www.Dharmakaya.org**)

The absolute goal of meditation is to reveal the fundamental nature of mind. Right practice allows us to realize and respond to life from a radiant, innate space of compassion and wisdom that is mind. Eternally present and obscured by habit.

Relatively, meditation calms our mind and trains us how to recognize our thoughts, find the gap between them, and

194

then expand it. Within this gap, the arising and dwelling of thoughts ceases. Clarity, calm and happiness are.

Selflessness is.

Cumulatively, my work at TIA, ALC and Green Leaves, saw me stress myself down to an unhealthy 135 pounds. I regret poor management decisions borne of frustration, as well as any suffering and pain caused by my words and deeds. I got angry with people who did nothing more than want to help. The most telling example of my missteps was my bungled firing of a teacher.

I reacted rather than responded to her actions and unwittingly caused so many unnecessary distractions. Throughout these and other situations, my intent was always good.

Personally, my *sathi* practiced avoidance. The energies of rejection and despair shook me so. I felt waterlogged. I was tired and made mistakes. I was angry. Parts of me still hurt.

By 1999, the ALC was closing so my visa was revoked. After six (6) wonderful years, it was time to move on, but, where to next and why? Having lived so close to Tibet but never visiting, the journey called. I trusted that answers would arise. Trust is a good thing.

Donning my backpack, I flew to Hong Kong (HK) and stayed with Kiki before embarking on a three (3) month, counter-clockwise journey up and through western china, down into Tibet and back to Kathmandu.

From Day One, crossing the orderly HK border into the frenzy of Shenzen reminded me how frustrated I could became when navigating mainland China. Immediately, mis-directions had me running full throttle to jump on an already moving, albeit slowly creeping, train.

Journal Entry (7/11/99)

"China has begun. I'm on a train just moving in order to connect to my Guangzhou-Kunming train. Getting on this beast had me hearing, 'No ticket,' 'No seat,' 'No train.' Pushing. Shoving. But a smile is on my face and in my heart. What a difference on Xing the border b/w HK and China. The people are noticeably less fashionable (polyester & nylon), the place dirtier (but not at all filthy) and overall feel of thing less cultured. At the immigration booth, inspectors are donned in pale, olive-green, Army-like following sign: Hell is the religion of fear."

"Amelia. Amelia. Amelia – you local bus rider you. You would have loved / hated last night's 15 hour sleeper bus journey. Road under construction. Bump. Bump. Bump. Sleeping space for about 30 people with filthy mattresses and pillows and everyone VERY close. While I met some nice people who were wanting to practice their English. I also managed to get ripped off at some point during the night, though I can't figure out just when. Not much, luckily."

Arriving in Kunming then Dali, I was disappointed by the over-development. The ensuing years had tarnished the magical and mystical aura that I had once found so alluring. I feel the following story speaks to the changes.

I had brought with me an 8x10 photo of Jim (from Jim's Café) and his then, infant son. When I did find and present him the photo, he barely registered a thank you. Sadly, Jim was cloaked in sadness. Divorced with his son elsewhere, I felt bad that I had caused him more suffering with my gift. With this inauspicious start to my journey, I knew I wanted to get to Tibet sooner rather than later.

First, however, I wanted to see the historic cities of Lijiang (an UNESCO World Heritage site) and Leshan, and travel through Kham, formerly the eastern region of Tibet. Here, I would unexpectedly experience a powerful lesson in impermanence.

Journal Entries (7/15/99)

"What a great afternoon! Lijiang, the old town, is an ancient treasure of cobblestone lanes, stone houses, and wooden carvings. Crossing over the stream from new to old is like walking back in time... hope the pics from my new camera can capture a glimpse of the magic and feel of the place."

After a few days, I proceeded north to Tibet.

"The trip here (about 6 hours) was a spectacular ride thru vast, rich, pine forests, along the bank of the raging monsoon Jinsha River which soon becomes the Yangtze. It's similar to the Khumbu Region, lacking only the backdrop of jagged, snow-capped, jagged Himalayan peaks."

"Xiangdian is a one street, plateau town whose Tibetan influence is strong. About two hours outside of town we started passing "chortens" (Buddhist shrines) and prayer flag bearing homes steeped in Tibetan architectural style"

"Early morning blue sky gives rise to the hope of a rainless day... An hour's walk to a Tibetan "gumpa" (monastery). Everything of my image. Spread about an expansive hill with 4/5 prayer halls, dozens of small houses for monks...

"Lots of construction amidst the ruins and remnants of those building destroyed in the Cultural Revolution... I could practice my language skills. It was wonderfully joyous. My spirit feels fresh and renewed."

Due to political uncertainty and tensions, the government required travel permits to proceed north. I wrote:

"Seems northbound is ok, EXCEPT by public bus. 'Don't sell tickets. No permit. You no go.' So, we'll try hitching in. Wish us luck... Actually, the whole scene is a bit surreal as conflicting stories abound about the possibilities and perils of travel. Things change daily. One never really knows, but, ain't that really the truth anyways."

Together with a German guy who spoke passable Mandarin (the main language of China) and a Swedish lady, we departed.

197

<u>Journal Entry (7/12/99)</u>

"With the exception of mud baths at Sunila's (yoga farm in KTM), I can unquestionably state that I have never been dirtier that I became today. Why? It was an incredible hitchhiking day north to Xianchang.... Left at 6am. Took a taxi ride outside of town and got a ride in 30 minutes... and travelled 60kms, 1/3 of the way, at a very quick, tail wagging, road sliding pace. Unfortunately, I puked twice into plastic bags and felt pretty poor. Although, getting in, I figured as such would happen since it was a jeep and I was placed over the wheel...

The ride ceased in a tiny village in a dense forest and on getting out, the general feeling was 'oh-no-what will pass thru here and when?' But, good luck, a big Toda truck passed by and we boarded. The fresh air and sun meant I felt fine and the views were spectacular. Infinite green expanses pierced the towering cliffs akin to 'El Capitan' in America. We stopped and switched rides at one point. The rest was a dust-ridden, bumpy journey that caked us in red clay."

On arrival, our filthy appearance attracted great attention as we walked through town searching for a room. We passed the police who pointed and laughed, knowing what we had done. Later that night, we met three (3) guys who had bussed in and suffered through a scary two (2) hour police interrogation that ended with the passing of cash.

My travels further north took me through the province of Shichuan where the food lived up to its' spicy reputation. Along the way, I visited a glacier park and hot springs and many other touristy things. In Leshan, the Cultural Revolution had spared an immense, 210' Buddha carved into a cliff.

By and large, it was fun. At one point, however, I found myself taking two (2) days for what should have been a straightforward, eight (8) hour journey. Everyone misdirected and lied to me. I was frustratingly furious.

198

Here is a sampling of ransom journal entries:

"This area of Sichuan is lush, virgin jungle. Glorious. Rich. Thick. Air you can taste."

"A lovely, sunny, hot spring morning under the expanse of a blue fresh sky... "A phenomenal buffet of Sichuan's finest."

"A drunk man yelled at the driver and he stunk. A child/infant – 2 months – shit and piss on the bus floor.... The train was packed with 60kgs bags of potatoes, stacked three/ four bags high. People are spitting all over..."

"I've now paid 3 TIMES to get to the same place... Arghhhh!"

Soon entering Kham, I passed through the far western province of Gansu and the town of Langmusri. The indigenous people were a Muslim minority whose hospitality and kindness were a welcomed change.

A rocky area with few trees and a green, rolling landscape, the region honored those who had died with a unique practice - a *"sky burial"* ritual. Given the difficulty in digging and scarcity of trees, bodies were offered to the vultures, falcons and crows.

As you approached this sacred, isolated area, the energy was subdued and odor unfamiliar. Random human bits – a finger here, an ear over there – were strewn about. In preparation, the bodies were stripped bare and clothes thrown into a hole. Monks chopped and mixed the deceased with millet and hand fed the birds.

"In bed 'til 11, reading and studying, then lunch, then a very moving and reflective trip to the sky burial location above and behind the Gansu monastery. Bones, flesh, body parts, axes, cutting blocks, discarded clothes, vultures, falcons and crows swoop the area....Too powerful...; Misty views and landscape."

Ashes to ashes and dust to dust. Stark impermanence.

199

As we gather for another day,
may all of us, and all beings
in the universe, be happy. Together,
with the help of our parents, teachers, families and
friends, may the light of understanding shine brightly in
our lives, so that the world may live in peace.

School prayer

The human body becomes the poop of birds. Our journeys really are quite extraordinary.

North to Xining, I boarded an overnight train heading west across the expansive western plateau to Golmund. From here, an overnight bus journey south to Lhasa, Tibet's capital, in search of answers: where to next and why?

They came in the form of an American, Communication scholar living in Hong Kong and vacationing in Lhasa with his partner. By chance, our rooms were adjoining.

"Come to Hong Kong," he said, *"and stay with us until you find a job. There is plenty of work to be had."*

Questions answered and decisions made, onwards through Tibet. The general direction of my post-KTM life was etching itself and it felt excellent. The next 60 days was a time of joyous, sacred, and carefree travel.

As for my tales of Tibet, perhaps another time.

> *QtoP16: What is my greatest regret in life? Would I act differently in a re-do?*

> *QtoP17: What do I think of school prayer? TIA's prayer?*

> *QtoP18: When do I most feel at peace? Out of sync?*

Years prior to this *"what next"* journey, my spiritual exploration included a fourth and final trip to Dharamsala in north India. His Holiness the Dalai Lama, the Tibetan Government in-exile, and Tibetan refugee families reside at the compassionate behest of the Indian government.

I taught English in a monastery here for two (2) months with my last full day being a source of perpetual blessings dedicated once again, right now as you read, on behalf of all sentient beings.

Journal Entries (9 &10/95)

"Dharamsala is a beautiful place. Green. Lush. Tucked in the hills and looking out over a wide flood plain. Behind, rocky peaks loom, turning red-orange last evening with sunset.... Dip Tse Chok Ling Monastery, where I am staying, is a 10 minutes down from the center of town, surrounded by forests, and overlooking the flood plain. Idyllic. Tranquil. Peace. It even has hot showers for the likes of me....

Life, as always, seems to be generating its' own pattern/structure these days. One week now into my stay. I arise around 7/8, eat b/w 8-9, plan, play, and occasionally meditate until 11, then lunch ensues. A break, and then a language lesson swap w/ Gyaltsen ..."

"My days have fallen into a lovely rhythm of teaching, writing, studying, peace and meditative practice."

"What a sight! Thirty monks all singing the Beatles 'Yellow Submarine'... and later the national anthem of America."

"I wish I could create & write pouring forth prose that would engender interest in others. How to tap into this?.... I find myself lacking in my ability to describe/detail with words the event. This is my weak point but impressions remain, perhaps, someday, they will make their way to print."

"Had a really good Tibetan language lesson today w/Gyaltsen."

"Morning's practice was difficult and arduous with my mind scattered and unfocused. In the early evening, however, thirty minutes passed as if in the blink of an eye. Illuminating, speaking to the power of mind."

"Visions of past lives passed faintly before my eyes as I sat in practice yesterday."

At the same time, I struggled.

"A morning spent rooftop, chatting w/friends. I feel I can't do anything right. My confidence and self-understanding is

205

whisked away as easily as the dried seeds of a dandelion take flight in the softest of breezes. I feel not grounded in anything. Jokes turn sour and cause pain. Perhaps I try too hard to be liked."

"I see a little puppy trotting down the street, its' ears dangling to and froe (?). It stops and pisses on my foot, then moves on."

"Sharing now a table with strangers who speak in hushed tones as if I cannot hear. Do I look stupid or what? One huge venture in ego. Embody Humility.... I feel unloved, lusting after things which I cannot have. Won't somebody please tell me, where has love gone? Has its flame been extinguished in my heart? If so, how to re-light it?"

Beyond my time in the monastery, the hilltop town and almost constant stream of shows and celebrations were enchanting.

***

"This afternoon, a walk to Bhagsu Waterfall and the road destroyed by a mudslide, up to my knees as I crossed it. Quite fun and very dirty.... On the road, an Indian family was performing an act – a little girl, perhaps 10, on a tightrope strung up b/w four bamboo poles about 12-15 feet long. Carrying pets on her head and balancing w/a stick, she made her way back and forth. At one point, stopping center, she shimmied and swung the rope beneath her feet, furiously left and right to the delight of onlookers....

Oh yeah. Last night, a trip to see the Tibetan Youth Congress in a delightful slow song and dance. Granted, production needs to be up-scaled as every number had some snafu or another. At one point, some guy was doing a rough quick step and his hat kept falling in his eyes and his boot was half coming off his foot when kicks were required. The audience was roaring w/laughter well before I could figure out what was happening....

One day, the Tibetan Children's Village celebrated its' 35th anniversary preserving and passing on Tibetan's rich spiritual and cultural heritage. *"What a beautiful event."*

My fellow foreigners and their stories, sprinkled throughout my journal, really informed my time in Dharamsala. We were a collective mirror that allowed for deeper insights. Each one of us, for our own unique reasons, found our separate ways to that healing and holy place and shared in co-creating the experiences.

Searching and seeking answers to whatever questions we sought to ask – in my case, family focused.

I share this next picture with the following aspirations for His Holiness, the 16th Dalai Lama, Tenzin Gyatso:

May all who see the following picture be inspired towards greater acts of selflessness on behalf of all sentient beings.

May each one of us more fully realize the value of a life drowning and drenched in loving-kindness and compassion.

Overflowing with boundless gratitude, I offer my thanks each day for creating the causes and conditions of your granted audience. You live within my heart. May your health be strong and life, long. May the teachings flourish.

May we all live each day in service to the gentler, kinder and more patient body, speech and mind which you embody and exemplify..

***

These were tales of my 30's in Nepal.

208

I encourage all groups to begin chapter discussions with the following three (3) questions, then reflect and share.

What is my overall impression of the chapter?

Which story did I most prefer? Least?

What is a theme of the chapter?

Reflect and Share: My 30's Nepal

A suggested way to proceed: *Someone call out a letter (A-Z). Read aloud that question and answer it until conversation is exhausted, then, continue with another letter. Enjoy.*

a) Do you agree or disagree? Why? (pg. 157) *"We truly hurt the ones we love."*

b) Do you believe that good things come to those who wait?

c) Is there a time in your life when you were particularly patient?

d) What three (3) words best describe your relationship with bugs and insects? Please explain.

e) How do you think significant, beneficial and lasting societal change occurs? Through what methods and means?

f) What is your opinion of the death penalty? Eating meat?

g) What do you think about the statement, (pg. 160), *"The sufferings of birth, aging, sickness and death apply universally?"* How is this important?

h) Who and what do you most trust? Distrust?

i) What is your favorite restaurant? Why? What role does food play in your life?

j) What is the most challenging health crisis you have ever faced?

k) On page 171, I describe encountering a four (4) year old Master. What was your reaction to this tale? And, our second meeting in Kathmandu?

l) Which stories from this chapter are most memorable? Why?

m) On page 174, I talk about, *"Being compassionate while not being a doormat."* Have you ever been someone's doormat? If yes, please share.

n) What is the best job you have ever worked? What did you like about it?

o) On a scale of 1-10, how assertive are you?

p) In describing our countries (USA and Russia), I wrote: *"Our countries had been drowning for far too long, under the muddied waters of fear and hate"* Is the creation of enemies an inevitable aspect of society? Humankind? Why or why not?

q) Have you ever visited a place that overwhelmed your senses? If yes, where? What happened?

r) Does this resonate with you? If yes, how so? (pg 184): *"Which part of me is real? Which part of me to bury? To reveal?"*

s) What role, if any, has real or perceived guilt, played in your life decisions? How has it affected your actions and emotions?

t) What is the most aggressive, social interaction you have ever experienced? What were the surrounding circumstances? Out comes?

u) Have you ever done volunteer work? If yes, please share. What drew you to it? What did you gain from the experience(s)?

v) On page 194, I list the six (6) negative emotions in Buddhism: *"pride, jealousy, desire, ignorance, greed, anger."* What do you think of this list?

w) What thing(s) frustrate you most in life? Why? How do you cope?

x) What is your reaction to my recounting of sky burials (pg. 199)?

y) What events in your life have most cultivated an attitude of gratitude?

z) Beyond food and lodging, how do you answer these questions? *(pg.176) "How much, and what do we really need, to survive?"*

Amusing Journal Entries

Reviewing my journals, I came across many wonderful descriptions, stories and memories that did not find their way into my tales so I share them here for your amusement. Please enjoy.

***

1) *"Padam, my guide, just said, 'My socks are clean.' When asked 'why?' he said, "because they are black.'"*

2) *"Streams of donkeys plod by, clopping hooves smack stone slabs, bells swaying to gong as their sullen faces gaze downwards. Across the way, a woman combs the same strand of hair, again and again, passing time."*

3) *"I have fucked my life up by speaking truth to fearful ears.... Trapped in a cycle of tragic love."*

211

4) *"Wilting pink flowers, highlighted by lime green leaves, droop themselves listlessly over the head of an angel. She has come and now floats near the table next to mine. Hovering and bobbing in a radiant blue, she glances to the right and gains awareness of my gaze to the left. Her eyes lighten and register surprise as I nod to acknowledge her presence and then return to their original placid green. She smiles. With that, her aura rises through the flowers, causing them to stir in fragrant motion and she is gone. I have always been able to see angels, as long as I can remember."* Comment: This is pure, fun fiction - just playing with words.

5) *"Hot water and cooled thoughts. Spiny smoothness. Random particulars. Funny solemnity and ancient contemporaries. Evening settles. I could stay here forever."*

6) *"An orange headed lizard climbs up and peers over the wall to my left. Then, it scurries away out of sight."*

7) *"Old men with thick glasses and wrinkled, aged faces stand near the door inhaling cigarettes as if such an act requires the last remnants of their energy."*

8) *"Grumbling giggles and gleeful stares. To love."*

9) *"I was tired and quickly receded into a world of empty, unremembered dreams.... I have mueslied, tea'd, peed, and tea'd again. The hour is now 8:30am and the sun is shining.... Cool feet cry out not to be returned to the sweaty tunnels of cotton. Slow life banked by receding ridges. I can't get you out of my mind. There is no answer to make me happy, bar one, but even then, I am responsible for my own happiness.... A breeze blows and chills my sweat drenched shirt."*

10) *"A bird just shit in/on my pack.... Sign of the day?"*

11) "Sunrise over the Ganges, seen from a gently rocking boat painted white. Even at 6:30am, hundreds of pilgrims were ritually bathing. From far right to far left, pilgrims wash and pray their way to heaven. Cold water laced with filth."

12) "People snored and farted with tremendous force throughout the night."

13) "Every aspect and every moment of one's life must be lived in harmonious relations to all and every other."

14) "An embittered shopkeeper musing to elicit shocked responses. Clinton. The US. Corruption. Sikhs. Punjab. The Peace Corps. Gays. The man sounds many dour notes on these and further topics." Comment: I found Indians love to debate matters political.

15) "The lady was middle aged, a softened version of Louise Lasser in that soap opera spoof which appeared on late night TV."

16) "Up to the village, at the head of the stairs, garbage thrown in a gully is attracting hungry creatures: two dozen crows perched in trees, five monkeys, four hawks and a puppy..."

17) "I've been trying to focus not merely on my breath, but also on a small mantra from A Path with Heart by Jack Kornfeld. It goes:

> *a.   May I be filled w/ loving-kindness.*
> *b.   May I be well.*
> *c.   May I be peaceful and at ease.*
> *d.   May I be happy."*

18) "My dreams have been astoundingly vivid the last two evenings, and, my sleep long – 10/12 hours. People, places and events of immensely powerful

213

delight. I saw into my hand, my right hand, as if it was cut open and peered into a cavern like construction. I also drove our old brown Chevy wagon into a Japanese department store but could not exit."

19) "How can we begin to forgive ourselves for the suffering we've caused others? And, how can we generate compassion for others when we have never experienced their level of pain and sorrow?"

20) "My days seem to move swiftly and my mind seems peaceful. Rhythms pulse as notes dance. The underlying snap and tap of a classical Indian drum."

21) "The cooing warmth of a small brown pigeon is quickly squelched by the swooping slap of a diving eagle's wings. Lunch procured."

22) "The pounding in his head continued from the night before and the angels which had guided him to sleep were now raging spirits beating to get out. Their voices screamed a singular piercing cry driving him to the place in which he now stands."

23) "Thoughts of things left unsaid to my family periodically crop up in my mind. Striving for balance."

Random Journal Book Reviews

a) "Just finished <u>All the Pretty Horses</u> by Cormac McCarthy. Boy is it terse. Succinct and staccato in its' style. Good, but unnerving in a way; it is underlied by an almost unbearable tension in which you wait for something to happen and yet nothing does. The plot? Three young guys on horse thru Mexico around 1920....Was overwhelmed by the ending. It was so thoroughly satisfying that it rescued the book from earlier reading struggles."

b) "Need to stop and indulge in a little <u>Siddhartha</u> by Herman Hesse.... Such a fine read."

c) "Started HH's (His Holiness the Dalai Lama) new book, <u>The Joy of Living in Peace</u>. Wonderful."

d) "I finished <u>Possessing the Secret of Joy</u> by Alice Walker and began <u>Jazz</u> by Toni Morrison. The former was a quite powerful, political story of genital mutilation among woman. <u>Jazz</u> is proving itself a wonderful, lyrical read but heavy on description and imagery. She has a profound way with words."

e) "Bought and read, <u>Congo</u>, by Michael Chriton. Simply fascinating blend of fact and fiction concerning primates and a lost city in the Congo. He weaves a marvelous tale."

Suggested Reads on Buddhism

I include the following list for interested folks.

1. <u>The Path to Freedom,</u> by His Holiness, the Dalai Lama; Basic overview/ foundational text

2. <u>The Miracle of Mindfulness,</u> by His Eminence, Thich Naht Hahn; Lucid guide for essential techniques to calm the mind

3. <u>Carefree Dignity</u>, by His Eminence Tsoknyi Rinpoche; More advanced text detailing core Mahayana concepts regarding meditation

4. <u>Cutting Through Spiritual Materialism</u>, by His Eminence Chogram Trungpa; Advanced underpinnings

5. <u>The Words of My Perfect Teacher</u>, by His Eminence Patrul Rinpoche; A complete overview of Tibetan Buddhist philosophy

Chapter 5: My 30's Hong Kong

Introduction

When I decided to relocate to Hong Kong, I was excited and uncertain about how the latter half of my 30's would unfold. While I felt blessed for all I had learned and experienced in Nepal, it is the relative nature of mind to have reservations about such impactful life changes. Where would I live? What about work and new friends? What if I didn't really enjoy my new surroundings? Moreover, how could it possibly surpass Nepal? As my mind churned, such ponderings proved themselves another needless form of suffering.

Hong Kong (HK) became a fortunate mix of East and West both in culture and my professional and personal lives. HK flowed into a welcoming series of events. The right people, the right places, and the right work: with the right causes and conditions, all things blended together beyond anything I had allowed myself to imagine. Sometimes – at all times – trust in yourself and remain true to your heart in acts of body, speech and mind.

By the end of four (4) years, I had made an array of exceptional friends from around the world while inhabiting a very small space. A taste of corporate life sat well on my palate and provided tremendously satisfying work experiences with a group of highly skilled and talented colleagues. The daily buzz of this working life contrasted nicely with a life lived on a small island overflowing with nature and devoid of vehicles. And, I began living openly in a supportive and caring environment. In time, infatuation gave way to a lovely man who found his way into my heart. Life lessons took form in many ways and I was open to all they offered.

These are more tales of my 30's.

"Ah, Hong Kong, a place of so many wild decadences. A decadence of nature and wealth, of spirituality, experiences and friends - so many, many different and wonderful things. Wasn't it though? Hmmm.... Quite," remarked my dear friend, Angela, in her lilting, wistful and proper British accent on hearing of this chapter. I completely agreed.

By the end of 1999, circumstances encouraged my departure from Nepal. I had journeyed through Tibet and perchance met Randall and his partner. Shortly thereafter, I found myself in a whole new part of Asia filled with understanding and insights from KTM (Kathmandu), among them being:

- the good fortune of my circumstances;
- beauty encourages spirituality;
- the benefits of simplicity;
- Existence amidst persistent, visible poverty and pollution;
- the difference between needs and wants, and;
- further realizing the Masters teachings and wisdom shared.

New lessons awaited in Hong Kong, a city of:

- vibrancy and wealth;
- opulence and contrast;
- opportunities, temptations, magic ; and,
- chaos that transformed circumstances.

Hong Kong (HK), means "fragrant harbor." Its' four (4) main areas total 427 sq. miles, including:

HK Island – skyscrapers rising from the harbor and buttressed by mountains creates HK's icon Harbor and Peak views; the Prince's Building sits Central;

The Outlying Islands that dot the start of the South China Sea; I lived on one of them - Lamma;

Kowloon – the southern part of the peninsula that extends from mainland China; Kowloon sits opposite HK Island and connect via the iconic Star Ferry; and,

The New Territories – the northern part of the peninsula bordering mainland China; Kiki, my Tibetan friend from Nepal, lived here with his wife and daughter.

With a population of 7.2 million, HK is the 4th most densely populated territory on the planet and has the highest life expectancy. Ninety percent (90%) of the population walks and uses public transportation. The remaining 10% have the highest per-capita ownership of Mercedes Benz and Rolls Royce anywhere. HK also has one of the highest per capita incomes, and the most extreme income inequality among developed economies.

My life swirled with two (2) wonderfully distinct and intermingled lives - the urban buzz and challenge of professionalism by day, the simplicity and tranquility of island life by night.

Monday through Friday, 9-5 was a corporate world of meetings, trainings, suits and ties. The weekday evening ferry and weekends became a life lived more personal, relaxed and open. Both were engaging, intriguing and expansive in their unique ways. Both allowed for greater feelings of openness, interdependence, and grounding. Fittingly, these interdependently separate lives merged via the waters of a swift sea channel that churned from HK harbor towards the South China Sea. As the city lights receded, slow moving cargo ships stacked high with containers and twinkling like Christmas trees passed with the watery right of way.

From the airport, to Lamma Island to Yung Shue Wan

218

(YSW) to Randall's, an affirming energy filled the air. Lamma was at once lush and beached, inspiringly green and seasonally arid, dry fresh – steeped in the sea air and populated by fine folks.

Down the gangplank to pier's end and left for 30 minutes was Pak Kok, sparsely populated. Five (5) minutes to the right was YSW, the island's largest village. The tiny main street bustled with great restaurants, including the Deli Lamma and Bookworm Cafe. Tourist shops and small businesses of general commerce thrived. On Chinese New Year's Eve (usually in February), powerful illegal firecrackers were strung in front of shops to ward off evil spirits for the coming year. Your ears rung for hours and the explosive remnants covered the sidewalk like paper snow.

Past the stores and upwards the hill was Tai Ping. Here, I took my first apartment. Along the way, people farmed small gardens. A creek trickled and sometimes streamed towards the harbor. A patch of lotus flowers bloomed annually.

One thing: I love lotus flowers and their symbolism. Arising from muck and muddied waters, the lotus unfurls radiating beauty. So to from our muddled mind unfurls wisdom and a palpable sense of compassion.

Cresting Tai Ping, the path crossed through thick jungle, past caves used for WW2 ammunition storage, and ended far at a secluded, harbor front restaurant. The 8,000 residents had no cars. With its' three (3) huge, smokestacks looming, a single utility road cut the island and serviced the coal-fired, power station that fueled HK Island. For a while, full moon parties were regularly hosted on Power Station Beach until tragedy initiated their halt. Folks knew folks and it was good.

Asian by day and Western by night, I straddled personal

and personal cultures whereby the ex-patriot community took on a much greater role in my life compared to Japan and Nepal.

Given the legacy of British control, English was the working language of HK. This made life considerably easier. Early on, I took Cantonese (HK Chinese) lessons for three (3) months but soon stopped. At markets, when I struggled to practice and speak, vendors would say, "*English, please*" and move to swiftly end our transaction - next customer.

One thing: After 10 years of living predominantly amidst foreign languages, it was a significant adjustment to once again, effortlessly understand everything being heard. I did not realize how accustomed I had grown to living within my own bubble - to zone out at will, to feign ignorance when questioned, to pretend to understand when convenient, or, to simply remain clueless. My options had dwindled dramatically. Engagement was largely required.

As far as settling in, the kindness and support of Rodney and his partner were invaluable. Though the house was small, I crashed on their couch until I got on my feet. After a range of interviews, including one that boomeranged in the best of ways, I accepted a job teaching English at a Japanese owned and operated school in Causeway Bay (CB) on Hong Kong Island. I worked there about nine (9) months. CB was a massive, gleaming area whose retail plazas pulsed with an almost kinetic energy.

Buying a translucent blue, Macintosh computer, I found living with home, internet access for the first time an exercise in mind training of a different sort. Navigating expectations and interactions was new on a different level. Living and chatting within the virtual world expanded my version of relative reality.

Initially, I stealthily explored gay chat rooms, coffee dates and hooking up. And, I worried about the negative karma of lying. Closeted and inactive was what it was. Closeted and active, though, meant consciously deceiving others with significantly more impactful, karmic consequences. I was grateful and fortunate when I came out. Boundless thanks to my dear friends, a lot of "*we knew*."

One thing: Living openly, some described my behavior as promiscuous. And, if enjoying an unexpected gropefest in the gym sauna when the lights went out, or, having fun against the 53rd floor, glass wall of a five (5) star hotel overlooking HK harbor fits your definition of promiscuity, then, yes, in hindsight, I was. Always safe, never scared, and occasionally embarrassed by performance anxiety, I was learning.

My apartment in Tai Ping was an inexpensive, month-by-month that well-suited my short terms needs. The two (2) small bedrooms, a living room, and a makeshift kitchen were devoid of direct sunshine. The glass balcony door was shaded by a huge, old tree growing directly out front. It brought me great joy. I love trees.

My neighbors in Tai Ping included Mamadu and Akiko, from Senegal and Japan, respectively. A lovely couple, he was an accomplished drummer who played various gigs around HK and lead Sunday beach drum circles. She taught Japanese. For whatever reason, he thought my name was Phil and I never bothered correcting him. One day, months later, he started calling me Peter. I still wonder the circumstances surrounding his illumination, as well as his surprise.

One hot day wearing only shorts, I answered a knock at my door. Two (2) young Christian missionaries said, "*Hello,*" as their faces looked suddenly discomforted. They politely apologized and left. "*That was odd,*" I thought. When looking next into my bathroom mirror, I understood their reaction.

Nearly naked, my face was speckled with white blotches of anti-blemish cream. In time, I moved into a lovely, 400 sq. ft. loft style home near the pier.

The new job was easy and paid the bills. I facilitated private and small group English lessons. My work colleagues from England, Canada and elsewhere were wonderful. My love of teaching and the students kept me in the classroom, though I was bored with the content and wanted more out of my work.

Further, being back amidst the Japanese mindset was challenging. Coupled with learning the Hong Kongese ways of being, the relative reality of situations often played games with my head. Patience and mindfulness were helpful neighbors when I relaxed into their visits.

Hong Kong Island is a masterful example of adaptation. Reclamation projects extended its' size, and land was scarce and expensive. The harbor met a shoreline built to protect from serious, seasonal nature. Wooden piers jutted as required.

The piers led out the station to a century old, double-decker tram, atop a road, atop a subway that moved people harbor side. The world's longest, outdoor covered escalator connected street level with Mid- Levels and the Peak. With its' record setting incline, the Peak Tram seriously angled you up to iconic views, and some of the world's most expensive homes.

Once settled, I joined an international gym chain where I befriended an inter-racial couple who invited me to an "*Underwear Only*" party on the Peak. "*No Sex Allowed*" signs hung on the living room wall.

The house and its' 25 Calvin clad, smooth muscled men were all wow. Several guests I recognized thru coffee dates and bars and still I felt somehow out of place.

222

One thing: To the straight men, I ask you to imagine visiting Hugh Hefner's mansion. What exactly would you do, surrounded by fantasies incarnate? How exactly would you feel? Ladies, comments? In my incubated awkwardness, this was my conundrum. My mind harkened back to:

- *"Doug - a sexy ball of testosterone. I admired him from afar, never really wanting to touch, preferring rather to simply gawk and stare, free from notice or reverberations (pg. 76);" and,*

- *the Playboy Playmate's house, "... being somewhat star struck and feeling out of place. A sense of, "Who is this guy and how did he get in here? (pg. 131)*

Speckled by the subtle light of an emerging dawn, I most enjoyed walking down to the ferry under the leafy, canopied trail.

In September 2000, 10 months after arrival, life was bountiful and flowing. Then, it all got better with a phone call. Before I knew it, a job interview from 1999 came to fruition in late 2000.

December 1999 (while searching for my first job)

Mr. George: *"Next, we will schedule you with Ms. Vance to discuss the specifics. She is our Assistant Director of Learning & Education (L&E)."*

Ms. Vance: (a week later) *"Sorry, your lack of accounting experience will hurt your credibility among the staff who you would be training. Good luck."*

September 2000 (the phone rings)

Me: *"Hello. Peter speaking."*

"Yes. Hello, Peter. You may not remember me. This is Ms. Vance, at PrinceWilliamCorp (PWC) I now direct the L&E Division. I have a position in which I think you might be interested. Do you have any time to come talk?"

Of course I did. She soon detailed her vision for a new *"English Writing Skills Coach"* position. From that initial hearing to my departure in mid-2003, I passed forward a program that included:

- Group workshops and private, writing tutorials;
- An intranet, self- study program;
- Document read-throughs for Partners;
- "Quick Topic," Public Speaking; and,
- Assistance in drafting and conducting company-wide, Needs Assessment surveys.

It was engaging, challenging and fun. I shared work with a talented and wonderful group of people. I am so grateful for their respect, support, insights and welcoming friendships.

It was my first and only, full time, corporate training experience – something I had always wanted to do. Years later, I felt a similar kinship with my Wilton spa family in Las Vegas.

Her reaching out reminded me yet again, of the need to always be mindful of our impact on others – the impressions that linger, those that dissolve and the depth of memories etched.

One thing: PWC agreed to my requested wage so I did not ask for enough – a lesson in undervaluing self.

Throughout my tenure, she randomly stopped by, questioned, guided and encouraged me, then, let me do my work. I responded exceptionally well to this management style.

Just prior to start, I had travelled to Bali, Indonesia and returned an itchy mess due to a case of tinea corpus, or *"crabs."*

Day One at PWC, I was shampooing my itchy groin in a bathroom stall. I also burned an essential oil diffuser and created a stunk-up, hallway mess. The powers that be quickly made themselves known. As I looked out the window of my tiny, 22nd floor office, I thought, *"Oh my, what have I done?"* It was all so very grand. Settling in, I enjoyed exploring the neighborhood at lunch.

Covered by cloth tarps, simple bamboo stalls lined the back streets. The expensive shoes of well-quaffed workers clip-clapped along sidewalks made of stone as they navigated small alleyways and steps. I found a vegetarian restaurant with Gyaltrul Rinpoche's picture out front and became a regular. That became my HK Island life. In my free time, I got officially certified at the gym as a Yoga instructor and started a class on Lamma.

Before getting on a ferry and chugging to life on Lamma, a weather comparison: Buffalo is to snow, as HK is to hurricanes. HK experiences seasonal typhoons that can cause quite a stir. Systems are in place to cope. Weekdays, as storms approached, the public warnings were issued as follows:

Category 1: elementary kids go home
Category 3: all school kids go home
Category 8: everyone goes home
Category 10: hold on

Yearly, categories 1, 3 and 8 were expected. One year, I experienced the first Category 10 in 17 years. Winds whipping at 110 mph shattered the highest windows of the Tax Bureau. Private paperwork spiraled skyward and drowned in the harbor. People rushed frantically en masse to the piers in the cold and pelting, horizontal rain.

226

Arriving at Lamma, the metal gangplank raised and lowered erratically at the whim of the ocean tossed ferry. It scratched and screeched loudly on the cement pier like a mis-calibrated metronome. Lining up three or four (3 or 4) at a time, we readied ourselves and scurried quickly down to the sopped, cement pier.

Safely home, we gathered at the Deli Lamma to celebrate the unexpected holiday. *"Have another drink and share with me your storm story."* Indian food and drinks replaced the hot cocoa and soups of a Buffalo storm. People danced on tables and stayed until sunrise.

QtoP1: Am I a good liar? Do I suffer guilt easily?

QtoP2: Over what do I obsess?

Qtop3: Have I ever danced on a table? Worked a pole? Shot the moon? Where is the best place I have ever had sex?

One year, the eye of a hurricane centered directly over Lamma. While the radio described the surrounding chaos of uprooted trees and falling signs, our sky was bright blue and the air still. The animals were eerily silent. Within two (2) hours, the storm's wind-whipping, backside swept through and damage ensued. I scurried to a mountain top and screamed naked at the storm.

The intensity of this rainy confrontation with nature contrasted sharply with the enveloping, womb-like warmth of an ocean swallowing you whole while scuba diving. I enjoyed them both.

Early on, I actively cultivated friendships on Lamma. I responded to a flyer calling for volunteers to *"fire spot"* during an upcoming, Chinese festival of ancestral worship. I am so happy I did. I soon found myself armed with a walkie-talkie and paired with a new friend, patrolling hillside gravesites. The ashes of burnt offerings, smoldering and windswept, sometimes ignited fires. It was our job to report back. Several people I met that day remain wonderfully in my life.

One thing: Elsewhere on the island and beyond the reach of this particular festival, the jungle overgrew homes that were traditionally abandoned the very day that someone died. Books on tables, cabinets opened, things strewn about: everything left as was - undisturbed by others - to hungry ghosts and creeping vines. I cultivated a proper reverence when exploring them on hikes, yet always felt intrusive.

I sometimes wonder, *"Will my world ever again coalesce around such a diverse and delightful group of people, all gathered for a time, in one magical place?"*

That was Lamma.

- Anni Zumma, a Tibetan Buddhist, Western nun;
- An extraordinary political activist (Duang Yang);
- An American poet, female;
- A man who sailed his catamaran around the world;
- An exceptional yogini;
- A Communication scholar, Rodney;
- A Lebanese restauranteur; male;
- A Palestinian computer pro, male;
- An Italian, stone sculptress, female, with five (5) young children;
- An inter-racial couple who met and have raised five (5) kids;
- A world level tennis pro, male;
- A lovely Kiwi (New Zealand) couple;
- A light and lost, Scottish wanderer, male;
- An innately gifted watercolor artist, female;
- A Special Needs scholar, female;
- A shark expert, female;
- A botanist who tended trees at HK's Disney Land, male;

- A Hawaiian surfer, female;
- A broadcast journalist won the *Edward R. Murrow Award for Journalistic Excellence,* female;
- Fresh juicers and vegans who opened a tasty shop;
- More and me.

Ahhh ... Lamma. Your memories tickle my mind and warm my heart. What to share and where to start? Experiences and emotions constantly swelled, crested and curled out of existence. Lives were continually upended and uprighted. That said, funny tales from the ferry pier, involving folks I did not really know, seems an excellent place to begin. Two (2) stories come to mind.

Monday thru Friday, I took the 8:15am ferry. A local couple sat window-side in the front left row. You had to see them unless you closed your eyes or looked away. They were mesmerizing. Every day, she turned left and picked his zits for much of the journey. My inquiring mind asks: How can someone have that much acne? And, can you please move that to the back corner and out of sight? Or better yet, just stop? Please?

A muscle ripped and handsome HK man always sat mid-center, right. One day he stopped coming. Asking around about my morning eye candy, I learned that he was HK's #1 bodybuilder. Months later, he returned. This time, his face was sadly dappled and permanently scarred. I felt so bad for him and the marked consequences of his actions.

Most weekday mornings, my best friend, Angela was joined by her dog, Wong Wong (WW), as they trotted down from Tai Ping to the pier. Like Amelia in Nepal, Angela was another strong, successful woman with whom I deeply connected. We shared, and still share, our lives.

WW was, far and away, the smartest most intuitive puppy I have ever met. After seeing Angela off, Wong Wong dined along a successful begging route then played all day.

Everyone knew and loved her. As you dis-embarked at day's end, WW often sat facing the on-coming crowd. If Angela was present, they left together. If not, WW would, or would not, choose to accompany you. It depended on her momentary, diva-like mood. On the weekends, WW and I often swam together at the beach. Her numerous, unintended scratches were a price joyously paid. One time, WW got into some herb laced edibles and frolicked thru the village in a goopy, loopy, *"can't quite figure this out"* energy. She was adorable and hilarious. I recently shared these stories with a Lamma friend, Jo, and she replied,

"Wong Wong was the most autistic human I ever met. I adored her. She took what she wanted from all around her, but did it with charm, poise and intelligence. A truly amazing creature. I remember my first morning on Lamma, jet lagged and hung over I took a walk. She met me on Yung Shue Wan main street – she was watching the butchery of a half pig – she smiled (a bit scary, she was a powerful dog) then guided me to Angela's front door. I loved her unreservedly from then on."

On a decidedly more impactful level, the suffering of friends rippled close. They struggled with the complications of an open adoption in which the adoptive parents reneged. Legal tussles ensued. In the end, the process sided in my friend's favor. They simply wanted to see their daughter once a year as had been originally agreed. I realize that in this life, I will not know the swirling emotions of parenthood. The power of jealousy, however, acquainted itself.

I befriended an interracial (Caucasian and Asian) gay couple with whom I spent much fun time. While I admittedly found Liang rather handsome, I liked and respected Ray tremendously and never wished to disrupt or challenge their relationship. It inspired me. Even when Ray went away on business and Liang and I hung out,

231

despite our unspoken attraction, he remained faithful and I acted appropriately. Given the small nature of the community, any such infidelity would have rippled destructively throughout.

One day, while we were enjoying a few drinks harbor side, Liang, who rarely drank, had a few too many and got very amorous. Standing with a wobble, he came over and started hugging, and caressing, laughing and playing with me. Boom! Another *"Sam in the Car"* moment, I froze. Ray's eyes pierced. Our relationship was never the same.

His jealousy towards me and fear of loss towards Liang manifested in several ways. At parties, he would disappear in a room and then pop out, believing he would find us somehow conspiring. Or at restaurants, he would insist that we sit next to each other as if to push a daring envelope. I heard happily they remain together. At the same time, another couple caused me to pause regarding acceptance in the face of unexpected revelations.

Darren and Laura were two (2) of the most beautiful people I had ever met. He was a swashbuckling man of adventure and she a buxom wench, all in the best of ways.

I easily imagined in them 17th century England – a manly man and a womanly woman. Both were so very kind and friendly to me. Now happy in their new and separate lives, my Lamma–time is filled with wonderful memories of us.

At some point, after years of marriage, she found that he loved to dress as a woman. Undeniably hetero in his attractions, he enjoyed nevertheless, donning a dress, wig and heels, and exploring this energetic side of his spirit.

QtoP4: How do I want to be remembered?

QtoP5: Am I a jealous person? Over what? Towards whom?

232

QtoP6: Do I really believe that, marriage remains
"Until death do us part"?

Big picture-wise, five (5) happenings best encapsulated the swirl of experiences that composed my Lamma life. They reminded me of, and re-affirmed, important life lessons. The first was a simple, Christmas Sunday walk. I do love me this particular holiday and its' generosity.

Maggie, the poet, her boyfriend, Chan, and I decided to cross the island for a special meal. Hugging the coast, we entered a patch of trees and stirred hundreds of small, yellow butterflies. Basking beneath the gentle sunshine, they swarmed silently, fluttering and flickering around us, dancing in an exquisite play of light and shadow, resettling elsewhere with evocative joy. Good friends, simple pleasures, and priceless moments of effortless, unaware awareness. Similarly, friends once phoned me to their jungle home. *"There is something surreal to be seen. Hurry!"* I did.

A teeming ant colony was moving, en masse across the living room wall. Within her mini-marshmallow sized, white spun home, the Queen swirled center, swept up in the fluid, organized chaos from bottom left to upper right.

Within minutes, it was all gone. Were they ever really there? All interdependent energies arise, dwell, and cease perpetually across hours, weeks and years, across countless eons, including the energy of ants.

The second happening originated with a dinner game and centered on trust and credibility. About 12 of us were harbor side, dining Chinese at one of those large, *"lazy susan"* tables that spin your food for sharing.

We played a simple game of *Truth or Lie* - someone stated something and you circle spoke if it was true or not. When my turn came, I spoke of the world famous, 1920's

233

Charleston dancer whose claim to fame was her lack of knees. She was born with entirely straight legs. Lie! A knee-less Charleston is impossible. Incredibly, everyone believed me. I was so floured at their gullibility; I chose to not reveal it as the whopper it was.

Days later, a stranger on the ferry approached me to confirm the story's veracity and I knew I had to set the record straight. People were so upset. *"We believed you, Peter,"* they argued, *"and you let us go on believing?"*

Some say, the only thing we really have in our life is our reputation.

The third happening became a simple, Sunday offering that grew. My personal desire to practice a new skill became a routine of great joy for many. Freshly certified, I offered a free yoga class. In time, we became a fourth floor, rooftop ritual of 15.

The jungle behind and the ocean inspiringly out front, the class became the highlight of our week for over a year. Friends began sponsoring me brunch afterwards at the Bookworm Café. I gratefully accepted and this too became part of our weekly routine. During summer, we expanded yet again with hikes and swims. Thanks to all who made these affirming Sundays so memorable.

Three things; one: I loved the Bookworm Café, almost as much as Green Leaves. The vegetarian food was exceptional and the space, owners and staff were bright and friendly. It was very much a community destination and often hosted various musical, literary, educational and spiritual events. My parents attended one.

A Protestant Minister/ Native American Holy Man held a seminar on the meaning and proper use of a peace pipe. My Dad loved it; he was open and receptive. I was so happy to witness this previously unseen side of my father.

high. Later, this man's wife, Lana, opened my mind to recessed and forgotten memories that helped refine and illuminate my self-perception.

Two: I am a vegetarian, technically, a pescatarian (seafood eater). Between the Bookworm Café and the fresh juice shop, becoming a vegetarian was almost effortless. In Nepal, seeing where and how the animals were killed, coupled with spiritual teachings, my consumption dropped dramatically. I quickly felt better, lighter and more energetic, too. I am not exceptionally particular about my diet - no red or white meats, a bit of fish, eggs and dairy are ok though infrequent, I can't be too fussed. If you cut a piece of meat with a knife, simply wash it before cutting my corn off the cob. I am fine with that. It is all about balance.

Three: Once, while dining outside the Bookworm, the HK animal rescue team came by with a cage housing their catch – an 18 foot python that had been eating peoples' pets. I was amazed and pondered how some folks would eat snake, just as it had eaten their pet.

The fourth happening foreshadowed tremendous suffering to be experienced by others once I departed HK for Sydney. The seeds of underlying discord became shockingly evident on December 31, 1999 - the arrival of the 21st century. On this auspicious night, my rose colored glasses were shimmering pink.

Being spiritual in Nepal was easy in the sense that it was all around you. Temples, monks, statues and ritual were daily on display just outside your door. Finding and maintaining a spiritual community elsewhere takes more effort. On this night, I felt strongly attuned with my new one, and, the new millennium. Then, I fleetingly saw something that reflected the truth of our relative existence, the pain we harbor and cause. The particular people involved are not important, it is the larger lesson.

That special evening on Lamma, I found myself overnight in a large, traditional, Native American teepee in a banana grove, filled with friends, food and life. We aspired that the new century be steeped in greater peace and understanding. At midnight, a cacophony of yells and honks and horns and cheers permeated our quiet space. *Smile and Be. Slow down. Fully breathe. Look around. Be and smile. Proceed.*

During one practice, we wrote down a thought and were asked to hold this thought in our mind until it connected with our heart, then, you burned the paper. Little did I know what was about to happen.

Glancing left, I accidentally read what my friend had written. I wish I could have unread it because my energetic perspective shifted and something good seemed gone. The message was simple, strong, and steeped in assorted angers; he had written:

*"What the f**k am I doing here?"*

He burned it and left shortly thereafter. His wife stayed. Relationships changed and continually presented challenge. Some survived and others did not. It depended on innumerable things. Boyfriends and girlfriends who became husbands and wives had shifts in their hearts and minds, divorced, and married yet again to the same of their former friends. Ignorance, anger and desire surfaced. Messy treachery joined love and anger and worry. Suffering energies flooded and transformed everyone involved. The Masters share:

- All birth, ends in death;
- All things stored, run out;
- All things joined, come apart;
- All things built, disintegrate; and,
- All things that rise, come down.

The fifth happening – a tale for shortly hereafter, brought the Lamma community together: candles, glow lights and a fire on Power Station Beach as someone paddled just beyond the surf line.

Throughout the year, HK celebrates many Monday/ Tuesday, and Friday/ Monday holidays. Used strategically, three (3) personal days stretched into nine (9) day vacations. I took several to Indonesia and Vietnam, where, in both cases, I was quite taken by the locals. In one (1) brief case, yes, I was a sugar daddy.

Two things; one: When it comes to money, never spend more than you can afford and never loan more than you are willing to lose.

Two: Indonesians are peoples and tribes with varied attitudes, institutions and beliefs spread across 13,000 islands. Indonesia is the world's: 4th most populated nation, 3rd largest democracy; and, largest Muslim country. Among its' 13,000 islands, Java is home to the capital, Jakarta, and 90% of the population.

In the 90's, I explored the city and the countryside with Amelia and Daphny, another ALC colleague. Journal pages recount my first solo trip to Sumatra where dormant volcanoes jutted forth sharply from the ocean floor leaving sparkling lakes in their wake and the equator was marked by a giant golf ball.

Journal Entries (summer, 1992)

"It's dark, pre-dawn, and the air is filled with sounds of life. Chants rise from voices raised in praise of Islam's God. Cars drive-by in low, uneven hums accompanied by the spits and sputters of an occasional motorcycle. A rooster crows ..."

"Traditional Bartok houses serve as my resting place

237

overlooking Lake Mananjau. In two words: Singularly spectacular! Add, pristine and unspoiled ... Mushrooms await but my feet hurt ... fruit fish and birds."

"A baby cries and is comforted with immediacy. Were I to cry, what and who shall comfort me?... the question begs the issue can I?""

"A splash of water is followed by a joyful scream. Life can be, at times, a simple experience, and, really, always is .... The cadence of nature's rhythms carries me on its waves, thrashing me to the shores of life, surfing me over its troubles."

"Write write," cries the teacher to her students, "good writers write, a need to be needed."

"Wow! magical day of intense sensitivity. mushrooms and their mystery work were conspired and consumed. views and vistas of unimaginable splendor."

"Just f**k me. Pound pound pound. A nearby carpenter constructs a house for leisure, rest and life.... My hand hurts, too intensely wishing for another."

***

One thing: Horrifically, in 2004, a 9.3 hurricane devastated much of the northern Sumatra. 250,000 people died in less than two (2) minutes. Peace to the departed and the saddened survivors who remain, proceed and succeed.

This 1990's trip to Sumatra contrasted sharply with my later, 21st century trips to the idyllic island of Bali.

I saw Bali's extraordinary tapestry as *"Nepal in the Tropics."* The statues, the clothes, the colors and culture, the iconography: Hinduism had blended with the indigenous inhabitants and reflected well in practice.

People and the environment were fluid and intertwined. I wrote:

"Last night I saw a fantastic display of local, tribal dancing... people dressed in silkened arrays of color doing an asst. of ritualistic dances. Just beautiful."

Forty-five minutes inland from the beachy part of Bali, Ubud was pure jungle magic. Cascading streams and waterfalls flowed through restaurants. Guest rooms floated in the green and leafy, rainforest canopy. Healing centers were many as the energy felt grounded, organic, healing.

I spent three (3) days at a health farm here, capping off a three (3) week cleanse and fast that had begun in HK. On day three (3), something putrid, old and fuzzy was freed from my large intestine wall. It flooded my blood with nauseating toxins that knocked me out for 14 hours. I awoke feeling terrific and spent the next day white water rafting. During this initial visit, I also discovered gay Bali in Denpasar, Bali's main tourist area.

Being new to an old game, I played catch up: the beach, the clubs, the boys, the dance floor and the drag shows - crowds and fun unto sunrise. When Aldy approached me and introduced himself, I melted. It was an interesting and expensive several months – my first, and last, as a "*sugar daddy.*" When I brought him to HK for my birthday, friends were kind enough to support my fantasy. My memories are so very fond and I felt so very, very.

Three things; one: While visiting Cambodia, someone carrying an iced coffee once offered me a hot coffee and said hello. Shortly afterwards, a spinning warmth crept into my brain and I realized I'd been drugged. Luckily, it was not enough to impair my faculties. It quickly passed as he swiftly ran away. In hindsight, I realized my guard was down because the man had looked exactly like, Aldy.

239

241

Two: Due to back pain, I sought an acupuncture treatment in Bali. Having placed and clipped the needles to provide electric jolts, the practitioner left the room and talked casually with a friend. I was so upset at his unprofessional manner. This taught me much about how to best behave when I later became a massage therapist. Not to be outdone, another therapist's small talk once included the question, "How many abortions have you been responsible for?" Shocked, I replied incredulously, "None," as I stared in utter disbelief.

Three: Angela and I once visited Bali together. Afterwards, she told me there was a betting pool on Lamma over the time between our arrival and my first hook up. Whoever chose seven (7) hours was the winner.

The Gilli Islands, west of Bali, were idyllic, perfection. Sadly, the four (4) days of tranquility quickly transformed into deep sadness on October 13, 2002.

On this day, I returned to Denpasar by boat. Unaware on arrival, I sensed a seriously quiet and unsettled energy. I soon learned that that on October 12th, followers of Osama Bin laden had bombed the city, killing 202 people, local and foreigner both, while injuring 209. Shaken, grief and panic overwhelmed the hearts and minds of a global many. Peace to person kind.

Vietnam is a breathtaking country of coastal beauty, inland splendor and some very lovely men, including, Mihn. I know karma is the reason some people access your heart with such ease. And yet, we can be so very unprepared, as was my case with Mihn. Before I knew it, he had accessed mine.

We made it work for about 18 months. Quite simply, I loved his energy, insightful comments and his laughter. I liked the way he smelled and tasted. I liked being with him and being together. We felt so good wrapped in each

244

other's arms. His anger, occasionally displayed at things I never fully understood, I could have done without.

Pre-cell phone days, he owned and operated a successful internet shop. His sister and adorable niece and nephew welcomed me openly on my numerous visits. One trip, we travelled to the coastal town of Nha Trang where we baked in mud and showered clean on jungle rocks. We lunched on shrimp and beer at a secluded beach. Sadly, it triggered an allergic reaction that cracked my fingers into an itchy mess. The saltwater provided great relief scuba diving the next day. One night, distant torches on the beach led to champagne and skinny dipping.

In Saigon, we watched New Year's Eve fireworks and went to secret, after-hours clubs. At 4am, we dined on noodles (pho) street side, and drank coffee until sunrise. I met many of his friends and they were very kind. I even interviewed with the local PwC office for a regional training position that, thankfully, I did not get.

Mihn visited HK and one Sunday we hosted a gay men only brunch. We both loved to cook. One night while out on Lamma, island police demanded identification so he brought them home. As he opened the door and I looked down from the loft, the police realized quickly his legality and left. Other adventures included:

- swimming at Repulse Bay;
- going shopping in Kowloon;
- sailing on a traditional Chinese junk out of Aberdeen harbor; and,
- walking down from the Peak at night on his birthday.

Another night, I found him cheating in a bathroom stall at a club. We once met in Bangkok and stayed at an exotic gay hotel/ bathhouse complex – a place of opulent fantasies, and, a bad choice for showing commitment. We

245

were equally to blame. There was something about our karma. From each fiber of my heart, I wish him the very best. We were both responsible.

Years later, I visited him in Vancouver where he has since settled. Sadly and with a sense of closure, unfortunate patterns repeated and forced my early departure – karma fully ripened, that fruit has fallen.

When later visiting Vietnam alone, I discovered how much Mihn had protected me from the many aggressive and trick-filled vendors. Heading north, Hanoi was markedly smaller. French influence imbued the architecture, culture and food. Much of the city had survived its' many wars.

Halong Bay was filled with limestone outcrops and caves where entire villages hid to avoid enemies. Two (2) hours south, the village of Nihn Bihn re-imagined nature's beauty by blending limestone and rice filled paddies. Visiting Hoi An was like stepping back in time. The mountain village of Dal Laht enchanted.

> *QtoP7: How fully and consistently am I aware of my intentions?*

> *QtoP8: What physically attracts me to a person? Mentally? Emotionally?*

> *QtoP9: What is violence? Is it ever ok?*

Driving motorcycles safely in Vietnam required faith and intuition. It was so chaotic. Families of four (4) all rode one (1) bike. To turn, you wove through the matrix of on-coming traffic. If you were walking, the same applied. It was at times, terrifying.

Once, while on a motorcycle tour, the driver wove our way through a traffic jam and stopped at the reason for its' existence. Without a helmet, someone's head had cracked like an egg. The tip of his spine was flinching and twitching spastically then I saw it stop. *"Drive slowly,"* I said, shaken as we proceeded home, wondering: *At just what point had the poor man's consciousness departed? And, where had it gone??*

Similar questioning led me to believe in the truth of reincarnation, which in turn gave credence to past life regressions via hypnotherapy. Tapping into and glimpsing past life actions of body, speech and mind can illuminate and provide insight into current life patterns. Like many of our actions, thinking is habit.

Lana, the hypnotherapist, and I met professionally five (5) times. Some recordings exist. The following transcription shares some of what I experienced. Brief commentary follows. *The italicized lines are me.*

Background

I got paper, a pen, and my cell phone as a timer.
Dug out my cassette recorder, inserted, *"Lana Notes Nov 99,"* and transcribed for 54 minutes.

My first hypnotherapy session, unheard in 18 years, from that to immediately this:

00-3:24: Relaxation techniques leading to a door

Lana: Relax your face, Use your imagination, Top of staircase, feel your shoes and socks, the handrail, Countdown 10-1. Imagine this level of relaxation and go deeper. There is a door.

3:25-18:32:   First rendering

"Outdoors sky, clouds and sun... Green moss on rocks... comfortable place but not familiar."

247

Lana: Move towards people you know.

"A group of young kids waiting for my arrival," "Scruffy dressed." "They are travelling."

18:33-28:00 Second Rendering

"A woman, my mother, to my left and I am sick," "Earth house...building a thatched roof," "From the pine trees, a man calls. A stranger is selling salt from bags that hang off his horse," "A sun-weathered face with welcoming eyes."

28:01-38:00 Third Rendering

"Feel like I am in a market," "Smells, animals and people who don't wash," "Prosperous and unfamiliar,"

"Streets are muddy and squish beneath my feet," "She's milking a cow... and has ponytails ... Life in a good place... all slow and meandering,"

Lana: Stay in this lifetime and go to the last day?

"dying peacefully and getting old."

38:01-47:27 Fourth Rendering

"An older woman missing a tooth...she is my wife: nice to me and kind, has let me live a simple life...grandkids,"

"I tend to animals for work and am tired. My hands are heavy,"

"She kissed my forehead and I went to sleep and died,"

Lana: Imagine another door. It will be a significant lifetime, perhaps about your current father.

47:28-54:00 Fifth Rendering

248

"On an island, ocean fishing with a friend... warm and sunny," *"Water is turquoise with many fish ... I actually do not like to kill all the fish but I understand,"*

"Nighttime and music... people in groups... one big man sits with paint on his face, not saying anything, not angry, sitting stoically... not someone to be questioned,"

"In this life time my older sister is a close friend... She's smart and we treat each other nicely."

54:01- Sixth Rendering

Lana: Anyone else in this life for you to meet?

***

Reading this over, certain lines give me pause. On immediate reflection and with heaps of wonder, it intrigues me to see what the mind connects.

"Feel your socks and shoes" takes me back to grammar school when my feet got tremendously hot in class and I was not allowed to take them off. I felt them way too much.

"Outdoor sky, clouds and sun ... green moss on rocks" are things that bring me great joy in this life. I have spent hours staring at starry night skies. I think of the moss covered rocks behind Grandma Trask's house. I have always loved a *"thatched roof."*

Talk of *"markets... animals... and smells"* and I recall the heavy odor of cows and rodeo dung that sometimes permeates the air in my Vegas neighborhood due to the Western themed casino across the street. I like the smell of zoos.

"Dying peacefully and getting old" and *"She kissed my*

249

forehead and I went to sleep and died," cause me to shiver with accommodating comfort. I like the feeling of familiarity this engenders. Truly understanding that death is universal and unavoidable calms your mind and spirit. I think of Grandma Feeley's passing.

"I actually do not like to kill all the fish but I understand," speaks to the Buddhist precepts of do not kill. In this lifetime, I was always uneasy gutting our catch during fishing holidays. Similarly, from a very young age, I ushered bugs and insects out the door rather than kill them. To this day, I remain a tad guilty about hanging a sticky strip near a light bulb in my Lake Cayuga camp cabin then turning the light on to attract insects. Hundreds of tiny lives stuck quickly to death.

"... not saying anything, not angry, sitting stoically... not someone to be questioned." Dad? I do not know, perhaps but I feel not.

Returning to the cassette, I continued in the same manner of first listen, first impressions.

***

54:01- 1:09:45 Lana: Anyone else in this life for you to meet?

"I am spear fishing and I don't like it. Am on a rock and they are telling me how to fish. The big man is there, with the painted face... he's just watching.,. I am asking, "Why? Why?"

Lana: Do you learn or resist?"

"I am fighting about it. I insist there are other ways to eat. Am told it is what I must do... the am told... I am getting angry."

Lana: What happens next?

"*I give in but refuse to kill, that's why I fish with a string.*"

Lana: I want you to sense if there is anything else important in this lifetime – something that makes a big impact?

"*Nothing there.*"

Lana: Ok. Go to the last day of that lifetime. How old are you?

"*About 50... "I've been stabbed. That's how I die.*"

Lana: Who stabbed you?

"*I don't know. Its' a bamboo pole, sharpened and I am impaled.*"

Lana: Was it a man or woman who stabbed you?

"*I think a man... seems like someone I know... they get me right in the middle of my chest.*"

Lana: Did anything happen before the stabbing? Was it a surprise?

"*I am completely shocked... Why are you doing this?... I am impaled but it is still beautiful.*"

Lana: For now, detach a bit from that life. Stay there. Relax and remove yourself and look back... why did this person stab you? Was it personal? Did they try and steal something? Were they angry with you?

"*They just got angry and I couldn't figure out why... I feel like he's angry because I questioned.*

Lana: Was it someone you questioned a lot in that life?

"Yes... I am getting flashes of a person I know in this life... I feel like he did it and that is that. What to do?"

Lana: Is there anything else to be learned about this lifetime? Where was it?

"I didn't like the island life... in the South Pacific."

Lana: I am going to bring you back now. Please remember these lifetimes... In the next few days, you may get further insights, sounds, smells, dreams and other lifetimes. I've opened the door and memories will bubble up... Become more aware... Slowly come back, gently opening your eyes. Coming back...

Immediate, post session discussion:

Lana: I love doing this. You are never sure what will come. I thought we'd deal with you as a monk in Tibet. And, yet, your lives were quite ordinary. What struck me was your feeling for your surroundings... your appreciation for the beauty around you... your spiritual, peaceful approach... a strong curiosity as well.

Me: *But no one close, and that fits in with this life... in the first life, I felt it wasn't exactly Tibet, more lower areas, more green and lush, like Gansu. And, the man who stabbed me with the spear... as soon as that came up, I got a friend in this life, Ray, whom I have had a rocky relationship..."*

My greatest connection was with Ray and our Annapurna trek – his anger and his rage, the pain in my mid-section and repeatedly asking *"Why?"* Did he really once impale me? May he and his family be well.

***

The fifth happening shocked and greatly saddened the Lamma community and sealed the end of an era.

Power Station Beach full moon parties were a monthly event for quite some time. Folks donated their equipment, tarps, time and hearts to ensure an amazing weekend. A bit of cash for generator fuel, and everything else was free. Sometimes word got out on the radio and hundreds of people arrived on the last ferries. Once, attendance topped 800+ partygoers. The three (3) island police briefly patrolled early on, and then let us be. Peace.

Cameroon was an integral, "*behind-the-scenes*" man for every party. With his thick, Scottish brogue accent and hearty laugh, everyone knew and loved him, as far as you can know and love anyone in a passing sort of way - everyone, in this case, except Natalia.

An Italian, stone sculptress and mother of five (5) young kids, she lived in a secluded, Pak Kok house where numerous unfinished pieces were always on display when visiting. I enjoyed seeing her creativity manifest. Looking at a rock, seeing something more, then, chiseling the vision into reality, I find this a boggling talent.

One thing: My cousin, Jon, once took me to the courtyard of a Houston sculptor who made 12' busts of US presidents and famous rock stars, including an extraordinary, 60' rendition of the Beatles.

Cameroon and Natalia swirled in love's current until he drowned. His self-strung body was found dangling from a triad of bamboo poles on Power Station beach. We were devastated and distraught. The inevitable "*why?*" had no definitive answer, no note to explain. In hindsight and commiseration, we failed to fully recognize and heed the signs which had signaled his intentions.

Two (2) days prior, I sensed something amiss when he

attended a party at my place and was oddly calm in his speech. It was infused with a somber energy and he was noticeably reflective. I assume by then he had made his decision. Friends echoed similar sentiments.

Natalia was overwhelmed by guilt and consternation. The community held a vigil on the beach for a week, raised money for his cremation and organized a memorial. Nearly 100 people gathered to mourn, commiserate and celebrate. Hands joined at sunset, our thoughts and prayers ascended as a lone surfer paddled out and sprinkled his ashes. May the compassion and loving-kindness of our energy that evening forever resonate on behalf of all suffering beings.

Shortly thereafter, a journalist from the *South China Morning Post* newspaper visited with an eye to write a story. Fortunately, we dissuaded him. Anything written would have been a wildly inaccurate depiction of what actually transpired and cast an unfavorable light on the community.

After four (4) years in HK, workwise, I found myself restless. One day, I squeezed into a busy, corporate elevator and the sullen, unsmiling faces suddenly spoke volumes. *"Wake up, people,"* I thought, *"This is your life!"*

Arriving at my office, I pondered my predicament and realized that alternative medicines and massage were real for me across my travels. This insight soon became the basis for my new career path in Massage Therapy.

I thought initially to study Ayurveda and move to southwest India to obtain a degree that was non-transferable for practice in the USA. So, I shifted my focus and googled, *"alternative health Australia."* The first listing was for Nature Care College (NCC) in Sydney.

In six (6) months, I was there.

My going away party was a blast! Reports forecasted a hurricane so I slung a plastic tarp improperly. It pooled water in a massive bubble that became a swaying shower head. Onwards we partied, inside my home and out. The vibe was magical. Thank you one and all.

With that, my time in Asia drew to a close. An entirely new existence awaited that, in some ways, was not new at all - a country quite familiar, a language I effortlessly understood, and my return to student life. First though, I went home to tell my family about my new direction in life, and, to come out. The news on both counts was well received and it got uncomfortable.

Dad: "*Are sure you can make a good living?*"
Mom: "*I always knew.*"

One thing: Mom did once let slip that she was more worried about my Buddhist beliefs than my sexual preference as far as eternal salvation and/or damnation goes.

I returned to HK, packed, and moved.

These were tales of my 30's in Hong Kong.

***

I encourage all groups to begin chapter discussions with the following three (3) questions, then reflect and share.

What is my overall impression of the chapter?

Which story did I most prefer? Least?

What is a theme of the chapter?

Reflect and Share: My 30's Hong Kong

A suggested way to proceed: *Someone call out a letter (A-Z). Read aloud that question and answer it until conversation is exhausted, then, continue with another letter. Enjoy.*

a) What do you define as decadent? Why?

b) What is your favorite flower? Why? What memories does it evoke?

c) Have you ever struggled to fit in somewhere? What was the situation? What made it difficult?

d) Have you ever undervalued your worth? When? In what manner?

e) After recounting an underwear party, I said: (pg. 222) *"I ask you to imagine visiting Hugh Hefner's mansion. What exactly would you do? How would you react? Surrounded by fantasies incarnate, what would you do?* Comments, anyone?

f) Professionally, do you enjoy your work colleagues? In a social setting, would they be your friends?

g) Which creative activity most touches your heart?

h) What is your favorite season? What special memories do you have about this time of year?

i) Have you every participated in any extreme sport? Would you do it again? Why or why not?

j) When moving to a new town, what is your best suggestion for meeting and making potential friends?

k) On page 229, I mention the traditional Chinese practice of immediately abandoning a home when the patriarch passes. What did you think of this?

l) Have you ever regularly taken public transport? If yes, what? Where? Why? Do (Did) you like the experience?

m) Are you a "*people watcher?*" Who, or what, is the oddest thing you have ever seen? Funniest?

n) What is your opinion of parenthood? What are its' greatest joys and challenges?

o) What is the most helpful emotion? Harmful?

p) On page 232, I recounted the non-sexual joy a male friend found in wearing female clothing and going out. What did you think of this?

q) What talents do you possess? Admire?

r) Which stories from this chapter are most memorable? Why?

s) Do you agree or disagree? (pg. 234) *"Some say, the only thing we really have in life is our reputation."*

t) What is the most spontaneous thing you have ever done?

u) Where were you when the 21st century arrived?

v) Is there anything you wish you could "*unsee?*"

w) Does this mirror any person in your life? (pg. 244)

"Who really knows why some people access your heart with such ease, they simply do. Before I knew it, Mihn had accessed mine."

x) What was your reaction to the transcription of my hypnotherapy sessions?

y) Do you feel that, at some point in life, most folks give pause to, or ponder, suicide?

z) What is the best party you have ever attended? What made it so great?

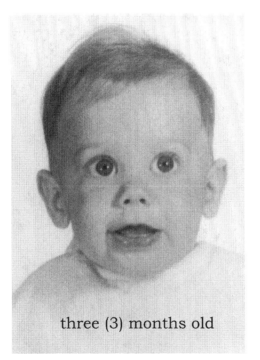

three (3) months old

Chapter 6: My 40's

Introduction

After 14 years in Asia, I was both anxious and excited to rejoin Western society. Granted, I was doing so in a foreign country, Australia, but still.

The anticipations of changing my career and being back in the classroom churned my spirit in wonderful ways. The current of my choices felt strong and upright. For four (4) years, Sydney did not disappoint academically, professionally or personally.

Returning then to America, I aspired that my 40's would be a decade well lived, rather than the strained one it became. Negativity bubbled to the surface and created causes and conditions whose consequences created an unwanted future.

It was my karma, of course, the truth of cause and effect.

With right view, accepting this truth promotes a more welcoming attitude towards, and greater responsibility for, the actions that can overwhelm our suffering minds. At least my parents were pleased. I was no longer around the world, just across the country.

These are tales of my 40's.

***

I was a much different person returning to Australia in 2003 than I was when first visiting in 1988. Sydney, though, remained the same in its designed splendor.

Temperate throughout the year and built around a stunning harbor, it is one of the most gorgeous and accessible cities in the world. Buses and subways easily

260

connect you with parks and nature. It is city built for walking and outdoor activities.

The coastal walk between world famous Bondi Beach and Maroubra, a place where I worked after graduating, was stunning. The trail hugged its way along rocky cliffs and through one of Australia's oldest cemeteries. It was dotted with little cafes and beaches. Small tidal pools were built ocean side for free, public swimming. Over the years, I explored many places around the city, including clothing optional beaches.

Aussies have a healthy and carefree body image. Even larger men commonly wear speedos, though, word is, board shorts are gaining in popularity.

One thing: The first time I went to a Vegas swimming pool, I wore my Speedo; it was also the last time. People stared and audibly snickered. I was somewhat shocked.

Conwong Beach, two (2) buses and 50 minutes from my home, was a family friendly beach where folks of all ages enjoyed swimming without suits. It reminded me of the hot river in Japan.

Oblesik Beach was more secluded and more risque. In the middle of a national park and surrounded by jungle, folks of all persuasions did things about which your mother does not want to know.

Closer to home, the iconic Sydney Harbor Bridge linked the north and south sides of the city. Together with 750,000 people, the cascading fireworks show on New Year's Eve was breathtaking to behold.

The Opera House and surrounding Botanical Gardens were a calm oasis amidst the high rises, while Hyde Park sat city center in tall tree, beauty.

Here, I joined 250,000 folks in a peaceful and powerful, anti-war protest. Our collective strength can be palpable.

My daily routine included 90 minutes of walking from home through Hyde Park to the subway and school. Even in the rare rain, it was wonderful. Let's work to better organize our lives, such that simple exercises, like walking, are more easily integrated into our daily habits, as was the case in times past.

One thing: Towards this end, I am a big fan of taking the stairs that always parallel an escalator. Sometimes I run up and down and up again. Try it.

Oxford Street, linking Hyde Park to Taylor Square in central Sydney, is the focal point of Australia's LGBTQ community. Between these two (2) points is everything gay, lesbian, bi-sexual, transgendered and questioning with most shops, restaurants, clubs, bookshops, outdoor cafes and drag shows staffed by LGBTQ folks.

Much like the Castro district in San Francisco, it was extraordinarily liberating to walk down the street and feel to be in the majority, to be open and comparatively comfortable in one's own skin. Taylor Square, the epicenter, sits at the crest of a small hill and has water spouts splashing about. If aliens arrived and judged us from this location, they might assume that same sex coupling was the norm if they recognized gender at all.

One thing: Tour companies would unload busloads of Chinese tourists at Taylor Square. They then strolled down Oxford Street, taking pictures and gawking at us as if we were creatures in a zoo. Really? Then again, I suppose I have done similar things to others. Peace.

Oxford Street hosts the annual, Mardi Gras celebrations. Established in 1978, it is one of the largest festivals in the world. Thousands of international and local visitors enjoy three (3) weeks of shows, lectures, discussion panels and parties, culminating in a parade viewed by approximately 300,000 people and a dance party for 20,000+. It is an extraordinary series of events for all things LGBTQ.

Each year, I attended the dance party as a volunteer.

I helped set up venues, painted things, moved furniture, etc... whatever was required. The night of the party, we were paired and patrolled the crowds approaching folks who might need medical assistance. As I did not favor party drugs, it was a great way for me to both enjoy and give back to the community.

One year while setting up, I watched the dress rehearsal for a performance of *"Somewhere Over the Rainbow,"* by Judy Garland from *The Wizard of Oz*. Song, singer and film – all iconic in the gay community.

I could not help myself from shedding tears.

During another Mardi Gras event, this would happen again. Only this time, it was an *"ugly cry"* born of someone special.

Two (2) blocks from Taylor Square, I rented a small studio apartment on the 5th floor of a six (6) floor walk-up. It was a cute little, 500 sq. ft. place. The most extraordinary thing about it though, was the large tree just outside my kitchen window.

Annually, dozens of migrating cockatoo birds – a large, white bird in the parrot family (*Baretta had one)* – called it home for about a week.. Their squawking was deafening.

One day while watching them, one flew to my window sill and we spent several minutes saying hello as it peered in and looked around. It was magical.

Once, I heard what I thought was loud music from a neighborhood party. I soon realized it was the Boss himself, doing an afternoon sound check for that night's nearby show. Thank you for the free concert, Mr. Springsteen.

Settling in, I returned to the classroom and loved it. Nature Care College (NCC) was everything I had hoped and more. Opened in 1973, NCC had 4,000+ students in a beautiful, north shore suburban location and a highly dedicated staff. I enrolled in the Remedial Massage program and expanded it to include Reflexology.

Reflexology posits that each organ in the body has a corresponding reflex point on the foot. Proper foot massage therefore, can impact accordingly. Further, my program also included a certificate in Iridology – the study of the iris, or colored portion of your eye.

Iridology posits that the entire body is mapped onto the iris (the colored part of the eye) via fibers. Reading properly the patterns, color and characteristics of the fibers illuminates weaknesses within. I found the discovery of this discipline fascinating.

In the 19th century, while being hospitalized, a Hungarian doctor noted that the iris fibers of an owl camped outside his window changed as the result of a broken leg.

A dark, brown spot appeared then slowly receded as the leg healed. Intrigued, he started mapping out the irises of patients who had broken various bones and established a correlation and pattern akin to the owl's eye. My instructor had 20+ years of personal, anecdotal evidence of its' effectiveness as a diagnostic tool.

From January 2003 to May 2004, I immersed myself in studying. I was grateful that PwC afforded me enough to cover my expenses. Only on graduation did I have to work.

My courses included:

- Swedish Massage;
- Lymphatic Drainage;
- Anatomy;
- Iridology;
- Pathology;
- Reflexology;
- Sports Massage;
- Aromatherapy;
- Professional Ethics; and,
- Clinical hours.

Australia requires all Massage Therapists to take a semester of Basic Counseling Skills. This impressed me greatly, Clients share highly personal details and it is important to navigate such discussions professionally.

In today's society, I feel touch depravity is an unrecognized source of many problems. It disturbs me greatly to know that some schools now ban student contact – touching - entirely. The long term, personal and societal implications of such policies are significant and deserve healthy questioning.

One thing: While working at a sports clinic, a middle aged woman became my client. She was stressed out caring for her stroke ridden, wheelchair bound husband whose only two (2) slurred, repetitive utterances were, "Shit" and "F**k."

What began as monthly appointments soon became weekly. Her physical condition improved and her pain subsided. I was pleased with her progress. Then, she started bringing me gifts and inviting me out to lunch. I always politely declined.

My on-going naiveté soon dissipated when I realized that she had cultivated an unhealthy emotional attachment and challenged professional boundaries. When I left the country, she missed her final appointments and called full of malcontent. May she be well.

My clinical work required 70 hands-on hours for massage and 50 for Reflexology. Years later, these experiences were invaluable when I supported and guided my students through their clinical trials and tribulations.

QtoP1: Am I comfortable naked? What is my best feature? Would I change anything?

QtoP2: Am I comfortable in large crowds? Why or why not?

QtoP3: Am I a touch deprived person?

In the case of the later (Reflexology Clinic), the power of this modality became evident. A diabetic client, whose lower leg was to be amputated, visited as a last resort. With regular sessions, a healing circulation was restored and his leg was saved.

For a Reflexology class project, I had to select an ailment and give three (3) sufferers, one (1) session a week for 10 weeks and elicit feedback, noting any changes. On one client, I noticed that the heart reflex section of his foot felt vacant; it almost collapsed on touch and felt empty.

I soon learned that four (4) weeks prior to our first session he had tried to commit suicide, something he neglected to mention. By the end of our 10th session, he reported significant improvement in his mood and the corresponding foot area felt stronger.

While in school, I befriended yet another strong, wonderful woman – Caliste. Like Amelia and Angela before her, we got along swimmingly and shared many fun adventures.

At one point, we discussed getting married for visa

reasons but that fell away when she met someone and fell in love. I look forward to the day when my relationship with a man is as easily profound as they were/are with these three (3) ladies and Judi, Veronica and Penelope who followed.

Once graduated, the next phase of my life beckoned. What to do? The answer was: stay in AU by transferring my student visa to the International Wing Chun Academy.

Here, as a full-time student, I could take any class, any time of day, as long as I accrued 20 hours by week's end. This flexible schedule made work convenient.

The Academy had an amazing lineage. Its' founder, Jim Fung of Hong Kong, was a student, first removed, of world renowned practitioner, Yip Man, Bruce Lee's teacher.

Sadly, Master Fung passed of cancer in 2007 but left a tremendous legacy in his wake.

One day, I floated the following proposal to staff: I would teach two (2), one (1) hour yoga classes per week in exchange for double the attendance marks. They agreed.

Before I knew it, I had 50 classmates enjoyably doing yoga. Most classmates were of Eastern European or Asian heritage and I soon befriended a terrific Italian guy, Diego.

He was travelling the world as a genuine pizza maker. We got along great. His English was good and mind sharp. Our conversations were worldy and fun. We remain in contact and I hope to one day visit him in northern Italy.

Through Caliste, I met a man who certified and contracted yoga teachers out to various venues for one-off or regular classes. One day, he sampled my class at the Academy and I was soon teaching at the University of Sydney gym, as well as the University of New South Wales.

Twice, I had the humbling joy of substitute teaching 7am staff classes at the Art Gallery of New South Wales. Per their web site:

Established in 1871, the Art Gallery of NSW is proud to present fine international and Australian art in one of the most beautiful art museums in the world....Modern and contemporary works are displayed in expansive, light-filled spaces, offering stunning views of Sydney and the harbor, while our splendid Grand Courts are home to a distinguished collection of colonial and 19th-century Australian works and European old masters."

As I write, words cannot capture the imprint these classes etched permanently within my heart and mind – to do yoga surrounded by such breathtaking art, such examples of human creativity and passion, such history and grandeur - all dappled by the silent, streaming rays of a nourishing sunshine as we began together a new day.

Just down the street from the Academy was The 487.

Four (4) stories of showers, saunas, private rooms, a coffee bar and movie theater, it was a wonderful gay place to relax and perhaps get lucky. The underbelly, however, taught me much about rejection and attraction.

It was the kind of place to go when you already felt positive about yourself and were not seeking affirmation.

If I entered unhappy, I left, feeling even more so, depressed. It took me years to better understand the dynamics of this lesson and how it repeats in other, similar situations.

Immediately after graduating, I advertised in a local paper for in-call sessions. Most folks were fine but it got increasingly uncomfortable as some odd characters entered my space so I soon stopped. One man saw the

268

Buddha picture on my wall and yelled at me about the evils of religion, then left.

In time, I worked for the Hotel Massage Service (HMS) and worked at five (5) star hotel spas around Sydney harbor.

The owners were a lovely couple who visited me years later in Vegas. I also joined the team at a Maroubra sports clinic. Getting exposure to these very different sides of the industry was invaluable.

QtoP4: Do I allow myself to experience fully my emotions?

QtoP5: What types of situations appeal to "my higher self"?

QtoP6: Do I surround myself with friends who support me?

While I had many extraordinary massage experiences working for HMS, two (2) spring to mind, one opulently great, the other one?

Well...

I did an in-room, couples massage at an exclusive, three (3) story hotel under the Sydney Harbor Bridge. As we worked on the couple in their $1,500 per night room, a gentle breeze blew the balcony curtains open revealing the iconic, Sydney Opera House just as a fireworks display ensued. It was a stunning confluence of events and remains my most memorably, decadent massage session. The beauty of it all in all regards.

In sharp contrast, I once got called to an in-room treatment elsewhere that haunts me still. I knew something was amiss when the door opened and the client remained behind it and out-of-view.

The first thing I saw was a floor strewn with peanut shells and a table covered in empty beer bottles. Cigarette smoke lingered. Cautiously carrying in my supplies, the door closed behind me and the client appeared.

No exaggeration, the poor man looked like Golum from *Lord of the Rings*. He was short, had a bulging eye, hunched shoulder, and talked in a slurred manner. I set up, helped him get face down and began.

After 10 minutes, he had a coughing fit, sat upright, got off the table, moved to the couch, and lit a another cigarette. I patiently waited. Soon, he took out $200 dollars, put it on the coffee table, and said, "*Just touch it. Please. The money can be yours.*" I felt pity, hesitation and concern.

He moved to the bed where he proceeded to stare at me as I stood at attention. I was watching *Troy* on the television and waiting for my hour to end. My thought process was this:

- I was in no way threatened or in danger;
- Leaving early would have required a written report and in doing so, embarrass the man; and,
- I would make good money for watching Brad Pitt in Roman leather. Be still my heart.

Three (3) weeks later, I was walking home and saw the same man, homeless and living on the street. What was going on that day in his life?

Years later, during a job interview in Vegas, I was asked: "*What was the most difficult massage/ client experience you have ever had and what did you do?*" Stupidly, I recounted a softened version of this story.

Halfway through, the interviewer's energy shifted and I knew immediately that I had just lost the job for overtruthing. I have subsequently developed a bland, simple story if the same question surfaces again.

Working at the sports clinic meant seeing clients over time and drafting treatment plans with colleagues to encourage healing. I worked in a massage room upstairs while Physical Therapists worked downstairs.

Two (2) clients stand out for affirming the power and beauty of massage.

My first was a grammar school teacher in her late 20's who was rehabbing from a terrible car accident. Most of her issues were successfully addressed except for a nagging pain in her mid-back. Her Doctor told her she would *"just have to deal with it"* the rest of her life. To which she replied," *Doctor, you are in your 60s. That is easy for you to say, but I refuse to accept this."*

After three (3) sessions, her pain was gone. In todays' *"pill popping for pain"* environment, massage has so much to offer. I look forward to the day when the profession's potentialities are recognized and shown rightful respect as a healing option.

The second experience was the pregnant store owner from two (2) shops down. From her fourth (4th) month through to birth, I massage her nearly weekly. It was a wondrous experience to lay hands on her ever changing body. It taught me so much about the resilience, strength and adaptability of the female, physical form.

Birthing a 10+ pound baby, she sourced massage as a main reason for her trouble free pregnancy. Your bodies are amazing.

Personally, Sydney became a place of great learning as far as integrating back into Western society as a gay man, while manifesting the blessings of my time in Asia. Soon after arrival, I found a Tibetan Buddhist center under the auspices of Sogyal Rinpoche, the author of, *"The Tibetan Book of Living and Dying,"* (see *My 30's: Nepal*).

271

A 25 minute walk, I attended weekly meditation sessions and met a like-minded man who became a dear friend and social mentor. Ming was a middle aged, gay Asian man.

His partner of many years had died and left him as a man of leisure so he travelled and traversed a spiritual path. Our genuine compassion for one another, and lack of sexual attraction, made it easier to navigate our relationship. From my eyes, we were very much *"older/ younger brother"* friends.

The good fortune of his financial situation co-existed with the challenges of his hiv+ status. Infected during its' onset, the preciousness of his human life took on a realer, starker urgency on a daily basis than most of us regularly encounter. Thankfully, he remains radiantly alive and well. Knowing him dispelled my fear of the disease, though due caution still remains.

One thing; Buddha taught that pondering the following truths can calm and balance our body, speech and mind by cultivating truths.

- *The preciousness of human life;*
- *The truth of impermanence - the constancy of change;*
- *The truth of karma – all thoughts, words and deeds have consequences; and,*
- *The pervasiveness of suffering among all sentient beings.*

Suffering is a key Buddhist concept. It is born of our ignorance about the true nature of reality. Buddha's teachings provided remedies for the negative consequences of this misunderstanding. Suffering is much more consequential than the fleeting impact of physical pain.

The sting of a slap quickly passes, but hearing "You are stupid and will never amount to anything!" just once, from the lips of someone you love, can generate lifetimes of suffering.

Ming helped me better understand the dynamics of gay culture and ways to cope with issues like rejection. He offered a perspective that transcended "*being gay*," and spoke to the larger issues of our common suffering as sentient beings and the negative habits we engender, the labels we may place on ourselves, our mental habits.

He helped me understand Buddhist practice along the path of gay life. My sense of self was realized along a continuum of what it means to be human – of where I fall along the broad and colorful spectrum of humanity in all its' expressive forms. In my naiveté, I thought the gay community would be more understanding, more rainbows and unicorns.

We are a lovely lot. At the end of the day, however, we are just people - struggling with our comic foibles and incessant judgments, doing our best to get along and make sense of it all. And in that, we each are the same.

Friend-wise, together with Caliste, a Japanese man, Kenichiro, became my "*go to*" friend – the person with whom you hang out and enjoy a coffee or movie.

I dated on-and-off. I was enamored by a lovely man from Djbuti and fell twice in love. In both cases, my ideal of love clashed with reality in ways familiar to many. Thanks to Boon and BJ for these experiences.

Boon was a lovely, educated, well-travelled man of Malaysian descent. Formerly a middle school teacher, his smile melted my heart on first meeting. He worked at an iconic gay bookstore and lived in a stunning little, split level, studio home. I once house sat for him and experienced binge watching for the first time – seasons 1 & 2 of *Six Feet Under* – my how television had changed!

I loved our conversations over coffee and walks through the parks. We enjoyed a Mardi Gras together and went to the theater; his blended tastes and smells lingered with his kind heart and smile.

Within a year, he embarked on a 10 month world tour. One day, he sent me a message from northern England/ southern Scotland and said my family name was everywhere.

During the next Mardi Gras, I was working as a bartender at a harbor side party. My shift completed, I was watching a performer descend a staircase when I turned to my left.

There, beside me with his gorgeous smile, was Boon. He had returned the day before and perchance we met. For the first time ever, I broke into Oprah's ugly cry. It was the best hug and kiss of my life, without compare.

Distance and longing can have that kind of impact.

> *QtoP7: How do I respond to memories of my suffering?*

> *QtoP8: On a scale of 1-10, how romantic am I?*
> *What best captures my idea of romance?*

> *QtoP9: Have I ever "ugly cried?" When? Why?*

BJ was an entirely different type of man and our relationship became a testament to the phrase: *"Hindsight is 20/20."*

Karma unfolds in a myriad of ways and my time with BJ drained. From personal blind spots to public presentation, I painfully learned much about myself.

We met as my visa expiration approached and he was completing a two (2) year, overseas work assignment.

Slick and highly successful, I fell fast for his energy and swaggy confidence. Like Mihn before, there was that intangible something that defined our attraction. We dated in a romanticized way with an energy that inevitably shifted once the mundane aspects of life were re-realized.

We spent a lot of time together and I avoided the truths revealed by his occasional questions about our possible future. If I had listened more clearly, free from my attachment to the idea of *"having found the one,"* then, I would have avoided the heartbreak that would follow. For the time being, I saw things as good and was convincing.

Eventually, it was time to leave Australia so I heeded my parents' request to return stateside. BJ's presence became new matters to unravel.

After 20 years in the cold (Buffalo) and 18 years in tropical humidity, I was happy to try desert life. This meant: New Mexico, Arizona, southern California or Nevada.

Las Vegas it was.

Return to America

When I left America in 1988, Ronald Reagan was finishing his second term. And, while I had found much of his rhetoric unsettling, it was nothing compared to the political and social atmosphere that was post-9/11 America.

Returning in May 2006, I envisioned my 40's as a positive decade. I believed that the relative, open and individual nature of American society would be an intriguing place to explore and experience as a Buddhist.

During the decade, good things occurred alongside other things not so much. Relationships were challenging. I was happy to find Ms. DeGeneres, Mr. Cooper, Ms. Maddow, *Will & Grace* and public others propelling acceptance.

I was grateful for experiencing eight (8) years of integrity, civility and calm focus under President Obama's governance.

Mrs. Obama, the seeds of your grace intelligence, and inspiration will blossom amongst the next generation of young ladies, and gentlemen.

The professional and the personal blended as work colleagues, and some graduated students, became good friends. Knowing where to begin in unraveling the lessons and maintaining some semblances of order is a tenuous task.

I proceed as follows:

- Initial return and BJ
- Starting again in Las Vegas
- Spiritual grounding and unmooring
- Blending the professional and personal

One thing: Shortly after returning, my parents celebrated their 50th wedding anniversary. We gifted them unlimited Amtrak passes for a vacation of their choice. It was an unexpectedly sad reminder that this milestone would not mark my life.

Initial return and BJ

Arriving in Vegas, BJ's friend, Keith, kindly hosted me while I found my footing. He showed me the city and helped me sift through housing options. Within two (2) weeks, I found a room on Las Vegas Boulevard via a Craigslist posting.

My roommate was a Hong Kong lesbian who claimed her daily noon to night beer consumption was to quell the pain of throat cancer. She said that she had a child in Hong Kong whom she was forbidden to see, and in fear had left the city. Shortly thereafter, I came home to an empty apartment – she and her things gone, no note.

I wondered why I attracted such people into my life. I did know that she was kind to me.

BJ soon arrived. We stayed until the day the power went off and got a weekly until we found a lovely, two (2) bedroom apartment.

It soon became apparent that the currents of our respective lives did not well blend.

The confluence of my desire to please at the expense of my own emotional well-being, and BJ's ways, I swirled endlessly in an emotional eddy of uncertainty and self-doubt.

In any meaningful discussion of us, I ended up capitulating to his whims. I found myself unable to defend myself or satisfy my own needs.

These are so many stories that sound so very petty now in their re-telling, even something simple, like a phone.

We got a joint plan with a set number of minutes and he constantly monitored my usage. I was back in America and felt lost in many ways. I wanted to talk to family and reconnect with old friends, yet, he was in my ear about, *"I need to call around and launch my new business. I need the minutes."*

This was prior to unlimited plans. And, I know – *"Just get your own plan"* – was the simple, but in my mind elusive, solution.

278

My life felt filled and frustrated by so many little things like this. Ways of being that stymied and confused. Anger.

One thing: Shortly before his shenanigans, BJ had moved his elderly mother to Vegas from a city where she had lived her entire life. She had visions of travel and fun that never materialized. Instead, she struggled with brain and lung cancer, and family.

I offered support by visiting her in the hospital, attending rehabilitation sessions, and reading aloud her favorite Bible passages.

It was my honor to be part of her journey, and it was heart breaking. She was buried alone, somewhere in a Vegas cemetery. I was unable to attend.

QtoP10: Have I ever allowed someone to control or dominate me?

QtoP11: On a scale of 1-10, how do I rate my sense of self worth? Self control?

QtoP12: Do I take people at face value? Why or why not?

Work-wise, my first job was at a private gym in an opulent, high rise complex. Opening in 2001, it was a Vegas first and sparked a building boom that would soon go bust in the crash of 2008 – a situation that worked to my advantage.

I served as a front desk/ gym attendant and Yoga Instructor while I waited for my state massage license.

Overall, I enjoyed the job, though I was initially taken back by daily exposure to such wealth and its' accompanying attitudes. BJ refused to meet my colleagues and new friends throughout my time there.

One thing: One day, I struck up a conversation with a member and soon found that we had met as teenagers at the nearby Pizza Hut. He and his partner were now millionaires hosting sex toy parties. It is a billion dollar business.

From 2007 until 2015, I happily worked part-time for the Wilton chain in a petite, boutique spa on the Strip. My boss was friendly, talented and accommodating. When *Life Choices: It's Never Too Late* was released, she sold it in our retail area. I was so grateful for her support and learned a lot working for her. Moreover, here I met my *'younger sister,"* Sandy.

We connected instantly and remain close friends. Over the course of our friendship, I saw her realize and embrace her true sexual self in being a pioneer and warrior. She is now happily married to a lovely Australian woman.

Starting again in Las Vegas

Early on, BJ kicked me out on my birthday so I returned to Craigslist in search of accommodation. Fortunately, it worked out well. I rented a room in a condo from Timothy, my new gay friend. We got along and had much in common – politics, movies and food were our top three (3) things. I lived with him for two and one half (2 ½) grateful years.

We lived in the northwest section of the valley, at the base of the Spring Mountain range, and I quickly learned about the extreme contrasts that define life in Las Vegas, even as it relates to weather.

One day I was on my way to work at 3:30 when I got caught in a snowy, white-out worthy of a Buffalo winter. I could not see 10 feet a head on the highway.

Classes were cancelled as four (4) inches fell on the Strip

and 10" in our location. We spent the next two (2) days hot tubbing, knocking heavy build-up off fragile tree limbs while laughing naked and uncontrollably at the joyful absurdity of it all. Snow days in the desert!

One thing: Vegas is a surreal, desert city that ranks among the world's most famous. It is extraordinary. When you live here and truly appreciate this image, you have to laugh. It is all so very loveably odd in its '24 hr. way.

On the one hand, stunning nature fills the valley and surrounding areas. The Red Rock Conservation Area became my go to place for hiking and re-connecting with nature. I had my favorite spot atop Calico Basin.

Within a 45 minute drive I could be at 8,000+ feet hiking around Mt. Charleston or skiing four (4) months per year at Lee Canyon. I could also:

- walk the Wetlands Park;
- go swimming and cliff diving at Lake Mojave;
- visit Gold Spike & Tecopa Hot Springs to soak in glorious mineral baths; and,
- enjoy Floyd Lamb and Spring Mountain State Parks, with the latter hosting Broadway shows.

There are so many beautiful outdoor activities to enjoy. Most folks have no idea such beauty abounds for it is the iconic imagery of the world famous Vegas Strip that defines perceptions. And, yes, it is surely an experience.

Memorialized countless times in music, films and on television, the Strip is truly something to behold in all its' illusionary glory - dazzling in its' array.

- The Eiffel Tower;
- The Statue of Liberty;
- an Egyptian pyramid;
- an erupting volcano;

- dancing water fountains;
- lights that flash with imagination; and,
- so much more.

The façade radiates with a pervasive energy of impermanence. Nothing is as it seems. Everything changes. Moving billboards with barely clad women and their telephone numbers ply the streets. Places and people shift at a rate unlike any in my experiences. Sometimes it is a challenge keeping up. Which begs the question: *Do you have to?*

Those of us who live here rarely visit the Strip. It can be a bit too much. We go when hosting friends or celebrating something special, like a birthday or a show. That said and to be clear, I love it all. I genuinely enjoy calling Vegas my home. And, what makes life tenable is finding a spiritual balance.

Spiritual grounding and unmooring

From 2006 until 2010, I conducted a weekly meditation group in service to Gyaltrul Rinpoche and all the blessings he has bestowed on my life.

Originally, we met at someone's home, later the public library, and then my new home. I really enjoyed manifesting our spiritual community.

Over the years, we were fortunate enough to host three (3) public teachings by Rinpoche, as well as a teaching by Kenchen Rinpoche, my teacher's teacher. My skills for successfully surfing life's circumstances however, waned.

My actions were not aligned towards more beneficial ends.

As my practice faded, folks went elsewhere and I feel guilt for allowing it to drift apart. I got stuck in the muck of mind, in angst and discontentment.

282

At a shallow level, I got lost in the energies of drinking, gambling and sex. That can be Las Vegas. Granted, I did not do anything stupid or get in trouble. I never lost more than I could afford. I maintained my integrity by speaking my truth and avoiding any situation that caused discomfort. Dating was a challenge.

I did have to deal with the embarrassment of calling folks and informing them that I had a 100% treatable STD and they needed to get checked. I was unkind to people in the sense that I simply stopped contacting them without good cause, a level of depression, perhaps, I think.

My earlier self had been living in a better place. Numerous times, as real as the light of day, Rinpoche appeared in my dreams and offered guidance. At one point in my late 40's, I called him and ugly cried my way to sleep. Thank you, Rinpoche.

QtoP13: Am I ever a "fake" person? Do I put on pretense? When? Where?

QtoP14: Do I consider myself "grounded"? How so?

Qtop15: Have I ever suffered from "performance anxiety" in the bedroom?

At a deeper, more expanded level, I felt an underlying lack of gratitude amongst folks. They seemed not happy with what they had, and were always wanting more. I felt a pulsing energy of fear. A fear of:

- "the other;"
- of loss; and,
- out-of-control changes in how we live.

We seemed a culture adrift in uncertainty and drowning in an obese anxiety. The unrecognized consequences of

283

endless war continued to permeate, swell, ripen and overwhelm without a proper recognition of their persistent impact.

Further, my academic side acknowledged a devaluing of science, both its' necessity and validity – a maligning of logic and argument. Public policy discussions require facts not opinions or emotions.

It exhausted me.

Regarding decision making, I found that the single, most impactful change on society during my time away was the technology of immediate communication - the Internet and cell phones.

The technology, itself, promotes mental behaviors that are antithetical to the goal of meditation. The goal being a peaceful, placid yet ever streaming mind that is not fixated or attached to any one thing and realizes the illusion of self.

Instead, we are training our minds to be forever distracted and tumultuous, never calm or able to simply "*be.*"

Linking back to my Wake Forest days and the works of Meyrowitz and Portman – *No Sense of Place* and *Amusing Ourselves to Death (pg.107)* - folks now sit together and are individually immersed in their phone – mentally elsewhere, a place removed.

The 24-hour, profit and opinion driven news cycle reports in reality show fashion rather than encouraging a properly informed citizenry. Immediate access to an overabundance of information is new in human history.

It is shifting our social reality in ways not yet understood. At its' best, this new age has the ability to highlight our interdependence and common humanity.

For nearly a year, I logged, daily onto a website where my friends from Nepal – Ramesh and Jessica, the couple who hosted our book club – detailed Jessica's sad untimely passing. She was an exceptional human being.

The outpouring of support from around the world was inspiring. Ramesh's constant updates bound us as close as possible to this tragedy and the compassionate impact was profound. Thank you for creating a truly global space for our shared grief. Peace.

<u>Blending the professional and personal</u>

The full-time focus of my professional life was mainly teaching massage. With it, my personal life became entwined. Part-time massage work at the Wilton remained, and I also tried two (2) independent business ventures.

In 2008, I wrote five (5) workshop curriculi and became nationally certified as a continuing education (CE) provider for massage therapists. Soon, I was teaching my workshops at the Wilton and La Cagio spas, as well as privately and in small groups.

My workshops included: Reflexology, Table Thai, Pregnancy, Polarity Therapy, Integrated Stretching, and Aqua Stretch.

Aqua Stretch, was a ground breaking therapy based on weight assisted stretching in a pool. I apprenticed with its' creator for over a year. I continue to conduct these workshops and love when former students attend. It makes me happy to hear of their successes in the field.

I also got involved in a MLM (multi-level marketing) venture with a terrific ayurvedic health product.

As I learned about the business building activities required for success, however, I realized this type of endeavor was clearly not for me. I could not generate appropriate levels of attitude or action.

Through this product, I extensively explored a business partnership with a friend. While the details are irrelevant, once again issues of "*being a doormat*" arose. In time, I spoke my disappointed truth and we have not spoken since.

Compassion, where forth art thou?

Over the course of nearly 10 years, I taught Massage Therapy at two (2) different, for-profit, schools. In both cases the classroom experiences were terrific.

My love of teaching was fulfilled. Life was content and challenged.

I felt my actions were benefitting others and the rewards I received were positively impacting mind and heart.

Students touched my life in ways I had never before experienced. Many folks came to massage feeling the need, but not understanding the why, of their enrollment.

As odd as it sounds, many students initially refused to disrobe for practice. As instructors, we knew that earlier physical abuse was commonly the reason for this attitude.

It was one of our jobs to help students confront their negative pasts and navigate their journey to self-healing.

Much of the crying and many of the breakdowns that occurred in the healthy and supportive space of our classrooms saved students from years of therapy and unhealthy behaviors.

In time, students realized that they sought their own path to self-healing by aiding others

Regardless of whether or not they ever became therapists, their time in the program wrought tremendous benefits. Many students come to mind though one stands out.

She was a young lady married at 14 and a mother of two (2) by 17. Her husband forced her into stripping to pay bills and she desperately wanted out so came to massage to make this happen.

Along the way, she periodically came to class with a black eye and cry. Eventually, we found a half-way house to help here escape her situation after the husband appeared threateningly outside the school with a gun. I do not know what has become of her but her final words to me are some of the kindest I have ever heard. She said,

"Mr. Peter, I can't believe you came from the other side of the world and met me. What are the chances of that? You will never know how special you are to me."

Wherever she and her family are, may they be well.

And, while this is one of the most extreme examples of student situations I faced, it is indicative of many. I felt blessed to be there and serve them in whatever manner I could. They allowed me to put into practice the teachings I had for years received – Buddhist thought manifesting in compassionate action to the best of my abilities. That is how I viewed my time in the classroom.

In the hallways and back office, however, I was challenged to apply different aspects of the teachings. Countless situations arose that forced me to practice patience, forgiveness, and anger management.

During my time abroad, many vocational schools and colleges had been overwhelmed by the drive for excessive profit and created a vast labyrinth of dubious means by which to achieve it.

288

The mid-2000s saw numerous schools face lawsuits and close. Some have reformed and remain.

After five (5) years, my first school decided to phase out the Massage Therapy program. We had to teach out the remaining students and call it a day. Towards the end, the school Director approached me five (5) minutes before my class and told me to pack my stuff; I was being fired. He left my office and returned five (5) minutes later and said, *"Oh. Sorry, Peter. I didn't mean to fire you yet. My mistake. Can you stay?"*

The second school was better, though not by much. Towards the end of my tenure, we got a new Director. At our initial meeting, my colleague turned and whispered, *"Watch out. They're evil."* And, they were. My tipping point between job satisfaction and poor management was reached. I quit soon after.

Negativity aside, my professional life did, at times, swirl positively into my personal life. I worked with some terrific people. One colleague and dear friend, Randall, sailed the world for eight (8) years while working on a private yacht. Ms. Kanda was a Jamaican beauty. Penelope travelled as a young lady and spent time at the Playboy mansion.

Through a training seminar, I am grateful for having met my mentor, Judi Moreo. And, for years I befriended another strong woman, Veronica. We made great strides together in improving our program.

Two things; one: She was also a realtor. After the 2008 crash, she was instrumental in helping me buy my first home - a two (2) bedroom, two (2) bath, attached garage, loft style town house. Thank you so much, dear lady.

Two: Just like the dire economic circumstances that saw the government bailout Chrysler in 1979, thereby precipitating *an argument with my Uncle, so to the dire situation of 2009 saw the government support the tumbling housing industry by offering a $8,000, first-time buyer incentive.*

I applaud such targeted interventions when enacted appropriately and with clear focus. I love my home and am very grateful for both the joy it brings me, and the sense of community ownership engenders.

It seems to me that our binary vision of government as a "yes or no" option is not helpful. For me, the role of government is granted and necessary.

Therefore, focusing on efficient, effective and transparent government is paramount. We must be vigilant in our civic duty to observe, participate and oversee the actions of elected officials. As envisioned, our institutions are to serve, not control.

Inside and outside of the classroom, Veronica and I were best pals for years until one night it all changed in an instant. A person does something and you never seem them in the same way again. It is as if the friendship switch simply clicked itself off, despite all the wonderful times we had shared. We were subsequently distant and eventually talked but things did not improve.

May she be genuinely healthy and happy.

QtoP16: What is the kindest thing anyone has ever said to me?

Beyond the confines and constraints of work based relationships, I did enjoy several positive dating experiences. For a brief while, I dated an extraordinary doctor. We enjoyed our time together. I loved his intellect and his manner of being - the way he carried himself – such handsome dignity.

He was articulate, fit, informed and wildly sexy to my way of reckoning. I know exactly when my heart energy shifted warmly. We were at an indoor water park and he lost himself in the swirling joy of an inter-tube ride. Oh my, that smile. I melt under the radiance of a good one. Emotionally, however, our needs and the ability to openly express were misaligned. Sometimes, despite best efforts, we move on, and yet the heart still sadly sags.

Another, more decidedly carefree man also captured my heart. Bill was a lovely Southern gentleman with a quick wit and seemingly encyclopedic knowledge of everything culturally 80's. He was so funny. For me, one of the highlights of our relationship was as follows:

We both had Friday's off and rotated planning "*date days*." One week you planned the date, the next you received. They included exciting unknown adventures and creative, joyful endeavors. We did this for over a year and never went to the same place twice, excepting movie theaters. It taught me the importance of actively investing in a relationship - cultivating memories by prioritizing us time.

Eventually, in the end, we made much better friends than lovers and the intimate aspect of our relationship ceased. After years of no contact, we are now dear friends.

These were tales of my 40's.

Reflect and Share: My 40's

A suggested way to proceed: *Someone call out a letter (A-Z). Read aloud that question and answer it until conversation is exhausted, then, continue with another letter. Enjoy.*

    a)   Are you a beach, mountain or desert person?

    b)   Would you prefer to live in a different time / era? When? Why?

c) Do you believe in alternative medical therapies? Have you tried any?

d) If you could go back to school, would you? To study what?

e) What people or activities affirm your positive sense of well-being?

f) Are you a more emotionally or logically motivated person?

g) Who has been a mentor in your life?

h) What do you think of this statement? (pg.268) *"At the end of the day, however, we are all just people struggling with our incessant judgments and comic foibles."*

i) Has this ever happened to you? (pg. 268) *"my "ideal" of love clashed with reality."*

j) What was the best kiss of your life? What made it so special?

k) What were the emotional high and low points of your life thus far?

l) Do you feel compelled to *"keep up with the Joneses?"*

m) Have you achieved a *"spiritual balance"* in your life? How so, or not?

n) Who is your best friend? Best memory of them?

o) What are the top three (3) qualities of a best friend? Lover?

p) Has this ever happened to you? (pg. 287). *"It was as if the friendship switch in my mind simply clicked itself off, despite all the wonderful times we had shared."*

q) What is your opinion of workplace romances?

r) What is your opinion of this comment? (pg. 280) *"We seemed a culture adrift in uncertainty and drowning in an obese anxiety. The unrecognized consequences of endless war continued to permeate, swell, ripen and overwhelm without a proper recognition of their persistent impact."*

s) What was the best date you ever went on? What made it so special?

t) How do you know you have found someone special? What are your tell-tale signs?

u) How do you keep intimacy alive in a relationship?

v) Which stories from this chapter are most memorable? Why?

w) What does society demand of a woman in a relationship? A man?

x) Each chapter recounts a story marking death. Which one brought about your strongest reaction? Why?

y) What are the best ways to ensure good, healthy communication habits in a relationship?

z) What is happiness? Where is mind?

Chapter Seven: My 50's

In the summer of 2015, an overseas teaching experience refreshed my perspective and reminded me of my potentialities. My 50s were still young.

It shook me from the frustration and general disgruntlement that I was feeling towards my life. While still teaching massage, the disrespectful practices of management eventually overwhelmed the positive joys of teaching.

More poignantly, a colleague in his mid-40's was diagnosed with multiple cancers and painfully faded before our eyes. Estranged from his family, we cared for him throughout his profound journey. May his beautiful spirit be at peace. With his departure, it was time for mine. I soon found myself teaching Shiatsu in Costa Rica for two (2) weeks.

Beachside and backed by jungle, the classrooms had no external walls. My first day, I was leading students through a guided meditation when a three (3) foot, rainbow colored lizard peaked its' head into class. It only got better after that.

At night, the local bar and banter with travellers reminded me how glorious was travel, so too, did the zip lining adventure. Amidst the jungle canopy, 50 feet above, tree to tree we zipped. It all went so fast and it renewed my spirit in so many ways.

The final night was a magical dance of moonlit shadows reflecting on the watery ebb and flow of a shallow, receding tide. I returned to Vegas and put in my letter of resignation the next week. The very day I left, a former boss called me in search of employees. *"It just so happens..."* I said, and soon had a new job.

Working full-time at four (4) days per week, time availed. One day, I took out a poster sized pad of post-it sheets and "*memory streamed*" childhood experiences. Filling the paper in less than five (5) minutes, I looked at the results and *Bing*! If I connect these ideas with sentences, I will have a book – so began *Life in Tens* in March 2016.

One thing: My parents celebrated their 60th wedding anniversary in August of 2016. To honor their love, my brothers and I surprised them with a life sized cardboard cut-out, placed in the narthex of their church. I found the picture in my bag of journals and no one could identify the time or location it was taken. The wife of the founding minister helped us arrange its' placement one Sunday morning and they loved it.

My new massage job at the airport was surprisingly fun. The days went quickly through a variety of modalities. It was fast paced and I always met interesting people. Working amidst the transient energy of the airport suited me - the hustle & bustle of thousands, the comings and goings of staff and travellers, alike. When not working, I mostly wrote.

October 11, 2016

It's Tuesday. I'm so excited. Angela, my dear English friend from HK now living in London, is visiting tomorrow for eight (8) days. My vacation has begun. I am cleaning, mopping, vacuuming, and doing everything necessary for her arrival. First and last nights she is at my place. In between, we will be posh-ing it up on the Strip.

Also, we are going to take a helicopter ride into the Grand Canyon and land for champagne and nibbly bits. She wants to drive on the iconic Route 66 so I am taking her to Arizona. These are both on her bucket list. More importantly, for me, I am glad she will be here to help me deal with my shock, grief, and disbelief.

Please note: What follows is stream of consciousness, first writing. Reading aloud helps.

<u>October 10, 2016</u> (written on the 11th)

It was a beautiful fall night. the 6:30 PM temperature was around 75° the air was crisp sun had set and I was just leaving Boulder Station movie theater on my way to pick up my car at my mechanics -10 min. away. Basic checks and fluid changes to make sure everything will be okay. going on a road trip with Angela i checked my phone in the parking lot and saw dad called so I paused to call back

Me: *"hi dad how are you I see you called I was in the movie so couldn't answer what's going on I'm worried you never call me I always call you. Is something wrong"*

Dad: *"yeah a bit of a chuckle sorry about that I suppose is it true. Anyways, something from the last couple days I've had shortness of breath and difficulty moving so last night your brothers and mother took me to the emergency room I had a whole bunch of tests the CAT scan and blood test and the doctors say I have one maybe two months to live so I'm hoping to make it through the holidays I began getting my financial affairs together this morning and I just wanted you to know that."*

It was all so matter-of-factly. He sounded good and said he was in no pain at all, just a bit winded. He said the doctors seemed to be surprised by this. The stark reality of life telescoped front and center as a state of shock and quiet quickly trickled then froze my body, speech and mind.

In the parking lot of a casino along a dodgy stretch of an iconic Vegas highway, I felt so small, distant and shrinking. I asked some questions and we talked a bit. I told him that just two (2) days prior, I had mailed the first three (3) chapters. How fortuitous. I added that I had

299

wanted to come home and read it to them. I am not sure if that will happen now. I suggested that perhaps Adam could read it to everyone.

I am lost in the colliding layers of karma and consequence.

Dad said he envisioned his final days lugging around oxygen in order to live. The doctors had suggested chemo and he added, *"There is not much quality of life in that really, afterwards. You are so sick."*

To a certain extent, I had been bracing to experience such a phone call regarding Mom. Not Dad. And now, what of her?

My heart is starting to ache. I am feeling a shortness of breath. I need to stop writing.

Note: I stopped until November 18th. On the 19th, I took out a calendar and briefly ordered events before my memories fogged. Exactly as written, I wrote:

Oct 14 Adam down the pharmaceutical rabbit hole, found by kind police, off to detox. Poor Dad- his own worries

Oct 16 mom fall with walker and leg gash

Wed Oct 19-22 trip home, Adam also there, just released,

- Nov 4 dad to hospital
- Nov 11 mom n dad move into home
- Nov 12 dad dies 6 hrs later, knowing she's ok
- Nov 17 call to mom, hear exact details
- Dec 3 memorial planned, post T'day

Oct 19-22 trip home

Wed Oct 19th 2016

"fading fast" No buy my groceries. Faint house smell of urine wow Mom morphed into gram. As usual til dinner done – elephant acknowledged Chemo/ lawyer n will talk

Thursday 20th

lawyer mtg. In middle "not doing chemo"
announced and arranged will to alleviate me of burdens,
"are we good?" no reply

Friday 21st

Dad sleeping in bedroom chair After Dinner talk and 'are we good" again; Dad says *"into a home"* mom grabs his hand and professes her deep love and ensuing loneliness in missing him. Mom with "Christ coming" and dad turns to me our Buddhist talk

Saturday22nd

Just dad n I to airport
Hand shake becomes hug, love u and take care of mom

Only other contact: call that was cut short
I am done

***

I ceased writing until 2017.

Note: It is Monday, February 13th. 2017. I have just re-read the above for the first time and immediately remark below.

Wed Oct 19th

"fading fast"
No buy my groceries

Dad and Todd picked me up at the airport. I had never seen Todd drive Dad who now preferred to be driven. Heading home, we stopped, as always, at the supermarket so I could buy my meals. It was easier that way. Mom no longer knew what to cook for me and I often took joy in cooking for everyone. In the parking lot, I asked Dad how he was and he replied, *"I'm fading fast, Pete."*

As we shopped, numerous cashiers and floor people said hello. Dad smiled as he responded. He introduced me to a golfing buddy, too, and then got quiet. At the cashier I paused before I paid because Dad always paid. This time he did not. He was so very much elsewhere. The suffering of expectations no longer applied. Simply be.

**Faint house smell of urine
Mom morphed into gram**

I was excited to see Mom. She was sitting in her favorite living room chair with a blanket and cat on her lap. We cheek kissed and she smiled as we held a long, sad, knowing gaze. *"How are you my Son?"* she asked. *"Ok"* I replied. I wasn't. We weren't.

My presence scared the cat away so I sat on the floor with my head in her lap. It felt like the proper thing to do. She put her left hand on my head and we were together; sometimes talking, mostly not. After a time, we got up for dinner and I saw in front of me, my Grandma Feeley. Mom's hair and eyes and especially her hips, now leading left while walking, were her Mother's being re-realized, saturated in an energy of descent and transformation.

**As usual til dinner done – elephant acknowledged
Chemo/Lawyer n will talk**

At times, I felt myself nearly drowning in the poignancy of our final, family dinners – over 5,000 served and shared. From our positions at the table, to the manner of our talk or silence, habits enabled one last time. Meal complete, Dad said,

"I need your opinion on getting chemotherapy."

We talked and asked and answered questions until everyone had their say. Dad put the topic to rest and we continued with things that I do not remember. To finish, he told us about tomorrow's 10am, family meeting with the Attorney to discuss the will and related things.

Thursday 20th

Lawyer mtg
In middle "not doing chemo" announcement
Arranged will to alleviate me of burdens

The lawyer was a fellow founding member of their church. His office was modern and flashy with glass walls and a green view. We were seated in an office and while waiting, Dad announced,

"Based on our talk last night, I want you all to know that I won't be getting chemo. It doesn't makes sense."

There was not much to say so not much was said beyond acknowledgement and solace.

The lawyer soon arrived.

Dad had originally drafted his will in 1997. Today was for updates and clarification. The *"Do Not Recessitate"* decree was affirmed and HIPPA access clarified. Dad shifted the Power of Attorney and we discussed the responsibilities. My job was simply to ensure that Dad's wishes came to pass. In his meticulous and foresightful manner, he had arranged and aligned all matters legal and financial.

Eyes opened, Mom sat so sadly throughout.

303

"are we good?" no reply

That evening, I had hoped to create a private moment between Dad and me. In the quiet of his bedroom, when the moment felt right, I held his eyes. Gesturing in a reciprocal hand motion and asking in an uncertain tone that was seeking affirmation, *"Dad, we are good, right?"*

With his head slightly tilted, he looked at me and silence ensued. The moment for reply passed. I left the room, my mind awash, striving to let it be – not reading any more, or less, into it other than what it was: a question gone unanswered for reasons to me unknown.

Friday 21st

Dad sleeping in bedroom chair

Early the next day, I knocked on his bedroom door. Unanswered, I slowly opened it and entered. In the far corner, Dad was sitting on his favorite chair in front of the cherry wood desk he had stripped and refinished decades ago. Head hung and arms crossed, he was sleeping. His energy draining as his aura dimmed. I quietly backed away. An image deeply etched.

After Dinner talk and 'are we good" again
Dad says "into a home" mom grabs his hand and professes her deep love and ensuing loneliness in missing him

Dinner was poignant and painful in its' finality. It would be our last dinner together as a family. We ate and sporadically chatted about not much until the time felt right and I asked again, *"Dad, we are good, right?"* Dad paused with a look and replied,

"You know, you asked me that last night and I didn't know how to reply. Of course we are right and I am so very

304

proud. Your education and experiences are extraordinary and the life you lived tremendous. We are just fine. Always remember that." I will.

Towards the end of our meal, Dad announced,

"*Carolyn, I am sorry but we have to put you in a home. I can no longer care for you. I am simply too weak.*"

With that, Mom opened her eyes.

One thing: Mom had taken to closing her eyes for long periods of time to lessen eye strain. You never knew if she was awake and aware, or, asleep. In this case, she had heard every word.

She reached across the table and grabbed Dad's hand, saying, "*I know, Bob. I am going to miss you so much. You know I love you. I tell you every day.*"

They looked silently at each other with love, recognition and resignation.

Mom with "Christ coming" and dad turns to me, Buddhist talk

Mom continued, "*I know Christ is coming again soon and we shall meet in heaven. I love you, honey.*"

Dad squeezed her hand as Mom looked down and away, tears falling. It was all happening and forever underway. A poignant and powerful pregnant pause filled the room. What more could be said? And with that, Dad's next utterance transformed the resonating energy as he turned to me and asked,

"*So, I assume you disagree with what your Mother just said about Christ's return. Any comments?*"

Honestly, Dad. That utterly, unexpected query? It was pure him. And, I realized, it was a ripe and final opening – an opportunity bursting with potential for our fullest sharing as father and son.

"Well, you know I do. I disagree. And, you know I respect your beliefs. They just don't resonate with how I see the world."

In the heartful, stream of conscious thought that followed, I talked about things I never thought I would. I shared with Dad and Mom my views on:

- Reincarnation and my beliefs;
- His and mom's role in my life as if chosen not assigned;
- How I have had periodic visions of him in monks robes; and,
- The gentle manner of his being the embodiment of Masters I have met.

Through it all, he listened intently, not with a smile, but with a face of knowingness, an expression of contentment. When I finished, exhausted, relieved and somewhat astounded, Dad simply said,

"That's what you believe? Thanks for letting me know."

And it was over.
That was it.
I felt that he already knew.

Gratitude without regrets.

Saturday22nd

Just dad n I to airport
Hand shake becomes hug, love u and take care of mom

The next day, Dad drove me to the airport. As we pulled up to the passenger drop off area, we began our goodbye ritual as I shook his hand and my words faded into finality. We smiled and I got out. Pausing at the curb, I turned for one final look as Dad put the car into park and got out. He swung around the trunk, approached me and said,

"Give your Dad a hug, son. I love you. The next part of your life will be amazing. Take care of your mother."

I had nothing left to say.
A lifetime of waiting. A first.
A last. Just words. Much more.

I watched as he drove off.

Only other contact: call that was cut short

Several days later, I called and Dad answered, *"Pete,"* he said, *"I am taking your mom to the doctors. We'll talk later."*

We never did.

On Friday, November 11th, 2016, Dad transferred from the hospital to the home where Mom had moved in the very same day.

After 60 years of love and one (1) last night together, Dad died, surrounded by his Minister, his wife, two (2) each of his children and grandchildren.

As Mom recounted, the Minster was reading Dad's favorite Psalms as she told him to *"Keep reading, keep reading!"* then eventually, *"Stop. He's dead."*

Tricia told me Dad squeezed her hand as his eyes opened and swept the room just before his final breath. It was over and had begun.

***

Per his request, Dad was cremated. Due to the upcoming Thanksgiving holiday, his memorial was held on Saturday December 13 at 9am.

I flew in on Thursday the 11th at 11pm. My brothers and I hung out together, talking more than we ever had in decades, Todd in particular. His awakening, his awareness, his actions: they reflected a man who was switched on. He talked of Dad and Mom and bills and policies, the house and things to know. He surprised everyone and it was wonderfully heartwarming amidst the sorrow.

Friday morning I went to see Mom. It was a somber encounter filled mostly with silence and sadness. Later that night, family and friends arrived and we hosted a get together at my parents' house where we cut and pasted three (3) montage posters themed *"love, family and memories."* We laughed and talked bittersweetly until the early hours.

Saturday's memorial was just as had been planned, ending with a favorite hymn, *Joy to the World*, our last Christmas Eve. A reception in the parish hall followed.

Together with my brothers and two (2) Ministers, I was honored to speak of my Father.

EULOGY

My Dad, Robert Kenneth S., was an:
- open-hearted;
- patient; and,
- loving man who grounded his life in faith. And, lived his life with gentle integrity and genuine kindness.

This sacred space and the Good Shepard family of faith sustained him for over 35 wonderful years. Thank you to everyone for contributing to this truth.

And, for your support of our family at this sad, sad time, family members including Mom, Adam and Todd, Tricia and Tony, Kat, Ron, Jude, Elsa, as well other family friends. I would like to honor my father by reading something I wrote a few months ago.

I know surprisingly little about my parents' childhoods. My dad was born in December 1930 and raised in Niagara Falls, New York.

His biological father died of a brain tumor when he was 12; his mother married twice again. He had two older sisters, one of whom has since passed.

Their upbringings were profoundly influenced by overcoming the challenges of both the Great Depression and WWII. On this side of the family, our ethnicity traces to England and Scotland.

My father served in the Navy between World War II and the Korean War and later went to Cornell University where he attained his Bachelor's degree in Industrial Relations. He worked as a human resource manager with the same company for over 50 years.

I know Dad loved his mother, Violet, very much. Every Sunday evening at her house, for17 years, I witnessed his devotion. To this day, his voice fills with warmth when he speaks of her. He was a good, and only, son.

Through his compassionate words and deeds, through his 60 years of love with our Mother, he has passed on to my brothers and me, the fine, caring, respectful manner of his youth.

What Dad taught us, - what Dad taught all of us - by the manner in which he lived, was:

- Live your faith and love your family;
- Cultivate friendships and care for your friends;
- Respect and recognize the worth and dignity of people you have yet to befriend;
- Listen, laugh, Be thoughtful. Be fair;
- Speak without swearing and do not speak ill of others;
- Whenever and wherever possible, help wisely;
- Enjoy life. Be grateful. Give back; and,
- Have fun.

Today, we honor all these lessons, and everything more, that was my father - Mr. Robert Kenneth S.

I love you, Dad.

***

If your parents are still with us and your hearts are strong, why not call them now and tell them that you love them.

If your parents have passed, please pause and allow their good spirits to enliven, embolden and expand your mind and heart with memories and grateful smiles.

If you are/ were estranged from your parents, please pause and allow compassion, loving- kindness to envelope your heart and mind so that a space for greater understanding and forgiveness may arise.

311

Epilogue: May, 2017

There is a sense that putting these final stories to paper, etches an immutable history as to how I will forever remember my Father, my family. It would, in a way if I let it, become my truth, but never in its' entirety. Words can only reach so far, can only reflect so much. Beyond them are matters for the mind and heart.

Mom is adjusting to her new surroundings while my brothers and I sort through legal issues. I started out 2017 with a 30 day, Hot Yoga challenge and I feel good. At the moment, my own suffering is all a bit too real, too raw and too close. It is hard. Perhaps I will of it one day write. For now, I am grateful we have come this far and I will end where I began.

"Knowing that no one, at any time or place, has ever experienced life in the exact manner by which you have lived yours, or, me mine, We are all swept up in the streams of our experiences whatever their rage or saturation.

We all thrive and survive in this state where being is the constancy of change.

I share my stories so that you may dive deep into your memories then surface and recount tales of your own.

"For a life examined," some claim, "is a life well lived."

Thank you.

Be happy.
Be healthy.
Peace.

Good in the End
Dedicate

To all Readers right this very moment, may the currents of your compassionate hearts stream steady and strong.

These stories are dedicated to teachers everywhere, in all their forms across time, for their wise guidance and caring support.

- To the realized Masters among us, and for their long lives;

- To all Parents and brothers and cousins, aunts and uncles;

- To all nieces, nephews and friends;

- To lovers and strangers alike; and,

- To all the kindred selves whom I have met along the way.

Thank you for being and becoming the pages of this book.

Together, may we spark personal insights and meaningful conversations for the benefit of all sentient beings.

Please note

I encourage any reading of this book to end with your personal dedications. Ensure that your efforts and energies are spoken aloud on behalf of others.
Thank you.

Acknowledgements

- To P Po: For your unflagging support and feedback;
- To Jeremy W: Your initial and extensive feedback pointed me in the right direction regarding content and purpose;
- To Judi: The journey remains grand;

- Steph V, Susan R & Chris M: Your comments were so insightful and improving;
- Jen T, Angela A and Amelia R: You are the best; these pages reflect my love towards each of you;
- To Ryan W: Your friendship is priceless; thanks for all your help and *all the Costa Rica pics, too!!*

- To Rick T: Appreciate you, our love and friendship;
- To April: Your kind hearted comments were great;
- To book club members: Thank you so very much;
- To my spa colleagues: Thank you for your patience in listening to my constant jibber jabber;

- To the staffs of Zen Shin, Sunrise Coffee House, Green Valley Grocery, Office Max (Krystal and Sara);
- Photo Shack and Michelle Poe at *Triple 4 Creative*;
- To Doc Randall and Jesus for self and auto care;

- To the Sydney Mardi Gras organization and Lexi & friends: Thanks for photo use approval; and,

- Finally: Thank you to all who took the time to read and identify with this journey and offer their loving support.

Our essence is compassion and wisdom.

Peace to all.

Travel Maps

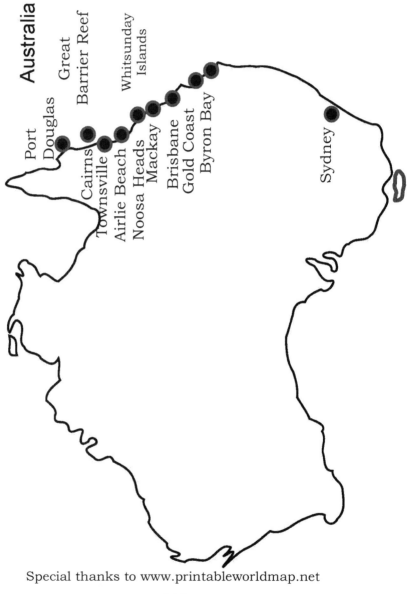

Australia

Great
Barrier Reef

Whitsunday
Islands

Port
Douglas

Cairns

Townsville

Airlie Beach

Noosa Heads

Mackay

Brisbane

Gold Coast

Byron Bay

Sydney

Special thanks to www.printableworldmap.net

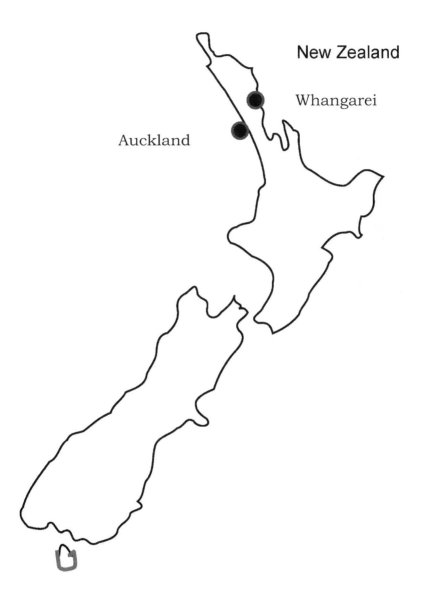

New Zealand

Whangarei

Auckland

Special thanks to www.printableworldmap.net

317

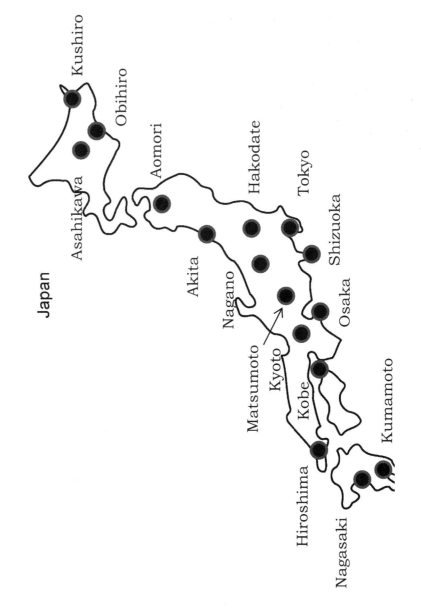

Kushiro

Obihiro

Asahikawa

Aomori

Hakodate

Tokyo

Shizuoka

Akita

Nagano

Osaka

Matsumoto

Kyoto

Kobe

Kumamoto

Hiroshima

Nagasaki

Japan

Special thanks to www.printableworldmap.net